**SIXTH EDITION**

# The Ultimate Job Hunter's Guidebook

Susan D. Greene

Melanie C. L. Martel

**SOUTH-WESTERN**
CENGAGE Learning

Australia • Brazil • Japan • Korea • Mexico • Singapore • Spain • United Kingdom • United States

**SOUTH-WESTERN**
CENGAGE Learning™

**The Ultimate Job Hunter's Guidebook, Sixth Edition**
Susan D. Greene, Melanie C. L. Martel

Vice President of Editorial, Business: Jack W. Calhoun

Vice President/Editor-in-Chief: Karen Schmohe

Senior Acquisitions Editor: Erin Joyner

Developmental Editor: Theodore Knight

Marketing Manager: Michelle Lockard

Content Project Management: PreMediaGlobal

Senior Manufacturing Buyer: Kevin Kluck

Senior Marketing Communications Manager: Sara Greber

Right Acquisition Specialist (Text, Image): John Hill

Production Service: PreMediaGlobal

Copyeditor: PreMediaGlobal

Senior Art Director: Stacy Jenkins Shirley

Internal Designer: PreMediaGlobal

Cover Designer: Lou Ann Thesing

Cover Image: ©iStock Images

Photo Researcher: PreMediaGlobal

Part opener image credit: Part 1, 2–Pixland/Jupiter Images; Part 3: Pete Saloutos/UpperCut Images/ Getty Images; Part 4: George Doyle/Stockbyte/Jupiter Images

For product information and technology assistance, contact us at
**Cengage Learning Customer & Sales Support, 1-800-354-9706**

For permission to use material from this text or product, submit all requests online at **www.cengage.com/permissions** Further permissions questions can be emailed to **permissionrequest@cengage.com**

Library of Congress Control Number: 2011927308

ISBN-13: 978-1-111-53176-8

ISBN-10: 1-111-53176-5

**South-Western**
5191 Natorp Boulevard
Mason, OH 45040
USA

Cengage Learning is a leading provider of customized learning solutions with office locations around the globe, including Singapore, the United Kingdom, Australia, Mexico, Brazil, and Japan. Locate your local office at: **www.cengage.com/global**

To learn more about South-Western, visit **www.cengage.com/ South-Western**

Purchase any of our products at your local college store or at our preferred online store **www.cengagebrain.com**

Printed in the United States of America
1 2 3 4 5 6 7 15 14 13 12 11

# CONTENTS IN BRIEF

# CONTENTS

# PREFACE

J ob hunting—particularly when the economy is tight and unemployment is high—can be a daunting task. For many students, just the thought of beginning the job search process can cause more butterflies in the stomach than final exams.

*The Ultimate Job Hunter's Guidebook* demystifies the job hunt and provides specific, easy-to-implement and creative strategies for achieving a successful outcome. Broken into its simplest parts and tackled methodically, a job search can be a rewarding pursuit that helps the individual grow personally and professionally.

## Organization of This Book

A theme that weaves its way through each chapter of this book is that job hunting should be looked upon as a marathon, not a sprint. Whether in job hunting or marathon running, success requires hard work over time, steadfast dedication, and a never-give-up attitude. In that light, *The Ultimate Job Hunter's Guidebook* breaks the job search process into four basic parts.

The first, *Setting Your Course*, encourages job hunters to take time to strategize and then organize their search. They must have an understanding of their strengths and the direction they plan to take.

The next section, *Gathering Your Tools*, helps arm the job seeker with a powerful job hunting arsenal, including effective cover letters, a strong résumé, letters of recommendation, and a personal website or portfolio.

*Hunting for an Employer* follows, providing information on the best ways to be resourceful in unearthing all available positions. It includes many specific tactics that incorporate social networking. It also covers the exploration of career alternatives and nontraditional strategies for finding satisfying employment.

Finally, Part Four, *Beginning the Search*, focuses on the crucial steps of applying and interviewing for the job. It concludes with guidance on evaluating job offers and learning a new position.

Each section of *The Ultimate Job Hunter's Guidebook* offers practical advice delivered in a straightforward style along with action-oriented examples that can easily be followed. Students will find this text useful as they embark on their new career and in years to come as they progress in their chosen profession.

## New Features

In addition to updating the material in *The Ultimate Job Hunter's Guidebook, Sixth Edition*, we've added some important new features. This edition includes an information-packed chapter on using such social networks as LinkedIn, Facebook, and Twitter in the job search. It also explains how and why today's job seekers must actively manage their online reputation.

At the beginning of each chapter, students are asked to take a "What Do You Know?" quiz. This lets them test their current knowledge of the topic to be covered. The quiz is followed by the "Chapter Focus," which lists 4–8 key points that will be examined in the chapter. Finally, "Real-Life Relevance" explains why the information in the chapter will be useful in the job hunt.

The end of each chapter also includes some interesting features. Students will enjoy "Success Stories," brief anecdotes detailing the many paths other job hunters have traveled to reach their career goals. Their stories are inspirational, motivational, and, most of all, educational. "Chapter Follow-Up" concludes the subject matter by offering a bulleted summary of the key points that were covered.

As in previous editions, the text includes many samples of job hunting tools, such as résumés and cover letters from a wide variety of career fields. Students can use these samples as virtual templates, substituting their own information into the established format.

The text also offers many hands-on activities and thought-provoking questions for the job hunter to consider either alone or in group discussions. And throughout each chapter is heavy emphasis on employing the latest technologies and online tools at every phase of the job hunt.

## Companion Website

Because we believe that one of the keys to a successful job hunt is to gather as much information as possible, we've created a comprehensive website as a companion tool for *The Ultimate Job Hunter's Guidebook, Sixth Edition*. The website expands on many of the subjects covered in the text to enhance teaching and learning. To aid in classroom lectures, downloadable PowerPoint slides and discussion questions are available on the Instructor Website.

The Student Website offers chapter summaries and self-tests to deepen understanding of the *guidebook's* material as well as direct links to many other useful career websites. You can visit the companion website for the text at www.cengagebrain.com.

*Susan D. Greene*
*Melanie C. L. Martel*

# Part One

## Setting Your Course

# Chapter 1

# Planning Your Job Search

## What Do You Know?

### Short Answers

1. What do you think are the first three steps of the job hunt?

   _____

   _____

2. What tools do you think a job hunter needs?

   _____

   _____

3. What role do social networking sites play in the job hunt?

   _____

   _____

**Chapter Focus**

In this chapter, you'll learn to:
- Identify the steps in the job hunting process.
- Begin to create a strategic plan for successful employment.

**Real-Life Relevance**

A job hunter with an overview of the big picture of the job hunt always knows what action item to tackle next. Approaching the job hunt as a step-by-step process makes it more successful and less stressful.

# Job Search Step One: Setting Your Course

The first few steps of the job hunt focus on choosing a direction, setting goals, and deciding on a strategy for reaching those goals. Although some new job hunters may be eager to get started, careful planning at the outset will ensure better results. The sections that follow outline these preliminary measures in detail and point to the chapters that offer even further explanation and clarification.

## Conducting a Self-Assessment (see Chapter 2)

The first step in job hunting is to find out about yourself and your desires. Decide what you'd really like to do. What are your skills and capabilities? What are your values and interests? A little soul-searching at the start of your job hunt can pay big dividends.

If you're still unsure of a career direction after your first attempts at self-assessment, explore the many career self-assessment tools that are available to you, and if necessary, consider enlisting the help of a career professional from your community or your college. After you've learned about yourself, you'll be better able to determine the type of employment you're seeking.

When you've a sense of your own strengths and skills and what kind of work you'd like to do, begin focusing on what you'd like in an employer. How large a company would you like to work for? What geographic area would be best? What work environment do you envision?

Begin the search by compiling a Top Ten List of job possibilities and then prepare for the next step: targeting and strategizing your job hunt.

## Targeting and Strategizing for the Hunt (see Chapter 3)

Now that you've developed a list of potential careers that interest you, the next step is to research those possibilities to narrow the list. Determine what you need to know about your potential career and then develop a list of research questions. Search online and perhaps at your library to find the answers to your questions.

Research different fields to find a career that matches your skills and your desires. Visit your college's career planning and placement office, gather facts and statistics about various careers online, and conduct informational interviews and job shadow people whose careers are potential options for you. If you're still unsure, continue to expand your base of information. Use all the resources available to you to gather as much information as possible about different careers. Choose one or two careers to start your research, and take some pressure off yourself by remembering that very few people stay in the same career over their lifetime. The job you're seeking now is only the first step in a series of career moves.

### Organizing the Job Hunt (see Chapter 4)

Once you've determined a career direction, take some time to create a job hunting headquarters and then map out a plan. Realize that your job hunt will progress more smoothly if you're organized. Assemble your organizational tools, such as to-do lists and spreadsheets, so you can locate and use as many job hunting documents as you need. Have a plan to maintain a positive attitude and avoid job hunting burnout.

Evaluate how you want to manage your time, noting the time management and organizational habits of people you consider to be successful. Decide what job hunting strategies will yield the biggest results.

Finally, be sure to take care of your physical and emotional well-being. Job hunting can be stressful, and in order to reach your goals, you must learn to make your stress work for you.

## Job Search Step Two: Gathering Your Tools

The next phase of the job hunt involves composing and finding all the documents you'll need to best present yourself to potential employers. Having a well-prepared résumé and some glowing letters of recommendation as well as a few samples of your work will give you a sense of confidence before you begin interviewing.

### Preparing Your Résumé (see Chapter 5)

If you were building a home, you'd use the very best tools available to you so the process would be easier and the outcome would be better. Similarly, when you build your career, it is important to use quality tools. Examine all the résumés you can find. Rely on your best judgment, but take into account the advice of those who work in your desired field. Make decisions about which format, font and wording you prefer. Write a few rough drafts, and get feedback from trusted friends and professionals. A neat, well-written, and error-free résumé will not only give you confidence throughout your job search but also get you in the door and provide you with the opportunity to sell yourself at the job interview. You may find it beneficial to develop several versions of your résumé tailored to the various jobs you'd consider.

### Writing Cover Letters (see Chapter 6)

You've all your tools—self-assessment, résumé, and research—and now you're ready to use them. Write a cover letter (also called a letter of application) to each employer with your résumé. Your cover letter will give you the chance to state which position you're applying for, mention your strong points, and ask for an interview. You'll probably need to develop several versions and review your drafts with others to double-check your wording and format. Be sure to address your cover letter to a specific person whenever possible. Remember that the best person to send your cover letter to is the person who would be your immediate supervisor, not the human resources department.

### Obtaining References (see Chapter 7)

What supporting documents can you supply that will support your assertion that you're a talented individual who is ready and able to work?

The most common supporting documents—letters of reference—can be valuable in convincing an employer to hire you. References serve as third-party endorsements testifying to the quality of your work and character. You can obtain letters of recommendation from previous employers, teachers, or anyone else you've known professionally. It is never too early to start soliciting letters of recommendation. You should also help potential employers to hire you by laying the groundwork for solid telephone references.

### Building a Portfolio or Personal Website (see Chapter 8)

If possible, also gather samples of relevant work, your writing, any special projects you've completed, awards you've received, or articles written about you or your work. Assemble these documents into a portfolio that you'll present to potential employers at the interview. Creating an e-portfolio for posting on your personal website is another excellent way to present your credentials and skills.

## Job Search Step Three: Hunting for an Employer

At this stage, you've amassed the self-knowledge and the tools so you can confidently present yourself to employers. Now you're ready to focus your search on specific employers and expand your network of contacts.

### Finding Potential Employers (see Chapter 9)

Who employs people with your skills? Which companies are best, and which positions within them are likely to fit you best? There are many places where you can look for answers to these questions.

Begin by networking. Your most valuable source of information is other people. Contact everyone you know to let them know about your career goals. Solicit names of others who might be able to help and keep track of all your contacts. Be persistent and thorough. Let everyone you know help with your job search. Ask questions of friends, relatives, and coworkers. See what you can learn from members of your church, health club, social organizations, or professional groups. Person-to-person contact will provide you with current information and the inside scoop on certain companies or careers. Talking with people is a great way to begin establishing your network. It is also valuable preparation for the interview and an increasingly important skill in the workplace.

Next, generate job leads by searching job boards and company websites, finding want ads, and researching companies. Check out manufacturing and industrial directories. Find the appropriate professional journals to see what newspapers and magazines have to say about a particular company or a general career field. Attend job fairs and trade shows. Libraries and college placement offices often have information on local companies and smaller businesses. The local chamber of commerce or professional and business associations can provide you with helpful literature.

All your reading and networking should pay off with a long list of possible employers. Narrow this list to employers that meet the requirements you set in the first phases of your job search. Set aside organizations that are outside your geographical range or do not employ people in the type of position you seek.

Now that you've a strong working list, do a bit more researching companies online and by writing to or calling potential employers to request any public relations information, sales literature, or annual reports they are willing to send you. Use these materials or your telephone skills to learn the name of the person who makes the hiring decisions at each workplace. This is usually the person who would be your supervisor if you were hired for the job. When possible, avoid sending materials to the human resources office; one of its primary function is to screen out applicants!

## Social Networking and Your Online Reputation (see Chapter 10)

Learn to make social networking work for you during the job hunt. Use LinkedIn, Facebook, Twitter, and other business networking sites to expand your circle of contacts and get job leads. Integrate social networking with traditional networking, and begin building your personal brand. Just be mindful of your online image; scrutinize your own sites and check mentions of you on others' sites to be sure your professional reputation stays professional.

## Have You Considered . . .? (see Chapter 11)

Unearth and evaluate all the appropriate job possibilities, including positions with the federal, state, and local government or with nonprofit organizations. Seek out smaller businesses or even start your own business. Finally, evaluate whether furthering your education or training would create better opportunities for you.

## Job Hunting in Tough Times (see Chapter 12)

Try accessing the job market by using nontraditional methods or by working in a different type of position from the one you originally envisioned. This may be a part-time position or a position remotely related to your main career interest. Explore achieving career success by working as an intern, a freelancer, or a volunteer.

Keeping an open mind and a multifaceted approach to the job hunt will increase your chances of finding a truly satisfying career.

# Job Search Step Four: Beginning the Search

You've decided on a career field and located an employer that offers you the best match for your skills, interests, and needs. You've created a résumé that highlights your strengths and written a cover letter that's allowed you to get your foot in the door. You've finally arrived for a face-to-face meeting. Now is the time to make a good impression, present your strengths, and land the job.

## Filling Out Job Applications (see Chapter 13)

Some employers may want you to complete a company application form before considering you for a job. This small first step is your initial chance to show the employer the quality of your work. Brush up on the information these forms require so you'll feel comfortable when the time comes to complete one. Be sure you know how to complete hard copy and online applications on job boards, on company websites, or at hiring kiosks.

## Interviewing (see Chapter 14)

Once the date has been set for your interview, begin practicing your interviewing techniques. Prepare a list of personal and professional references to bring with you. Research the company at which you'll be interviewing. Find the company or organization's website, and gather any literature it publishes. Also prepare your own list of questions about the company and the job. The more you know about the company or organization and the position you're interviewing for, the better prepared you'll be.

Arrive for your interview on time and looking your best. Be ready to answer the interviewer's questions intelligently and completely, presenting yourself with poise and confidence. Watch your body language, voice, and mannerisms.

Consider each interview a learning experience, and be prepared to evaluate yourself after each one. Whatever you do, remember that your work is not finished once the interview is over. Think of ways to improve your job hunting skills, and follow up the interview with a thank-you note, e-mail messages, and telephone calls to remind the employer that you're interested and qualified.

Because the costs of hiring and training new employees are so high, employers continually seek ways to weed out poor candidates. Some of the employment tests you may encounter are drug tests, aptitude tests, psychological tests, and medical exams. A prepared job applicant will anticipate this step.

When the preliminary phases of the job search have proved successful, a few long-anticipated steps remain. You'll need to evaluate the possibilities you've worked so hard to create, and after accepting a job, you'll need to be sure that your employment gets off to a strong start—all the while keeping an eye on your plans for the future.

## Evaluating Job Offers (see Chapter 15)

Once you've been offered one or more jobs, your job hunt may be over, but you now face a decision that will have a huge impact on your life. Learn to identify employment scams and how to negotiate salary offers. Then, carefully weigh all your options to make the career choice that is best for you.

## Learning Your New Job (see Chapter 16)

The first few months on the job are often fraught with challenges as you meet new people and begin to learn your specific responsibilities. You may want to adjust your work habits in order to fit in at your workplace. You'll need to hone your skills, manage workplace relationships, take in a tremendous amount of information, and learn about the corporate culture of your new workplace.

Review the four major steps of the job hunt outlined in this chapter and the many smaller steps described in each of the following chapters. Some of the steps may be new to you, but there may be others that you've already accomplished. For example, you may have a good idea of the type of job you'd like, although you may not have the tools you need to get it. Or you may have developed a draft of your résumé for a job search in the past, but you're no longer certain of what career path to take. No matter what stage you find yourself in, an exploration of the steps explained in the following chapter, "Conducting a Self-assessment," followed up by a special focus on the areas most in need of improvement—will make your job hunt a more efficient, less anxious, and more rewarding experience.

---

**EXERCISE**    **Step-by-Step Confidence Check**

In the blank spaces to the left below, indicate your own comfort level with each of the following job search steps. Begin by rating each step on a scale of 1 to 10, with 1 indicating a very low level of confidence or preparation and 10 indicating a very high level of preparedness.

| Rating | Job Search Step | Post-Exploration Rating |
|---|---|---|
| _____ | **1.** Conducting a self-assessment | _____ |
| _____ | **2.** Planning and organizing the job hunt | _____ |
| _____ | **3.** Preparing a résumé | _____ |
| _____ | **4.** Writing cover letters | _____ |
| _____ | **5.** Obtaining references | _____ |
| _____ | **6.** Assembling a portfolio | _____ |
| _____ | **7.** Targeting employers | _____ |
| _____ | **8.** Job hunting online | _____ |

| | | |
|---|---|---|
| _____ | **9.** Considering all career alternatives | _____ |
| _____ | **10.** Accessing the job market in nontraditional ways | _____ |
| _____ | **11.** Filling out job applications | _____ |
| _____ | **12.** Interviewing | _____ |
| _____ | **13.** Taking employment tests | _____ |
| _____ | **14.** Evaluating job offers | _____ |
| _____ | **15.** Learning the new job | _____ |

Now circle the three areas that you gave the lowest ratings. Skim the Table of Contents, and list the chapter numbers in this book that address your concerns.

Area 1: _____   Area 2: _____   Area 3: _____

After you've had time to explore your target chapters more deeply, review and renumber each item on the list again—this time using the column of blank spaces at the right. Note your areas of improvement as well as areas that still need more work. Which resources will you seek out or revisit in order to address your lowest-scoring areas?

## SUCCESS STORIES

Often, the greatest inspiration comes from those who have succeeded. Consider the following success stories from job hunters who were once like you!

I knew I had a great résumé, so why couldn't I find a satisfying job? I realized I had no plan and no solid idea of what else I needed to do besides write that résumé. I started reading everything I could find about job hunting, and I began to look at the job hunt as a project, with many specific steps and a very clear, desired outcome. I became more systematic in my approach and found I was much more relaxed at interviews. Once I became more informed about the process, everything turned around.

Liza
*Events Planner*

I suddenly realized that not only was I stagnating in my current position [at a small company] but also that if I left my current job, I had no real idea of how to find a new one at a larger company. I reviewed all the stages of job hunting, trying to gain confidence from the fact that although my résumé was outdated, I was very confident in my career goals and my job skills. I also discovered that I had a good sense of the best employers for people in my field. Suddenly, the task before me went from overwhelming to very specific, and I was able to get interviews in a relatively short time.

Colton

*Employee Assistance Program Specialist*

## Chapter Follow-Up

By familiarizing yourself with the steps of job hunting, you can better plan, prepare and organize your search. An overview of the process will give you more confidence about what tasks come next and which ones you've already completed, and it will ultimately help you be more successful in finding the right job.

# Chapter 2

# Conducting a Self-Assessment

## What Do You Know?

### True or False

\_\_\_\_\_ 1. The average worker focuses in on one career at an early age and continues to move up in that profession over a lifetime.

\_\_\_\_\_ 2. Most people are certain of which career they'd like to pursue by age 20.

\_\_\_\_\_ 3. Personal interests add variety and depth to life but aren't an important factor in choosing a career.

\_\_\_\_\_ 4. Personal values such as need for variety or personal time are not large factors when choosing a profession.

\_\_\_\_\_ 5. Many job seekers could achieve improved results if they made a few personal improvements.

\_\_\_\_\_ 6. Time spent gaining input from family and friends on their perspective of your strengths and weaknesses would be better than diving immediately into the job hunt.

## Chapter Focus

In this chapter, you'll learn to:

- Understand the importance of self-assessment in the career search process.
- Understand that the career search process repeats itself over a lifetime.
- Understand the different facets of self-assessment.
- Learn where to find different self-assessment tools.
- Look closely at your career interests, strengths, and temperament.
- Use the perspectives of others as well as your own insights.

- Formulate strategies for personal and professional improvement.
- Develop a Top Ten List of potential careers.

## Real-Life Relevance

A clear picture of your professional and personal assets is essential to choosing a career path. Without this basic understanding, your job hunt will lack direction and results, and even if it turns out to be successful, it could lead to a frustrating and unfulfilling career.

# Know Yourself

Self-examination is an important step in the job hunting process. It involves gaining a thorough understanding of your values, your interests, your support system, your temperament, your skills, the benefits you've gained from all your previous employment experiences, and a strong sense of your personal and professional goals. Although it may seem a time-consuming distraction from the task of getting your name out to potential employers, it will give direction and focus to your search. You'll be better equipped to zero in on the right kind of job, and you'll stand out to employers as someone who really knows what he or she wants.

## An Important First Step

Too many job hunters have a knee-jerk reaction to the intense pressure that accompanies choosing a major or choosing a profession after having completed a college degree. Some automatically fall into the family business, while others take the first job opening that comes along. Some who find themselves suddenly unemployed automatically seek employment in a field they've tried before, even though they may not have enjoyed their former job. Before choosing a career in haste, it is vital that you take some time to understand your own particular skills, values, and interests. Honest self-examination might also reveal some areas in your personal or professional arena that need improvement.

The ability to assess yourself in order to choose the next career step is not only important, but it is also a lifelong skill. The Bureau of Labor Statistics reports that the average baby-boomer worker holds approximately ten jobs between the ages of 18 and 42, and younger workers are predicted to hold even more (http://www.bls.gov/nls/y79r22jobsbyedu.pdf). The process of evaluating yourself and choosing the right career path repeats itself over a lifetime. So, the question to begin with is not which job would you like to do for life but which job would you like to do next?

**EXERCISE**   ## Where Do You Stand?

Complete the following exercise to understand how complete your self-understanding really is.

Mark an X on the line at the appropriate spot between 1 and 10.

*Self-Assessment Area*

1_____5 _____ 10
(Totally Unsure)                    (Somewhat Sure)              (Completely Confident)

My values

1_____5 _____ 10

My skills

1_____5 _____ 10

My temperament

1_____5 _____ 10

My interests

1_____5 _____ 10

My certainty about my career choice

1_____5 _____ 10

*Reflection*

Which area or areas are strongest? Which are the weakest? What do you know for sure? What information do you need to gather now?

_____

_____

_____

_____

_____

## Your Top Ten List

Perhaps you've always known which career was right for you or perhaps you've had a mentor or teacher who has already helped you create your career goals. However, for the unsure or undecided, rather than trying to make a quick choice of the perfect career that will provide satisfaction for a lifetime, a more realistic first task would be to develop your Top Ten List of potential careers. Your Top Ten List is a well thought out list of careers that match your values, skills, temperament, and interests. You may have not have exactly ten career possibilities on your list, but the principle is the same. Committing your options to paper is a simple, nonthreatening way to sort through a difficult decision. Eventually, after conducting some research and reevaluating your list, you'll be able to confidently narrow your list to one or two career goals.

## What You'll Need to Develop Your Top Ten

Determining the following pieces of the puzzle will help you form a complete picture of yourself, your top ten, and ultimately, your job objective. Begin by understanding the following items:

- **Your values.** What is important to you personally and professionally? What are your priorities?
- **Your skills.** What are you good at? What tasks can you perform competently? What are your natural talents? What have you gained from your education and training? What skills have you developed through life experience?
- **Your temperament.** What kind of person are you? Where do you find your source of energy? How do you gather and use information? What types of personalities do you enjoy working and spending time with?
- **Your interests.** What types of things bring you enjoyment and satisfaction?

## How to Develop Your Top Ten

After you determine which areas of your career goal puzzle you would like to learn more about, you need to decide how to gather the necessary information. There are three places to look to find the answers to clarifying each of the variables that factor into your career goal.

**Look Within.**   Begin by analyzing your own thoughts and experiences. Journaling, creating lists, or developing information webs can lead to important self-discoveries.

---

**EXERCISE**   **Uncovering Interests**

Write a brief journal entry in response to the following:

When imaging my future career as a child, I always wanted to be _____

_____

_____ .

If anything were possible, the one job I would truly look forward to going to each day would be _____

_____

_____.

If I had the time and money in the world, I'd most like to spend my time

_____

_____.

Some of the things that have always come naturally to me include

_____.

What do the statements you've written tell you about your dreams, interests, and abilities? In what types of careers could you put them to use? List these careers on your Top Ten List.

**EXERCISE**    **Drafting Your Top Ten List**

Now you've done some self-analysis. Have some career possibilities presented themselves? Perhaps as you've been trying to decide, one or two careers keep resurfacing as front-runners. Brainstorm and list all the possibilities here. Do not worry about the order of the items; just attempt to list your best options. After conducting an assessment of your career priorities, utilizing the Web to research different careers in addition to enlisting the help of family, friends, and career professionals, you can return to this list and begin shortening and prioritizing it.

1. _____

2. _____

3. _____

4. _____

5. _____

6. _____

7. _____

8. _____

9. _____

10. _____

**EXERCISE**   ## Summary of Strengths

Fill out the following questionnaire, and refer to it to help you choose a career direction or when you need a morale boost, such as perhaps just before an interview.

**1.** My best personality trait is _____.

**2.** The course in which I did best in school was _____.

**3.** I am good at _____.

**4.** A skill I mastered quickly is _____.

**5.** What I like best about working is _____.

**6.** Good things my teachers or employers have said about me include _____

_____.

**7.** I often receive compliments on _____

_____.

**8.** I have a special talent for _____

_____.

**9.** One obstacle I've overcome is _____

_____.

**10.** I received an award or recognition for _____

_____.

**11.** My most valuable work skill is _____

_____.

**12.** People enjoy working with me because _____

_____.

Re-examine your responses to the questions above. Below, write a brief, specific example of a circumstance that illustrates one of your responses. Focus specifically on the following items from the list above (the numbers correspond to those in that list):

**5.** _____

**7.** _____

**8.** _____

**9.** _____

**11.** _____

Does your skill set suggest any possible careers? After consideration or researching by speaking with others or searching for information, you may be able to make a connection between your skills and a suitable profession. List the possibilities on your Top Ten List.

**EXERCISE**   ## Setting Career Priorities: Evaluate Your Priorities

As you progress in your career, moving from your first job up the ladder of success, you may find that your priorities change. They may be influenced by such variables as your economic needs, your marital status, your career goals, your desire for personal time, and your family needs.

Take a moment to consider your priorities in life. For example, if you're seeking your first job, your goal may likely be to obtain a position that will give you good training and serve as a stepping-stone to more advanced positions. If you've young children, you may prefer a job that does not require any overtime or weekend hours so you can spend time with your family.

Look over the following list of job and personal variables. In the left-hand column, number them in order of priority to you. Renumber them in the right-hand column based on the priorities you anticipate having five or ten years down the road.

| Priorities Now | Job and Personal Variables | Priorities in Ten Years |
|---|---|---|
| _____ | Salary | _____ |
| _____ | Family (children/spouse/parent) | _____ |
| _____ | Personal time | _____ |
| _____ | Job location | _____ |
| _____ | Work-related travel | _____ |
| _____ | Potential for advancement | _____ |
| _____ | Commuting time | _____ |
| _____ | Friendly coworkers | _____ |
| _____ | Compatible supervisor | _____ |
| _____ | Job responsibilities | _____ |
| _____ | Personal hobbies | _____ |
| _____ | Prestige | _____ |

| | | |
|---|---|---|
| _____ | Benefits | _____ |
| _____ | Vacation time | _____ |
| _____ | Retirement plan | _____ |
| _____ | Security/stability | _____ |
| _____ | Personal growth/fulfillment | _____ |
| _____ | Exposure to new skills | _____ |
| _____ | Other | _____ |

## Look Online

Numerous self-assessment inventories are available online—some free and some for a fee. There is no harm in perusing the various websites and taking the free inventories and tests. Some people use these tools to learn more about their skills or interests or simply to find a direction they feel has potential. Several sites even review many of the available assessment tools, informing you of fees and limitations of each assessment. (www.quintcareers.com/online_assessment_review.html and http://rileyguide.com/assess.html are good examples of helpful sites.)

Unfortunately, there are no guarantees about the reliability of your results or the validity of these tests. Nor do the sites offering the assessments offer assistance with interpreting and piecing together the information you do unearth. In many cases, the old adage is true: You get what you pay for. On the other hand, you can maximize what you do get from these online assessments by completing several of them and trusting your own instincts. The same overall results tend to appear again and again and can yield some helpful information. List the suggested careers that are indicated in more than one test on your Top Ten List.

**EXERCISE**    ### Discovering Your Temperament

Personality inventories, such at the Myers-Briggs Type Indicator (MBTI), assess temperament, define how you relate to others, take in information, make decisions, and organize your world. People of certain temperaments tend to be most satisfied in careers suited to those temperaments. To uncover your temperament, you can see a career counselor or the career planning office at your college or university and take the MBTI to see what light it can shed on the type of career choice that might be right for you. A licensed professional will administer and interpret the MBTI for you. (Slightly less valid but still very helpful is a similar free version of the inventory called the Jung Typology Test, which can be found at humanmetrics.com.) Once you've determined your temperament, read the accompanying descriptions and lists of suggested careers carefully, and go back online to search for careers well suited to your type. Most people are surprised to see that some or more of the careers identified as suitable to their temperament are the very ones that they have long considered or wished for. Add the careers you find most suitable to your Top Ten List.

## Look to Others

Although you may find some information that your intuition and common sense tell you is worthwhile, another helpful way to learn about yourself is with the assistance of a professional career counselor, who uses effective assessment instruments in a controlled environment.

Many colleges and universities have career counselors on staff, and some offer courses in career planning and placement. Professional career counselors can also be located through your state office of employment security, phone directory, or online. These professionals use tests that have been carefully studied and proven reliable. They can also take the time to help you make sense of the results. A word of advice: Be sure to understand the fee structures before engaging a career counselor's services. The costs of career assistance vary greatly, according to the expertise of the counselor, the location of the counselor, the time involved, and the types of assessment used. For example, the services of the career center at your college are free to enrolled students, but the services of a credentialed psychologist trained to administer reliable career inventories can cost several hundred dollars an hour, which may or may not be covered by your health insurance.

**A career counselor can help you identify your strengths and focus on your career goals.**
(Kathy Sloane/Photo Researchers, Inc.)

Many job seekers also look to family and friends to offer advice and a more objective perspective. Those who know you well and offer support and useful viewpoints are valuable resources at every stage of the job hunt.

**EXERCISE**   **Valued Perspectives**

One step that helps many job hunters assess their strengths and goals is to gather the impressions of those they trust and respect. The perspectives of others are often eye opening, and those insights have special impact when several people note the same strengths or weakness. What do the off-the-cuff descriptions of others indicate to you? What themes emerge?

**Step 1:** Interview five people who know you well and whose opinions you value. Write their names below. Then, ask each person to list ten words to describe you, and write them here. (Be sure not to let participants see one another's responses.)

| Name 1 | Name 2 | Name 3 | Name 4 | Name 5 |
|---|---|---|---|---|
| 1. | | | | |
| 2. | | | | |
| 3. | | | | |
| 4. | | | | |
| 5. | | | | |
| 6. | | | | |
| 7. | | | | |
| 8. | | | | |
| 9. | | | | |
| 10. | | | | |

**Step 2:** List the words that tend to be repeated or that you feel are especially accurate.

**Step 3:** Add any words you think describe you that are not included in the above lists.

**Step 4:** Rank all the adjectives listed above as they relate to your career success.

1. _____    6. _____

2. _____    7. _____

3. _____    8. _____

4. _____    9. _____

5. _____    10. _____

**Step 5:** Examine the common themes and patterns of these responses. Usually, those who know you well will indicate whether your talents lie in dealing with people, data, or ideas. What seem to be the most common strengths listed by those you surveyed?

_____

**Step 6:** Brainstorm for connections: How do these strengths translate into job skills? Although answering this question is difficult, it is essential. For example, if your friends and family have all noted your outgoing personality or unflappable disposition, you might be well suited for a career that involves working with the public in a sales capacity or service industry. If they've noted you're detail oriented and logical, you might begin exploring a career in computer programming or technical support.

You may need the assistance of a professor, a business professional in one of the fields you're considering, or a career counselor, but be sure to carefully examine the links between your strengths and their workplace applications.

How do these personality traits translate into job skills?

_____

Or worded another way, list three to five job skills here:

1. _____

2. _____

3. _____

4. _____

5. _____

Understanding yourself through this exercise will help you when choosing a career, writing a job objective or summary of skills on your résumé, and preparing for an interview. List career choices that match your skills on the Top Ten List on page 15.

# Take Action to Be Your Best

One final step when assessing yourself is to determine what improvements you can make to increase your chances of success. When you feel good about yourself, others can sense your self-confidence. Probably no other quality will make you more marketable as you search for a job. As you begin your job hunt and are developing a sense of your individual strengths, it is also a good time to make some positive moves toward improving how you look and feel as well as how you perform in the workplace.

**EXERCISE**

## Areas in Need of Improvement

First, read this list, and check the actions that you would like to take. Then, write a strategy for how you plan to make a change. Remember that the first step in making a positive change is recognizing a problem. The next step is creating a specific plan to remedy it.

**Items I would like to change** (check all that apply):

*Personal Improvements*

_____ **1.** Exercise more.

_____ **2.** Lose weight.

_____ **3.** Improve my posture.

_____ **4.** Smile more.

_____ **5.** Upgrade my wardrobe.

_____ **6.** Speak more clearly.

_____ **7.** Clean up my language.

_____ **8.** Stop smoking.

_____ **9.** Become a better listener.

_____ **10.** Improve my manners.

_____ **11.** Pay more attention to personal hygiene.

_____ **12.** Become more comfortable speaking with others.

_____ **13.** Improve my health or dental health.

_____ **14.** Other:_____

*Professional Improvements*

_____ **15.** Computer skills

_____ **16.** Writing ability

_____ **17.** Public speaking

_____ **18.** Technical skills

_____ **19.** Other:

(You may need additional space to develop your plans.)

Now develop a strategy for improving each item you've identified. For example:

_____ **15.** Computer skills

Strategy: Add one small, measurable skill to my computer expertise each week. Learn to do spreadsheets or attempt a new word processing program. Start where I feel comfortable and visit my college's learning center, community education division, or local adult education center to get more help.

List your top three areas in need of improvement, along with a specific strategy for each:

Item number: _____

Strategy: _____

_____

_____

Item number: _____

Strategy: _____

_____

_____

Item number: _____

Strategy: _____

_____

_____

# Choose the Right Job for You

Finally, as you choose a direction for your job hunt, it's important for you to clarify your thoughts about the type of position you might like and the type of company for which you'd like to work. Once you've answered these questions, you'll be better prepared to market yourself and to find jobs that most appeal to you.

**EXERCISE**  **Evaluating Career Variables**

Answer the following questions. Refer back to this questionnaire when you're evaluating a particular position to see if it meets your desires.

**1.** I want to work for a company with
- ❏ under ten employees.
- ❏ under one hundred employees.
- ❏ several hundred employees.
- ❏ several thousand employees.

**2.** It's important for me to be in a position with potential for advancement.
- ❏ True    ❏ False

**3.** I want a job that requires
- ❏ a lot of creativity.
- ❏ some creativity.
- ❏ no creativity.

**4.** I want a position with
- ❏ a lot of responsibility.
- ❏ minimum responsibility.

**5.** I want a job with the following hours:
- ❏ nine to five
- ❏ part-time
- ❏ flexible scheduling
- ❏ potential for overtime

**6.** I want to work for a company that
- ❏ promotes from within.
- ❏ brings in new people regularly.

**7.** In doing my job, I think I would like to
- ❏ juggle a variety of responsibilities.
- ❏ be responsible for one main function.

**8.** I would like a job that involves working with
- ❏ people.
- ❏ data.
- ❏ products.

**9.** I would like to work for a
- ❏ public company.
- ❏ private company.

**10.** I want to work for a company that is
- ❏ growing rapidly.
- ❏ maintaining its status quo.

**11.** I want to work for a company located
- ❏ within walking distance of my home.
- ❏ no more than a half-hour drive away.
- ❏ no more than an hour's drive away.
- ❏ I will relocate for a job.

**12.** I want a position with
- ❏ a lot of structure.
- ❏ minimal structure and an informal environment.

**13.** I like work that is
- ❏ routine.
- ❏ full of variety.

**14.** I enjoy working
- ❏ in teams and groups.
- ❏ by myself.

**15.** I enjoy working with
- ❏ my hands.
- ❏ my mind.
- ❏ my hands and my mind.

**16.** I enjoy working with
- ❏ computers.
- ❏ machines.
- ❏ neither computers nor machines.

**17.** I want to work for a company that
- ❏ allows employees to dress casually.
- ❏ requires employees to dress professionally.

**18.** I want a job that has
- ❏ no stress or low stress.
- ❏ medium stress.
- ❏ high stress.

**19.** I want a job that entails
- ❏ no travel.
- ❏ some travel.
- ❏ lots of travel.

**20.** I enjoy work that involves
- ❏ talking on the phone.
- ❏ face-to-face interaction.
- ❏ mostly written correspondence.
- ❏ minimal interaction with coworkers and customers.

**21.** I want a job that requires a
- ❏ high school diploma or equivalent.
- ❏ college degree.
- ❏ graduate degree.

**22.** I want to work in an environment that
- ❏ does not allow smoking.
- ❏ permits smoking in specified areas.

**23.** To me, opportunities for training are
- ❏ very important.
- ❏ somewhat important.
- ❏ not important.

**24.** I want to spend most of my workday
- ❏ outdoors.
- ❏ indoors.

**25.** I want a position that pays in the following range:
$ _____ to $ _____

**26.** Medical benefits are important to me.
- ❏ True        ❏ False

**27.** I want to work for a company that encourages further education and offers tuition reimbursement.
- ❏ True        ❏ False

**28.** To me, having a job title with a lot of prestige is
- ❏ very important.
- ❏ somewhat important.
- ❏ not important.

**29.** When I picture myself at work, I envision myself doing

_____

_____

in an environment that is

_____

_____

with supervision that could be described as

_____

_____

and with coworkers who

_____

_____

_____.

**SUCCESS STORIES**

Often, the greatest inspiration comes from those who have succeeded. Consider the following success stories from job hunters who were once like you!

I have always been interested in working with children and come from a large family. I worried that I wouldn't be able to support myself on the salaries offered in the field. Finally, I decided to do what I love, despite my misgivings. I began teaching at a small private elementary school and was promoted several times in my first few years there. I feel I have been noticed because my true enthusiasm and commitment to the children are clear.

Ana Maria
*Elementary School Vice Principal*

After graduation, I took a position as a manager at a bagel shop, just so I could have health benefits and steady income after graduation. Out of sheer frustration, I got permission to paint a large mural on the wall inside the restaurant. I have always been an artist but never knew how to turn my talents into a job. When the owner of the building saw my work, he commissioned me to paint murals in several of his other properties, and my name is becoming well known. I will soon be able to paint full time!

Jean
*Muralist*

I was an international relations major who was not quite sure how to use my new degree. The career counselor at my university helped me see that my strong communication skills, along with my interests in political science and international events, made me a good candidate for a management position in a large insurance company with a lot of international accounts.

Elise
*International Accounts Manager*

## Chapter Follow-Up

Conduct a thorough self-assessment before choosing a career path:

- Evaluate your skills, temperament, values, and interests.
- Use a variety of approaches to learn about yourself, including journaling, taking various career inventories, and soliciting assistance and feedback from career counselors as well as family and friends.
- Make personal and professional improvements to improve your chances for success.
- Evaluate career variables to get a clearer picture of the type of job you want.
- Draft a list of career possibilities so you can begin to research and narrow it.

## Chapter 3

# Targeting and Strategizing for the Hunt

## What Do You Know?

### Short Answers

1. List three ways to research a career that interests you.
   _____
   _____

2. How does an informational interview differ from a job interview?
   _____
   _____

3. What is job shadowing ? What's the best way to make a good impression when job shadowing?
   _____
   _____
   _____

## Chapter Focus

In this chapter, you'll learn to:

- Research career options to narrow your focus.
- Conduct informational interviews in order to learn more about which career you'd like to pursue.
- Job shadow to learn about a career firsthand.

## Real-Life Relevance

Using research, an effective job hunter is able to hone in on the best career path from a variety of options. Research can take many forms, including online research or conducting an informational interview either in person, on the phone, or via Skype or e-mail. Job shadowing is another form of research that gives the job hunter extremely helpful information about the day-to-day duties of a particular career. Finally, re-evaluating career goals, with all the facts in mind, should allow you to set off in the right direction.

## Narrowing Your Options

Conducting Career Research

If you've been unsure as to which career direction to choose, now is the time to gather information and to eliminate items from your list of possibilities. Good research can make clear how your skills, your values, and your temperament match different careers. Even if you've already narrowed your options, current research prepares you for the interview and for salary negations. One very reliable and helpful option for conducting research is the *Occupational Outlook Handbook* produced by the U.S. Bureau of Labor Statistics. Its website, www.bls.gov/oco, lists careers alphabetically and describes education and training, earnings, typical duties, working conditions, and predicted employment growth for hundreds of different jobs. Many college career planning offices also provide career research databases—often available to students and the general public alike. Similarly, many state employment offices and professional organizations provide current, helpful research on the careers within their profession.

---

**EXERCISE**    **Creating Research Questions**

Brainstorm a list of six to ten questions you need to know about a career you're considering. Begin with determining answers to the basic facts about the career, such as:

1. What are the job duties?

2. What is the salary range?

3. What is the employment outlook?

4. What qualifications are needed?

5. What are related professions?

6. What education and training are required?

Add your questions below:

7.

8.

9.

10.

Now choose one of the jobs on your list of potential career options (return to your Top Ten List in Chapter 2) and then write answers to these questions. Circle careers that are still good options; eliminate those that are not. Don't worry if many careers remain on your list. There is still time to narrow it.

## Conducting the Informational Interview

Conducting informational interviews is another excellent ways to investigate your career options. Speaking with a person who is actually doing the kind of work you're considering provides many insights that can't be gained any other way.

If you'd like to know more about a particular job, why not interview—by telephone, Skype, or in person—several people who hold positions in your chosen field? As long as you make it clear to the interviewees that you aren't asking for a job but rather an informational interview, you should have no problem finding willing participants.

## Arranging and Conducting Informational Interviews

Through networking, cold-calling, or personal contacts, find someone who works in your area of interest. Call or write to this person, and make your proposal. Explain that you aren't asking for a job but that you would like to find out about his or her field. Ask for fifteen to twenty minutes of time, and set up an appointment. Be sure to keep your session to that length. Listen carefully during the interview. Jot down a few notes, but maximize your time by writing out most of your notes and impressions after the interview. Have a copy of your résumé with you should your interviewer request to see it or to pass it along to a personal contact.

Follow-up is crucial. Immediately after the informational interview, write your contact a brief thank-you letter expressing appreciation for the information and the names of any other potential contacts he or she shared with you. (Example 3.1 is a sample of this type of thank-you letter.) Within the next two to three weeks, call or e-mail your contact with an update on what progress you've made, particularly with regard to any contacts he or she gave you. Thank this person again, and ask if he or she has heard of any new openings you should pursue. You may want to touch base with this person every month or so to start your network and keep your contact strong.

118 Blue Street
Atlanta, GA 30305


September 4, 2011


Ms. Janet Korbett
Appraiser
River Company, Inc.
Atlanta, GA 30312

Dear Ms. Korbett:

I just wanted to take a moment to thank you for meeting with me last week. I enjoyed hearing about your many responsibilities as a real estate appraiser for River Company.

    As I pursue my own career in appraising, I will keep in mind the information you provided to me. If you should hear of any job openings in the field, I would greatly appreciate your letting me know. Again, thank you for your time and your advice.

Sincerely,

*Susan Johns*

Susan Johns

**Example 3.1    THANK-YOU LETTER FOR AN INFORMATIONAL INTERVIEW**

## Getting the Most Out of Informational Interviews

Although every informational interview you conduct will be different, there are some cardinal rules to keep in mind.

- Be prepared.
- Be brief and courteous.
- Do not ask for a job.
- Follow up with a thank-you letter and an occasional phone call or e-mail.

Successful informational interviews can help you feel confident that you're focusing your job search on the right career area and are supplied with fresh, appropriate information.

To get the most out of an informational interview, you need to be fully prepared. Research the company and field on the Web, at your local library, or through any other resource you've available. Prepare a list of questions to bring to your interview, but don't feel strictly confined to your list. Rather, in the interview, pay close attention to the conversation, and focus on the areas that seem most relevant and interesting to you. Here are some general questions you can use to get started.

## Sample Questions for the Informational Interview

1. Tell me about being a [name of profession].
2. What do you do in a typical day?
3. Which duties do you like the most? The least?
4. How did you get into this field?
5. How is this field changing?
6. How do most people prepare for this job? What skills are needed?
7. What are the entry-level positions?
8. What other jobs are related to this one? Are there any particularly interesting specialties within this field?
9. How do people in this position go about advancing their careers?
10. What education or training is necessary for this position?
11. What personality traits are needed to be successful in this field?
12. What range could a person starting in this field expect?
13. What individuals and which companies are prominent in this field?
14. Could you give me names of people I might contact about openings in this field?
15. May I use your name in my introduction to those people?
16. What advice would you give someone who is entering this field?

EXERCISE **Preparing for Informational Interviews**

Write a few additional questions—either general or specifically related to your career of interest—that you could ask.

17. _____

18. _____

19. _____

20. _____

As mentioned earlier, send a gracious thank-you letter after each informational interview. Example 3.1 may help you start your own draft.

## Phone and E-mail Informational Interviews

When an in-person informational interview isn't practical or possible, another option is to interview someone in the field over the phone or by e-mail. If you can reach someone by phone and engage them in conversation, you'll get a wealth of information in a short amount of time.

If you can identify someone who would be a good source of information for you and you're able to obtain this person's e-mail address by calling the company receptionist or searching for it on the company's website, send the potential contact a brief letter explaining that you're new to the field and would greatly appreciate a few minutes of his or her time in answering some questions. Ask a maximum of five questions because most recipients will be put off by a lengthy questionnaire. The recipient won't want to write you an essay. So, make your questions specific, such as, "What are your daily responsibilities and what skills are most important to doing your job?" If necessary, ask follow-up questions, but be aware that you may be imposing on your source. As always, be sure to send a gracious and sincere thank-you reply to anyone who responds.

EXERCISE **Conduct an Informational Interview via E-mail**

Compose a brief e-mail in which you introduce yourself to someone in your field and ask three to five key questions that would help you gather information useful in your job hunt or career.

## Job Shadowing

For a more in-depth perspective, spend an afternoon or two observing someone at work in your targeted field. A job shadowing opportunity requires time and effort to set up, but it may be the best way to ascertain that your field of interest is truly suited to your skills, needs, and wants. Here's how to go about it:

1. Find a contact person who works in your targeted career field. Teachers, relatives, friends, and networking organizations may be able to suggest names. Your goal is to locate someone who is willing to show you the ropes and let you follow him or her through an average day and observe his or her daily work routine.

2. Make it clear to him or her that you don't plan to interfere in any way. Remain a silent, unobtrusive shadow; listen and observe. This is not the time to ask for a job, although you may want to make note of contact names for the future.

3. If you're persistent and savvy enough to set up a job shadowing day or two, you'll find your efforts amply rewarded. The insight you'll gain by observing the workplace and employee duties firsthand will give you a real taste of the field and a sense of whether it is right for you.

4. Follow up your informational interviews and job shadowing days with thank-you notes to everyone who shared their time and expertise with you. Make lists of questions you still need to research, re-evaluate the pros and cons of the career, and write down contact names that might be useful in the future.

**Job shadowing is a career exploration activity. It gives you an opportunity to observe professionals in your field as they perform their daily work activities.**

(Lisa F. Young / Alamy)

## Returning to Your Top Ten List

Now that you've conducted thorough research on the careers on your Top Ten List, conducted informational interviews, and perhaps even job shadowed, you should have a better idea of what careers are better suited for your temperament and for the skills and interests you've identified earlier. Circle the careers that still seem to be good choices, cross off those that no longer interest you. What do you still need to know?

# Focus and Refocus—Setting Career Goals

Targeting your career direction is important before you begin your job search and after you've landed a position. By setting goals, you can work toward meeting specific objectives, measure your success, and achieve a feeling of self-satisfaction. Remember that the most effective goals are measurable, are meaningful, and have a specific deadline. Check that all the goals that you list below meet those criteria.

**EXERCISE**    **Goal Setting**

Fill in the following blanks with your current goals, your goals for five years from now, and your goals for ten years from now.

1. **Type of job desired:**

   Current goal _____

   Five-year goal _____

   Ten-year goal _____

2. **Responsibilities you wish to have in your job:**

   Current goal _____

   Five-year goal _____

   Ten-year goal _____

3. **Skills you wish to master:**

   Current goal _____

   Five-year goal _____

   Ten-year goal _____

**4. Salary desired:**

Current goal _____

Five-year goal _____

Ten-year goal _____

**5. Other accomplishments that would help you measure your success:**

Current goal _____

Five-year goal _____

Ten-year goal _____

Trying to brainstorm your goals may make it apparent that you need more information to continue. This is a good sign. If necessary, begin researching a few occupations to establish their potential.

List your additional questions about one of your potential careers here:

**1.** _____

**2.** _____

Write the questions you've been forming about other career paths here:

**1.** _____

**2.** _____

Often, the greatest inspiration comes from those who have succeeded. Consider the following success stories from job hunters who were once like you!

I knew I enjoyed working with computers. An avid gamer, I thought I might begin studying computer engineering at a nearby university. I really had no idea what "engineering" was, but it seemed to be the closest match to my interests. After I looked at the program description and course selection online, however, I found that in this field, I really needed strong math and science skills—two areas I had always struggled with. And the field involved no art—one of the things I enjoy most. I decided against entering this field but began researching the field of game design. I enrolled in an art and a developmental math course for the following semester, so I had the chance to study what I enjoy while strengthening my math background and giving myself more options for the future. Eventually, I did graduate with a degree in game design and got a great recommendation from my adviser. I had several job offers by graduation.

Raul
*Game Designer*

I was completely unsure of my career direction. I always looked forward to my violin lesson each week but didn't know how my love of music could ever translate into a career. Finally, my violin teacher offered me a chance to job shadow her at her other job as a music therapist. I was very impressed with her patience and focus on her young students and the way she used music to help them progress toward their goals. I knew I had found my niche and a way to make music and have meaningful work.

Zoe
*Music Therapist*

## Chapter Follow-Up

After conducting a careful self-examination, the best way to focus in on your career target is to research and gather information about each possibility:

- Conduct research online or at your library.
- Conduct informational interviews to get the perspective on someone who is successful in the career that interests you.
- Narrow your list of potential careers after re-evaluating your goals, and unearth any remaining questions.
- Job shadow someone whose career is on your list to see firsthand what the working environment is like.

# Chapter 4

# Organizing the Job Hunt

## What Do You Know?

### Short Answers

1. How much time per week should a job hunter use to look for employment?
   _____
   _____

2. List all the ways a cell phone could become a job search tool.
   _____
   _____

3. How could disorganization sabotage the job hunt?
   _____
   _____

4. Under what circumstances might it be acceptable to quickly check a text message during an interview?
   _____
   _____

## Chapter Focus

In this chapter, you'll learn to:

- Maintain and communicate the attitude that finding a job is your job.
- Establish a job hunting headquarters.
- Use a cell phone and voice mail professionally.
- Use such organizational tools as address books, planners, to-do lists, and calendars to keep track of job hunting information and progress.

- Create a filing system to manage documents effectively.
- Maintain a positive attitude and focus during the job hunt.

## Real-Life Relevance

Next, it is essential to cultivate and keeps track of many job leads at one time—all while handling a certain amount of stress. Organizing your work space and using the proper tools will minimize stress and maximize productivity while promoting confidence.

# Make Job Hunting Your New Job

Finding the perfect job is often as time consuming as a full-time job, and successful candidates have an orderly plan for their search and their time. You'll need self-discipline to work on your job hunt, and you'll need to be assertive with those who ask you to run errands or socialize during the time you need to work. If you aren't currently employed, it might be a temptation for you or others to think of the time between jobs as a mini-vacation. In fact, researching job opportunities, applying to companies, finding and following up on leads, and keeping track of the many details can—and should—be very time consuming. Approach your job search like the important project that it truly is, and communicate this attitude to those around you.

Choose a location that will be your job hunting headquarters, even if that means setting up a small desk or table in the corner of a room. Have your computer, chargers, notes, stationery, and all your paperwork assembled in that spot. If you prefer to take your laptop to another location, have all your supplies in your briefcase so your mobile office is never lacking. Become familiar with the organizing or time management software that may have come loaded on your computer. Get up early, and use your job hunting headquarters to plan your day. Set small, specific measurable goals for each day, and if you're the "out of sight, out of mind" type of person, write those goals on a large whiteboard or have the reminders pop up on your cell phone or computer.

# Organizational Tools for Job Hunters

Some basic tools that will help you in your search are the telephone, an address book, spreadsheets and planners, and calendars.

## The Telephone as a Job Search Tool

For many people, the cell phone has become an indispensible tool. Those transitioning from being full- or part-time students and those entering the workforce for the first time may need to rethink the tools on their phone and adapt them for the job hunt.

- Use the notepad for to-do lists and establish deadlines. Take down ideas to mention in the interview. Have and review a list of "elevator talking points" that you might present in two minutes or less to a prospective employer.

- Use the calendar for appointments. Set reminder alarms.

- Use the reminder alarm to make follow-up calls or to complete some other task you might be tempted to procrastinate about.

- Keep all your contacts in your e-mail address book, and categorize your references, prospective employers, and potential leads, assigning each a different ringtone.

- Use your Web browser to complete company research, to find job openings, and to double-check directions.

- Carry digital copies of your résumé or reference lists so you'll be ready to present them quickly if the need arises.

- Check your e-mail frequently for contacts from potential employers.

- Explore job hunting software applications that show job openings.

- Consider having job listings sent as text messages to your phone.

## Responsible Cell Phone Use and Etiquette

Part of using the cell phone for the job hunt involves using it responsibly:

- Remember your basic cell phone etiquette. Don't conduct business in a public setting, Never broadcast your professional (or personal) conversations in a public space.

- Don't answer calls you can't respond to politely and efficiently. Let the calls go to voice mail so you can return the call when you're in a quiet place and where you can give the caller your full attention.

- Keep your cell phone charged so you don't drop an important call.

- Password-protect information stored on your phone, and back it up frequently and insure the phone against loss.

- Keep your phone clean and in good condition, and consider purchasing a new faceplate if yours shows excessive wear. Set your background and ringtone to something neutral and professional. And although your phone is part of your professional image, when job hunting, never wear your phone on your belt.

- Shut it off. Never allow the phone to ring, and never take a call or text when meeting with an employer, when networking, or at any other professional event.

- Never show annoyance or disrespect if a prospective employer fails to observe telephone etiquette.

Create a professional-sounding voice mail message that is clear, professional, easily understood, and free of background music, slang, or profanity. An example of a brief yet businesslike message might sound like: "Hello. You've reached Brianna Simons. Please leave your name and number at the tone, and I will return your call as soon as possible." Do not use the default message on your phone, as prospective employers will be unsure whether they've reached the right person.

Be sure you've use of a telephone that's appropriate for professional use. If you're unable to get a cell phone of your own and share a phone with one or more roommates or family members, let them know that you may be receiving business calls. For example, you might work with the others in your home and ask them to simply rehearse this response: "Tom is unavailable right now. May I take a message?" Explain to them that you're waiting to hear from potential employers and that it is important that they take clear messages for you. Review telephone etiquette with any children at home, reminding them not to yell for you or bang the phone down on a caller.

## Address Book

Set up an address book stored electronically or in print. This tool could include such information as company names, contact names, mailing addresses, e-mail addresses, and website information (see Figure 4.1). Remember to back up your electronic files often and to update the information frequently.

## Planners and Calendars

Commit to using a daily planner or a monthly calendar, selecting the type that works best for you. Choose a format that you'll be likely to look at often and is difficult to lose. Notice the effective habits of some of your more organized friends, and try to copy the same strategies until they become habits of your own.

No matter what type of planner or calendar you select, begin each day by creating a to-do list and filling in a time planner. After you've brainstormed a list of all the tasks you must complete, prioritize each item, labeling those things that are the most important an "A," those of medium importance a "B," and the least important a "C" (see Figures 4.2, 4.3, 4.4, and 4.5). Develop the habit of checking your to-do list and filling in your planner daily, crossing off completed items and moving incomplete tasks to a new list. If you're unable to work on any of your top priorities, focus on keeping a forward motion, and try to complete several of your "C" tasks. This time management habit is one you'll likely use throughout your career and will make you not only a more successful job seeker but also a more effective employee.

**Figure 4.1**    SAMPLE CONTACT LIST

| Company | Contact | Phone | E-mail |
|---|---|---|---|
| Baehr, Inc | Lynn Baker | 371-5431 | LBaker@tds.net |
| Carozzi Systems | Chris Carozzi | 371-0908 | CSystems@bellsouth.com |
| Eaton Products | Barbara Ebol | 371-8712 | Ebol_Barbara@comcast.net |

**Figure 4.2   SAMPLE JOB HUNTER'S TO-DO LIST**

Date: 8/15/2011

*Check When*

| *Completed* | *Priority* | *Task* |
| --- | --- | --- |
| ❏ | B | Dig up more leads at the library by using newspapers. |
| ❏ | A | Make follow-up phone calls to J. Curaci at ABC Corp. |
| ❏ | A | Revise résumé objective to fit the ad in the *Daily News*. |
| ❏ | A | Write thank-you letter to Mr. Lee at Lee Tools. |
| ❏ | A | Write cover letter for job lead from Uncle Joe. |
| ❏ | B | Write thank-you letter to Uncle Joe. |
| ❏ | C | Buy more matching envelopes at the office supplies store. |
| ❏ | B | Call Barton's to find the name of a contact person. |
| ❏ | C | Stop by the chamber of commerce for brochures and leads about local industries. |

**Figure 4.3   SAMPLE JOB HUNTER'S TASK PLANNER**

Date: 9/21/2011

By today's end:

    ❏ Make phone calls for leads, follow-up, etc.

    ❏ Write letters and revise résumé.

    ❏ Read annual reports and brochures from the chamber of commerce.

By one week from today:

    ❏ Meet Jane for lunch to network.

    ❏ Stop by post office and office supplies store.

Within one month:

    ❏ Do further research at the library.

Within six months:

    ❏ Attend the Business After Hours meetings that begin in the spring.

Within one year:

    ❏ Double current list of contact names in database.

    ❏ Take a class in information technology to brush up on new software.

    ❏ Attend a Toastmasters club meeting to improve public speaking skills.

**Figure 4.4    CAREER SEARCH ORGANIZATION CHART**

Remember, looking for a job is your full-time job. Use the chart below to organize your search. Add dates to the chart as you complete each step. Before beginning, photocopy this chart for future use.

| Prospective Employer, Contact Person, Title, Address/Phone | Research Completed | Date Inquiry Letter Sent | Date Cover Letter/ Résumé Sent | Date of Follow-Up Phone Call | Interview Date/Time | Thank-You Note Sent | Remarks |
|---|---|---|---|---|---|---|---|
| | | | | | | | |
| | | | | | | | |
| | | | | | | | |
| | | | | | | | |
| | | | | | | | |

Figure 4.5    SAMPLE JOB HUNTER'S TIME PLANNER

**Date:**  May 23, 2011

## A.M. Tasks

8:00    Call the three new contacts from last week.

8:30    Revise cover letter to Barbara Ebol.

9:00    Draft cover letter to Sydney Bourassa for marketing assistant position.

9:30    Draft cover letter to Intex, Inc. Find out contact name.

10:00    Get ready for interview.

10:30 _____

11:00    Interview at Cyler's Advertising.

11:30 _____

## P.M. Tasks

12:00 _____

12:30 _____

1:00    Evaluate interview performance.

1:30    Write and send thank-you notes to interviewers at Cyler's.

2:00 _____

2:30    Work out at health club.

3:00 _____

3:30    Stop at office supplies store to purchase more stationery.

4:00    Go to the post office for stamps.

4:30    Call Mr. Edmonds to follow up on last week's interview.

5:00    Revise résumé for interview at Conton Hospital.

5:30    Attend Entrepreneurs Networking Dinner downtown.

6:00 _____

6:30 _____

Get organized and stay focused. Dedicate time each day to specific job hunting. A sense of accomplishment will help you remain optimistic until your efforts pay off.
(Lon C. Diehl / PhotoEdit)

## Managing Your Job Hunting Files, Documents, and Notes

Managing the many forms and electronic files that are part of the job search can be a challenge. Although most of your information will be stored electronically, you may also have hard copies of certain documents. Create a filing system that's comfortable for you so you can easily locate information you need. Label your files so you can find information quickly. Some files you might need to create include:

- **Company research:** Notes, articles, brochures, annual reports, website information, and other materials that provide information on the employers you're researching
- **Tools:** Your résumé, cover letters, letters of reference, lists of references, copies of professional licenses and certificates, and school transcripts
- **Networking information:** Your spreadsheet of contacts, along with dates and action items
- **Interviewing notes:** Notes about the names of people present at your interview, when your follow-up or thank-you letters were sent, questions or comments about information discussed during the interview, and comments to yourself about your own interview performance
- **Relocation information:** Data on housing, schools, transportation, realtors, churches, or the job market in an area to which you'd consider relocating
- **Salary research:** What local newspapers, online job boards, employment agencies, *The Occupational Outlook Handbook* (**www.bls.gov**) and other websites, such as **www.salary.com**, say you can expect as a salary range

# Managing Your Attitude During the Job Hunt

Your work space can be neat, your time management can be effective, and your documents can be in order, but if your goals are unclear or your motivation and self-esteem are slipping, your job search may be unproductive. Some job hunters find that keeping a positive attitude while job hunting is the toughest part of the process. The following pointers will help you keep your energy strong and your focus clear while looking for a job.

## Set Goals

Write down your short- and long-term goals, and review them periodically. Each goal you create should be specific (for example, "Lose five pounds" rather than "Lose weight"), and each should have a deadline. Your daily goal might be to make two new contacts. A weekly goal might be to send twenty résumés and cover letters. Decide on a way to reward yourself when you've achieved your goals. Ask yourself, "What action can I take today that will ultimately help me reach my most important short-term goal?"

## Get Past the Shame Barrier

Being jobless is not a reflection of anyone's character. It's okay to acknowledge that not having a job is an uncomfortable and sometimes embarrassing position to be in. However, realize that it's only temporary and that it happens to almost all of us at one time or another. Don't waste time wallowing in depression; instead, set up a plan that helps you take action.

Finally, recognize that your next job may not be your dream job. Employment depends on a variety of factors—only some of which you can control. At the very worst, you'll work in a less than ideal position for a little while. At best, you'll find something that's related to your career choice.

## Stay Healthy

Do everything you can to keep yourself healthy and calm, and do not let the stress of job hunting undermine your physical or emotional health. Keep up your workout routine, get enough rest, and maintain a healthy diet.

While you're planning your next employer contact, also make a plan for stress management, and develop a list of strategies to keep yourself calm and centered. Build a network of supportive friends and family members, and join online job hunting communities. If the pressure becomes too intense, see a counselor or visit your rabbi or pastor. To the extent possible, avoid people who discourage you or distract you from the goals you've set. Consult books and websites devoted to simple but effective relaxation techniques. Taking care of your mental and physical health will help you achieve all the small objectives that will lead to your larger job hunting goals.

**SUCCESS
STORIES**

Often, the greatest inspiration comes from those who have succeeded. Consider the following success stories from job hunters who were once just like you!

I was temping as an administrative assistant to a product development specialist at a large financial institution. She had been working for too long without appropriate support, and her office and her materials were in total disarray. When I interviewed for the permanent position, the topic of a competitor's new line of investment options came up. I reached into my own files and pulled out a relevant article from a banking journal. The interviewer's mouth dropped open, and she hired me on the spot, grateful for my drive and desperate for my organizational abilities.

Lydia
*Assistant Product Development Specialist*

After I graduated from college, my mom expected me to babysit my younger brother. For several weeks, I drove him to all his after-school activities, anxious to repay my family for all the support they'd shown me while I was in school. As the number of "favors" I was asked to do increased, however, I realized I needed to convey a more professional attitude at home. I set up a work space in our basement and began using it regularly. My organization became apparent, and I was very productive. I was always busy following up on leads, and I noticed that Mom seldom asked for babysitting favors when she saw me "working" in my home office. Soon, one of those leads paid off, and I got my first full-time job in a field I truly enjoy.

Richard
*Game Designer*

I had been hopeless about finding car keys, important papers, and my cell phone. I was always showing up at doctor's appointments without my health insurance card and the motor vehicles office without my car registration! When I began looking for a job after graduation, a friend gave me a simple portable plastic filing box with a handle. I tried to put every one of my important papers in it, and soon, I realized I was spending a lot less time searching for things. I set up my job leads on my laptop and developed ways to keep track of which employer I was going to contact next. What a relief to be able to find information when I needed it! Within a month, I'd followed up on thirty promising leads, but I know I'd never have been able to track down even one without starting with that simple plastic box!

Hope
*Media Specialist*

## Chapter Follow-Up

- An effective job hunt takes time and organization.
- Pick a location that will serve as your headquarters. Keep everything you need together so you can work on finding the right job easily and without distraction.
- Pick the amount of time and the time of day you'll devote to job hunting. Be protective of your time, and don't let others misdirect you from your goal.
- Rethink your cell phone as a job search tool, and use all its capabilities to your advantage.
- Remember that cell phone etiquette and responsible cell phone use will also help you in your job search.
- Use address books, planners and calendars, and spreadsheets to organize your dates and your tasks.
- Set short- and long-term goals to keep your hunt focused.
- Don't allow negative emotions or poor health to become an impediment to your goals.

# Part Two

## Gathering Your Tools

# Chapter 5

# Preparing Your Résumé

## What Do You Know?

### True or False?

After you answer this quiz, turn to the end of the book to check your knowledge of résumés.

_____ 1. It is never acceptable to use lime green paper for your résumé.

_____ 2. One of the most effective ways to draw attention to a certain part of your résumé is to leave space around it.

_____ 3. The most important thing an employer should remember after reading your résumé is your experience.

_____ 4. The descriptions of skills listed in résumés must be written in complete sentences.

_____ 5. If your health is excellent, you should mention that fact at the top of your résumé.

_____ 6. Your work experience must be listed first.

_____ 7. Your résumé must be written in complete sentences.

_____ 8. Your résumé must include an accurate accounting of every job you've ever held.

_____ 9. It is acceptable to list the name of a college you attended only briefly.

_____ 10. It is usually a good idea to use the most common résumé software exactly as is.

## Chapter Focus

In this chapter, you'll learn to:

- Compose a résumé that accurately reflects the assets you bring to a job.
- Organize those assets under résumé headings and then organize the headings themselves.
- Lay out the résumé in a way that leads the reader to the most important points while de-emphasizing the least impressive information.
- Follow the basic rules of résumé writing, including résumé format and language.
- Recognize the differences between chronological and functional résumés.
- Handle gaps in your job history on your résumé.
- Explore résumé alternatives.
- Make your résumé computer friendly.

## Real-Life Relevance

Your résumé is one of the most basic and most important tools of the job hunt. Certainly a brief summary cannot communicate the full value of your education, your skills, and your experience, but it can serve to display them effectively and instantly convey your strengths and skills. Almost every employer expects to receive a résumé as a first step in the hiring process, and ultimately, your skill at writing a résumé could determine whether you get interviewed and hired.

# How to Write a Résumé

How much time do you suppose the average employer spends looking at a résumé?

- Fifteen minutes
- Five minutes
- One minute
- Thirty seconds
- Five seconds

What does the length of time an employer looks at your résumé have to do with résumé writing? Everything! Recognize that your reader is making quick assumptions about you and often reading with the intent of weeding out undesirable candidates. This forces you as a writer to make some tough choices. What is your biggest asset as a job hunter, and how can you showcase that strength? What details can be omitted, and what gaps can be minimized?

Carefully choose every word on your résumé. To get in the proper frame of mind, try to imagine that you have to pay five dollars for each letter you use. If that were the case, you would choose powerful verbs and clear descriptors of your job duties. You would omit unnecessary pronouns and never lapse into a lengthy narrative. Finally, you would examine your format to be sure there was little visual clutter and that the eye was drawn to the most important sections of the résumé. So, how long *does* the average employer look at your résumé? Just thirty seconds!

What have you heard about résumés before? Eliminating common misconceptions can help you write a draft of your résumé with accurate information in mind.

**EXERCISE**    ## Check Your Résumé Savvy

*Multiple Choice*

**1.** Résumé software can
   a. create a generic-looking résumé.
   b. be a good starting point when drafting a résumé.
   c. be customized for different employers.
   d. do all the above.

**2.** When the job experience section of a résumé is constructed to highlight the dates of the applicant's employment, that format is called a(n)
   a. functional résumé.
   b. chronological résumé.
   c. abstract résumé.
   d. electronic résumé.

**3.** An applicant's high school should be listed on the résumé if
   a. the applicant has not yet been accepted into a college or university.
   b. the applicant has graduated in the last two to three years.
   c. the applicant has demonstrated some exceptional skill or talent during high school.
   d. all the above conditions apply.

**4.** As a rule, the résumé of a person with fewer than five years of full-time work experience should be
   a. one page long.
   b. two pages long.
   c. three pages long.
   d. written in paragraph form to expand on the limited experience.

**5.** The following items could be included in a résumé's education section:
   a. Participation in a corporate training program
   b. Achievement of dean's list or president's list status
   c. An expected graduation date
   d. All of the above

The answers to these questions can be found at the end of this chapter, but the expanded explanations for the correct answers can be found throughout the chapter. Some responses may surprise you, but all should help you focus on résumé preparation.

## Basic Elements of a Résumé

Arrange the parts of a résumé to illustrate your best assets. The heading and job objective usually appear at the top of the page in that order. References usually appear at the end, but other than these basic limitations, the locations of all other sections of the résumé are flexible.

Think carefully about what you'd like the reader to notice first. Remember: *Most employers look at a résumé for an average of only thirty seconds!* Develop a strategy. Which of your assets is the most impressive, the most recent, or the most relevant to the job you are seeking? Be sure not to strictly follow a model developed by someone else because it might not be the most advantageous to you.

You should have a specific reason for the content and location for each word on the page. For example, if you are a recent graduate, your education might be more impressive than your experience, and you might put it nearer the top of the page. If you have developed some important technical skills but acquired them through less than glamorous jobs, consider placing a summary of skills at the top of the page and listing your work history nearer the bottom.

**Heading.**   This is one of the most important elements of your résumé. Include your name (which should stand out above all else), your address (permanent and temporary), your e-mail address, and your telephone number. Be sure your e-mail address is professional and appropriate. Create a new one for the job hunt if your current e-mail address is suggestive or unprofessional.

**Objective.**   You might also call this "Job Objective" or "Career Objective." Write a one-sentence explanation of the type of position you are seeking. It usually appears beneath your name and address. Your objective should be as specific as possible and should *not* include your future career or educational plans. Note a specific job title, skills you'd like to use, and/or the location or size of the company for which you'd like to work. Change your objective to fit the job you're applying for each time you apply for a new position. Use the exact wording of the job title specified in the job posting or mentioned by the person who told you about the job. If you cannot narrow your objective, omit it. Note that not being able to write a job objective is a strong indicator that you have not yet adequately researched your career goals.

**Education.**   Include the names and locations of all the colleges you've attended and any degrees you have received. It is perfectly acceptable to list a college or university even if you did not complete a degree there. In most circumstances, any education, however brief, is considered a plus. Give the dates you attended college or the date you expect to receive your degree. Under this heading, list any certificates you've received and seminars or training programs you've completed. Be consistent when describing special training sessions, and list the information in the same order as the other educational experiences in this category. Some people also note special honors and awards, such as making the dean's list.

If you've been accepted into a college, it is understood that you graduated from high school, so there's no need to list it. In fact, listing your high school may immediately label you as an inexperienced job hunter—not the first impression you wish to make.

If you wish to stress portions of your education that are especially relevant or current, you might also include a subheading titled "Important Courses" or "Relevant Courses." Under this category, list all classes you've taken that will be of special interest to the employer (computer classes are especially important). This section is useful if your education fits your objective more than your work experience does.

**Experience.**   This can also be called "Work Experience," "Employment Experience," or "Experience and Skills." Here, you give your previous employers, their locations by city and state, the dates you were employed, and the position you held. You may have to create your own job title if you didn't have an official one. However, be sure to be accurate and clear when inventing your own job title.

If your paid employment experience is limited, consider describing any volunteer work, internships, or practica. List them just like your other work experience, but add the word *volunteer* or *intern* in parentheses

With each job held, you may list first the company name, job title, or dates of employment, as long as you are consistent throughout your résumé. The most important element of this section of your résumé is the description of duties, skills, and responsibilities of each job.

Even "unimportant" jobs have likely taught you valuable, transferable skills. For example, you may have been responsible for large sums of money, locking or securing a business, training other employees, or covering for a manager when she was away. You can list each job skill by how important each task is to your current goals rather than by how often you performed it. List your skills in order of importance to your prospective employer, not necessarily in the order that you used these skills at your former workplace.

**Summary of Skills.**   Some people include a brief paragraph or bulleted list outlining special skills they have that they wish to emphasize or that might not be apparent in their job descriptions. "Proficient with Visio and Quickbooks," "Type 90+ words per minute with complete accuracy," and "Fluent in French" are sample phrases that might appear in a summary of skills. Again, if your computer skills are extensive, this heading is a must. This heading usually appears at the top of your résumé—after the objective. Job hunters are presumed to be computer literate, so it is not necessary to list knowledge of MS Word or Excel as a skill. But if you have special knowledge of other programs or languages, you should be sure to make mention of it.

**Activities and Interests.**   You may choose to create a section on your résumé to demonstrate your interests outside school or work, especially if those interests dovetail with skills needed for your prospective career. Some employers like to see an applicant who is well rounded.

However, be aware that some may view this information as frivolous or irrelevant. Be careful not to include any activity that may cause someone to either deliberately or unconsciously discriminate against you. For example, avoid mention of religious or political affiliations.

**References.**   For your résumé, it is sufficient and customary to write "References available upon request" or "furnished upon request" at the bottom of the page. Be sure you can name three to five people who have observed your work habits and can speak about your character. Most people will not mind being a reference, but be sure you ask only those who will speak in glowing terms.

Compile a list of their names, addresses, telephone numbers, and e-mail addresses. You might also want to explain the nature of their relationship to you. Employers that request your list of references are definitely interested in you. (See more on letters of recommendation in Chapter 7.)

# The Language of Résumés

The language used in résumés is unlike that used in any other document. Your goal is to create a written summation of your skills, capabilities, and experience that is as brief as possible without omitting any of your strengths. Here are some guidelines.

*Tips on Résumé Language*

- **Use action verbs.** Describe your duties with strong verbs—for example, *coordinated, delegated, trained,* or *supervised.* (See the pages that follow for a complete listing of strong action verbs.)

- **Avoid using "I."** Each description of your responsibilities should begin with a verb—for example, "Assisted customers with product selection," not "I assisted customers with product selection."

- **Use telegraphic phrases.** The "sentences" on your résumé should sound like brief, powerful sentence fragments. That is, they should be concise, to the point, and all unnecessary words should be left out. Read the sample résumés that follow, and notice the wording of the descriptions of job skills and the job objectives. Note that such words as *the, and,* and *so* can often be left out, and the remaining fragment will still make sense. Each phrase starts with an action verb and ends with a period. For example, someone who has held a position as a customer service representative might write this:

  > *Assisted customers with questions and complaints. Completed weekly reports. Provided material and assistance for production of monthly newsletters.*

  Spend extra time brainstorming all the skills you learned at each place of paid or unpaid employment; this is one of the most important parts of your résumé. Practice describing those skills by using the strongest and most concise wording possible, and rearrange the order of those phrases you listed, making certain that the strongest, most relevant skills are first.

- **Minimize abbreviations.** Abbreviating words may seem easy, but it's best to avoid this habit. Very few abbreviations are understandable to all readers, so use only the most common: "St.," "Ave.," and the letters of your degree, "A.S.," "B.S.," and so on. If you are applying for a new position in a field in which you previously worked, you may use some abbreviations that are common in that profession. But when in doubt, write it out.

- **Use numbers that favor you.** It is fine to write "Completed opening and closing procedures of cash drawer." It is even better to add "Handled $15,000 in daily cash receipts" or "Trained 10 other employees." Being specific will enhance your credibility.

# Style and Impact

Because a potential employer looks at your résumé so quickly, some of the smallest details take on major importance.

**Format.**    Because your interviewer's first glance at your résumé will be a quick one, you need to be sure that your most important points will stand out immediately.

How do you make a part of your résumé stand out while ensuring that the whole page is still easily readable? Think of the techniques that advertisers use successfully:

- **White space.** Notice how the white space around a word catches your eye. Leave double or triple spacing above and below your name. Place headings in the center of a line. If your consistent employment dates are a strength, put those dates out in a margin. Readers are more likely to read a page with lots of white space than one crammed with text.

- **Font.** Avoid Times New Roman font, as it is used so widely. Experiment with others, such as Georgia and Tahoma, that are readable and professional looking.

- **Capitalization.** Use full capitalization for headings or job titles.

- **Underlining or italics.** This is a good way to make job titles stand out.

- **Bold print.** It can add a good touch to your name.

- **Punctuation.** Stars and bullets sometimes help draw the eye to items in a list.

Whatever techniques you use to organize and highlight your résumé, be sure that your layout is neat, consistent, and appealing. Study as many different résumés as you can to see what appeals to you.

---

**EXERCISE**    **Format Focus**

Study six to ten different résumés for thirty seconds each. Force yourself to glance at each one quickly. After you glance at one, put the résumé out of sight, and see which phrases or headings you can recall. What were your general impressions of each résumé (and job candidate!), and what adjectives would you use to describe the résumés you saw? This method often provides job hunters a way to quickly find an appealing résumé layout.

| *Favorite Résumés* | *Most Noticeable Feature or Heading* |
|---|---|
| Page _____ | _____ |
| Page _____ | _____ |
| Page _____ | _____ |

Elements I might include in my own résumé (layout? use of white space? effective language?):

_____

**A Note about Paper.**    Although your résumé will be sent and stored electronically, you should also keep several hard copies on hand to bring with you to an interview. The feel of these résumés in the prospective employer's hand conveys one of the first messages about you. Flimsy, shiny, unsubstantial paper sends a negative message. For this reason, avoid onion skin or shiny photocopy paper. The paper you choose should be sturdy and professional. Choose quality paper that has some weight and is marked "letterhead" or "résumé stock." Visit a local copy center or office supplies store to view samples of the great variety of résumé stock that is available.

The color of the paper also sends a message. In most cases, your résumé should appear conservative and professional. White, off-white, some shade of beige, or light gray paper is fine. Some people choose to produce their résumés on light blue paper, which is acceptable when applying for positions in less conservative fields—for example, early childhood education. Generally, the more conservative the business is, the more conservative the color of the résumé should be. Hot pink might work well for a person applying for a position in advertising, but white is better for someone applying for work in a bank. Again, unless you're trying to make a special point about your creativity, the paper should be a standard 8 1/2 by 11 inches. Finally, match your résumé paper to the cover letter stock and envelopes (if needed) to give a unified look.

## Résumé Do's and Don'ts

*Do*

1. **Customize your résumé for the specific job you're applying for**. Make sure to match your objective and your skills to the requirements of the position.

2. **Use strong action verbs to describe your skills.** See the following pages for a complete listing.

3. **List all your accomplishments, including relevant courses, volunteer work, internships, relevant interests, and professional affiliations.**

4. **Arrange your résumé to show off your assets.** Which heading should go first? Education? Experience? What information should go first in the experience section: your job title or the company name? Which would carry more clout?

5. **Make it perfect.** This is a cardinal rule of résumé writing. Ask someone with a fresh perspective and a sharp eye to also look at it.

6. **Keep the résumé to one page—two if you've had extensive experience.**

7. **Use telegraphic phrases.** Keep it short, simple, and to the point.

8. **Proofread carefully.** Ensure that your grammar and spelling are impeccable.

9. **Use professional type and layout.** Avoid gimmicks or unusual colors or fonts.

10. **Experiment with several different formats and layouts.** Are your skills best highlighted by using the functional or chronological format?

11. **For hard copies use the best type of paper you can find**. Résumé, cover letter, and envelope paper should match.

*Don't*

1. **Don't exceed one page unless you've had the experience to merit the additional pages.** Many employers look only at the first page anyway.

2. **Don't be wordy.**

3. **Don't use the word *I*.**

4. **Don't use abbreviations, except for the most common ones.**

5. **Don't handwrite your résumé or cover letter.**

6. **Don't use unusual type, formats, photographs, or paper, unless they are commonly used in your field or you're trying to make a special statement about your creativity.**

7. **Don't include any personal data, such as height, weight, health, or marital status.** If this information is pertinent to the duties of the job, the employer will request it later.

8. **Don't include any information that could possibly carry any negative connotations or unnecessary personal information.** Be especially careful to omit information about your religious or political affiliations.

9. **Don't keep your résumé to yourself.** Solicit opinions about your résumé from a variety of people you trust. Use their feedback to create a dazzling finished product.

## Action Verbs for Résumés

Skim the list that follows to see whether any of these action verbs would be appropriate on your résumé. Remember that when describing your tasks in your current job, you should use verbs in the present tense. When describing previous positions, use verbs in the past tense.

| | | | |
|---|---|---|---|
| Accelerated | Advocated | Assigned | Boosted |
| Accomplished | Aided | Assimilated | Bought |
| Achieved | Allocated | Assisted | Brought (about) |
| Acquired | Analyzed | Assumed | Budgeted |
| Acted as | Answered | Assured | Built |
| Activated | Applied | Attained | Calculated |
| Adapted | Appointed | Attended | Catalogued |
| Addressed | Approved | Augmented | Centralized |
| Adjusted | Arbitrated | Authorized | Chaired |
| Administered | Arranged | Balanced | Charted |
| Advanced | Ascertained | Bargained | Checked |
| Advised | Assembled | Began | Clarified |

| | | | |
|---|---|---|---|
| Classified | Demonstrated | Financed | Interpreted |
| Coached | Designed | Fixed | Interviewed |
| Collected | Detected | Focused | Introduced |
| Commanded | Determined | Followed (up) | Invented |
| Commended | Developed | Forecasted | Investigated |
| Communicated | Devised | Formed | Joined |
| Compared | Diagnosed | Formulated | Judged |
| Compiled | Directed | Fostered | Justified |
| Completed | Discovered | Founded | Kept |
| Composed | Dispensed | Fulfilled | Launched |
| Compressed | Displayed | Functioned | Learned |
| Computed | Distributed | Furnished | Lectured |
| Conceived | Documented | Gained | Led |
| Conceptualized | Drafted | Gathered | Lifted |
| Condensed | Earned | Generated | Located |
| Conducted | Eliminated | Governed | Logged |
| Conferred | Employed | Grossed | Lowered |
| Conserved | Enacted | Guided | Maintained |
| Consigned | Encouraged | Handled | Managed |
| Consolidated | Enforced | Headed | Manipulated |
| Constructed | Engineered | Hired | Marketed |
| Consulted | Enhanced | Honed | Mastered |
| Contacted | Enlisted | Hosted | Mediated |
| Contracted | Ensured | Hypothesized | Merged |
| Contributed | Entered | Identified | Minimized |
| Controlled | Equipped | Illustrated | Mobilized |
| Converted | Established | Implemented | Modeled |
| Cooperated | Estimated | Improved | Modified |
| Coordinated | Evaluated | Improvised | Monitored |
| Correlated | Examined | Increased | Motivated |
| Corresponded | Exchanged | Influenced | Moved |
| Corroborated | Executed | Informed | Navigated |
| Counseled | Expanded | Initiated | Negotiated |
| Created | Expedited | Innovated | Netted |
| Critiqued | Experimented | Inspected | Nominated |
| Culminated in | Explained | Inspired | Observed |
| Cultivated | Explored | Installed | Obtained |
| Cut | Expressed | Instilled | Offered |
| Dealt | Extended | Instituted | Opened |
| Decided | Extracted | Instructed | Operated |
| Debugged | Fabricated | Insured | Optimized |
| Defined | Facilitated | Integrated | Orchestrated |
| Delegated | Fashioned | Interacted | Ordered |
| Delivered | Filed | Interfaced | Organized |

| | | | |
|---|---|---|---|
| Originated | Quantified | Screened | Taught |
| Outlined | Questioned | Searched | Targeted |
| Overcame | Raised | Secured | Tempered |
| Oversaw | Ran | Selected | Temporized |
| Participated | Rated | Separated | Terminated |
| Perceived | Ratified | Served | Tested |
| Performed | Received | Serviced | Tightened |
| Persuaded | Recognized | Set (up) | Totaled |
| Photographed | Recommended | Shaped | Traced |
| Piloted | Reconciled | Shared | Tracked |
| Pinpointed | Recorded | Shifted | Traded |
| Pioneered | Recruited | Simplified | Trained |
| Placed | Rectified | Sold | Transferred |
| Planned | Redesigned | Solidified | Transformed |
| Played | Reduced | Solved | Traveled |
| Predicted | Re-evaluated | Sorted | Treated |
| Prepared | Referred | Specialized | Trimmed |
| Prescribed | Refined | Staffed | Tripled |
| Presented | Registered | Standardized | Turned (around) |
| Presided | Regulated | Started | Uncovered |
| Prevented | Rehabilitated | Stimulated | Undertook |
| Printed | Reinforced | Streamlined | Upgraded |
| Prioritized | Related | Strengthened | Unified |
| Processed | Rendered | Stressed | Unraveled |
| Procured | Reorganized | Stretched | Updated |
| Produced | Repaired | Structured | Utilized |
| Programmed | Replaced | Studied | Vacated |
| Projected | Reported | Submitted | Validated |
| Promoted | Researched | Substituted | Verified |
| Proposed | Resolved | Succeeded | Volunteered |
| Protected | Responded | Summarized | Widened |
| Proved | Revamped | Superseded | Withdrew |
| Provided | Reviewed | Supervised | Weighed |
| Publicized | Revised | Surpassed | Won |
| Published | Revitalized | Supplied | Worked |
| Purchased | Revived | Supported | Wrote |
| Quadrupled | Saved | Sustained | Yielded |
| Qualified | Scheduled | Synthesized | |

**EXERCISE**    **Action Verb Review**

Carefully review the list of action verbs, and determine which verbs describe duties you've had at previous jobs. Write "1" to the left of any verb that you could use in describing your current job. Write "2" next to any verb that would apply to the job prior to your current position, and write "3" next to verbs that apply to the one before that.

Using the appropriate action verbs, draft a description of the duties you perform at your current job. For the moment, do not worry about the job title or company; just write three to seven telegraphic phrases you might include in a description of your duties.

_____

_____

## Skills Identification

Skills tend to fall into one of three categories: job related, transferrable, and adaptive. *Job related skills* are required of a specific job—for example, knowledge of a specific type of data, tools, machinery, or software. *Transferable skills* are those that are useful in many professions, such as the ability to manage people, troubleshoot problems, speak effectively, or write clearly. *Adaptive skills*, also called self-management skills, speak to your work style and how well you'd fit in at a particular workplace. Punctuality, resourcefulness, and the willingness to persevere are all adaptive skills that make even a less experienced applicant more attractive to employers.

**EXERCISE**    **Identifying Skills**

Make a list of all your concrete skills, such as your familiarity with computer programs and other specific talents you've developed and specialties you've acquired.

*Job Related Skills*                                            *Example of Mastery*

❑ _____          _____

❑ _____          _____

❑ _____          _____

❑ _____          _____

❑ _____          _____

Now think of the skills you have with people (such as training), data (such as record keeping), or such things as operating, assembling or repairing equipment. Add them to your list.

_____

### Transferable Skills

❏ _____

❏ _____

❏ _____

❏ _____

### Example of Mastery

_____

_____

_____

_____

Now think of your personality traits, such as reliability, ability to work on a team, and honesty. Add them to this list.

### Adaptive Skills

❏ _____

❏ _____

❏ _____

❏ _____

### Example of Mastery

_____

_____

_____

_____

# Types of Résumés

As you assemble your résumé, you'll need to decide which of two formats—chronological or functional—better highlights your strong points. Each type of résumé is good in certain situations and both are equally acceptable, although the chronological résumé is more common.

## Chronological Résumé

This type of résumé highlights the sequence of jobs the applicant has held. A chronological résumé is better for those who have clearly progressed toward their job objective. For example, this format would highlight a job hunter's progression from a clerical, to a supervisory, and then to an upper-managerial position because the job titles and the dates of employment would be clearly listed down the left side of the résumé.

This format is also a good choice for those who have had no gaps in their job history and want to stress the fact that they have been consistently employed.

The experience section lists jobs in order of dates, giving the most recent position first. After you've listed each employer, location by city and state, and job title, write a brief job description using strong action words. You may place the dates in the left margin or after each job description, depending on how much you want to highlight them. Be sure you present dates consistently throughout your résumé, such as "5/09–present" or "May 2009–present" or "2009–present."

## Functional Résumé

This type of résumé stresses skills, not dates. A functional résumé is better for those who have held a variety of unrelated jobs. For example, if you have worked in a shoe store and a fast-food restaurant, a functional résumé would allow you to stress the fact that you've had experience waiting on customers, regardless of the setting. This format is a good choice for job hunters who have gaps in their job histories.

After a clear job objective at the top of the résumé, the next heading listed is "Skills." Three or four broad skill areas should be identified, each of which should relate to the job objective. For example, if your job objective states "Seeking a position as an office manager," you might decide to create such categories as "Office Skills," "Managerial Skills," and "Organizational Skills." In each category, you could describe how you demonstrated those skills in previous jobs. You would have to draw on your experience from all the positions you've held—paid and unpaid. Dates of employment are still listed on the page—but later; they are not the first thing an employer sees.

Look carefully at the sample résumés shown on the following pages. What do you notice first? How have these job hunters magnified their assets and downplayed their weak points? Does one format appeal to you more than others? Examine each résumé to see which format—chronological or functional—and which layout is best for you. Then, it's time for you to begin preparing a first draft of your own résumé.

# Suki Noguchi

22 Catanga Way
Colby, OH 46119
(803) 555–2642
SMN774@aol.com

**OBJECTIVE**

Position in technically oriented writing or editing.

**SKILLS**

Excellent writing skills.
Keyboard 80 words per minute.
Thorough knowledge of Atom, Soap, and Epic Editor.

**EDUCATION**

B.S., Journalism/Technical Writing, expected May, 2012. Dixon College, Colby, OH.

Relevant Course Work: Advanced Technical Writing, Magazine Writing, Copyediting, Technological Reports I and II, Desktop Publishing, Introduction to Information Technology.

**EXPERIENCE**

2010–present       *Publications Assistant,* Alumni Office, University of Ohio (part-time). Produce bimonthly medical reports; write copy and take photographs for faculty and alumni newsletters.

2009
Summer             *Marketing Assistant* (intern), NEC Development, Inc., Osborn, Ohio. Wrote sections of proposals; copyedited manuals, brochures, and correspondence.

2008
Summer             *Office Assistant,* Department of Humanities, Cumberland College, Hartford, Connecticut. Prepared mailings, updated computer records, assisted students with registration, performed general office tasks.

**ACTIVITIES/INTERESTS**

Editor, *University News,* school newspaper, 2009–2010, Assistant Editor, 2008–2009, Copyeditor, 2009.

Secretary, Alpha Phi International Sorority.

References available upon request.

**Sample 5.1    CHRONOLOGICAL RÉSUMÉ**

# JASMINE SINGH

**PERMANENT ADDRESS**
(after 5/30/11)
196 Chestnut Rd.
Taylor, PA 15215
(513) 555–0932
Jassingh@media.com

**TEMPORARY ADDRESS**
(until 5/30/11)
Taylor College
212 Metcalf Hall
Taylor, PA 15211
(513) 555–3387

## CAREER OBJECTIVE

Seeking employment as an officer in an urban police department.

## EDUCATION

A.S., Criminal Justice (to be awarded May 2012), Taylor College, Taylor, Pennsylvania. Dean's List, 2009, 2010. Degree includes courses in Human Relations, Contemporary Social Problems, Report Writing, and Spanish for Law Enforcement.

Farnsworth Community Technical College, Farnsworth, MD, 2006.

## EMPLOYMENT EXPERIENCE

| | |
|---|---|
| 2009–present | Taylor College, Taylor, PA. CAMPUS SECURITY ASSISTANT. Assisted Coordinator of Security with patrolling hallways, admitting visitors, and reporting incidents in residence halls. |
| 2010 | Parker's Photography Studio, Farnsworth, MD. PHOTOGRAPHER. Photographed family portraits and weddings. Assisted customers in choosing among proofs. Worked in darkroom. Closed and secured studio. |
| 2008 | Smith's Burger Cottage, Farnsworth, MD. COUNTERPERSON. Responsible for cash drawer averaging $2,000 daily. Took customer orders and delivered food. Trained six new hires. |

## PROFESSIONAL AFFILIATIONS

| | |
|---|---|
| 2009–present | Treasurer, Association for Students of Criminal Justice. |

## REFERENCES

References furnished upon request.

**Sample 5.2  CHRONOLOGICAL RÉSUMÉ**

# JASON ALLEGIA

312B Black Brook Road
Pearson, KY 55162
(504) 555–9066
Portfolioprimo@roadrunner.com

## JOB TARGET

Seeking entry-level employment at a large hotel where I can use my technical and customer service skills.

## SPECIAL SKILLS/COMPUTER SKILLS

Fluent in written and spoken Spanish. Extensive knowledge of BarSim and Optiikeeper systems.

## EDUCATION

Pearson Community College, Pearson, KY.
A.S., Hotel Restaurant Management, expected 2012.

Important Courses: Front Office Procedure, Hotel Computer Systems, Hospitality Security Management.

## EXPERIENCE AND SKILLS

Mile-Away Motel, Pearson, KY. *Desk Clerk.* Registered and checked out guests. Trained three new employees. Took reservations and processed payments. Assisted guests with questions and information about local sights. 2010–present.

Krystal Kleen Dry Kleening, Franklin, KY. *Clerk.* Assisted customers with problems and questions. Processed orders: Completed special-order forms. Operated cash register. 2009–2010.

## RELATED INTERESTS AND ACTIVITIES

Member, Pearson Community College Hospitality Club, 2010.

Certified by the American Hotel and Motel Association Educational Institute, 2010.

## REFERENCES

Available upon request.

**Sample 5.3    Chronological Résumé**

# Sienna Naccach

726 Teaberry Way, Collinsville, IL 47630
(304) 555–4671
Orangepencil@excite.com

**Career Objective**

Administrative Assistant position in a growing corporation.

**Summary of Skills**

- Excellent communication, organization and time management skills
- Keyboard 75 words per minute
- Thorough knowledge of all office equipment, including BlackBerry devices, fax machines, postage machines, photocopiers, and switchboards
- Well rounded, experienced with multitasking and troubleshooting in high-traffic workplace

**Education**

Collinsville Technical College, Collinsville, IL. Business Administration major. 2011–2013.

ITX Industries, Highland, IL. Completed 15 hours of in-house training in areas of Customer Service, Information Technology in Business, and Telephone Techniques. 2010.

**Experience**

ADMINISTRATIVE ASSISTANT (Internship). Wellspring Commons Medical Center. Marissa, IL. Provided administrative support as needed in busy twelve-physician office. Assisted with correspondence, newsletters, invoices, insurance forms. Answered patient questions and assisted receptionist with appointments and telephones. 2011.

RECEPTIONIST. ITX Industries, Highland, IL. Greeted clients. Answered phones. Completed data entry and filing. Assisted office staff with completing travel arrangements, mailings, and projects. Participated in all relevant in-house training sessions. 2009–2010.

CHILD CARE AIDE. Little Rainbows Daycare, Bella Vista, FL. Planned and supervised daily activities and field trips. Conferred with parents and lead teacher. Assisted with meals. 2010.

**References**

Available upon request.

Sample 5.4    CHRONOLOGICAL RÉSUMÉ

# Nora Viktor

2411 Phelps Avenue • West Plains, MO, 63034 • (114) 507–1520 • NoraVkt@tec.mo.us

## OBJECTIVE

To secure a position as an airline ticket agent at a busy metropolitan airport.

## EDUCATION

A.S., Travel and Tourism, West Plains Community College, Rainham, IL. Degree to be awarded May 2013. Completed courses in Domestic International Travel Procedures (includes SABRE and Travelport training), E-Travel, Desktop Applications, and Conversational Spanish.

## EXPERIENCE

*Office Assistant* (Intern). Runaway Travel, Thayer, MO. Assisted agents with arranging and booking foreign and domestic travel arrangements. Special assistant for Medco, Inc., travel accounts, serving all 4,000 Medco employees, including management and CEO. Greeted customers. Responded to telephone inquiries. 2010–2011.

*Customer Service Representative.* Spencer Gifts and Novelties, Charlestown, IL. Assisted customers with selection and purchase of merchandise. Handled cash. Maintained appearance of all store displays. 2008–2009.

## EXTRACURRICULAR ACTIVITIES

Vice President, Wildcats Travel Club. Arranged club tours to Orlando and Niagara Falls. Responsible for publicity and financial arrangements for both trips. 2012.

## REFERENCES

Available upon request.

Sample 5.5    CHRONOLOGICAL RÉSUMÉ

# Joaquin Tomas

11 Regent Street
Tuttle, North Dakota
(612) 555–6443
Whitedeer@juneau.com

## GOAL
Seeking challenging position as Technical Support Specialist I for Laurie Corporation.

## STRENGTHS
- Ability to function as a team player and to work independently. Able to transition between worker and manager as needed.
- Strong oral and written communication skills. Authored Learning Center web page and brochures.
- Experienced in the repair and assembly of personal computers.
- Excellent technical skills, problem solving and troubleshooting skills.

## SKILLS
- Subnetting
- Access Control Lists
- Scripting
- Cisco Command Line Interface

## EMPLOYMENT
*Technical Support Representative* (Intern). Softex Software, Gibbon, ND. Provided effective and consistent technical support. Published and maintained technical support web page. Assisted operations division with installations. 2010–2011.

*Lab Monitor.* Bluewater Technical College, Gibbon, ND. Responded to student and faculty questions at large, busy Learning Center open lab. Maintained computing facilities and managed printers. Wrote articles for "Techie Tips" on Bluewater Learning Center web page and authored Top Ten Techie Tips brochures. 2008–2010.

*Customer Service Specialist.* QuikMart, Jolene, ND. Assisted customers. Operated cash register. Stocked shelves. Responsible for maintaining cleanliness and appearance of interior and exterior of busy market and gasoline station. Acted as manager when needed to cover vacations. 2008.

## EDUCATION
A.S., Bluewater Technical College, Gibbon, ND. 2011. Graduated magna cum laude.

**Important Courses:** Networking Theory I and II, Windows Server Operating Systems, Managing Information Systems, Technical Support Tools and Skills, Microsoft Project

## REFERENCES
Available upon request.

**Sample 5.6    Chronological Résumé**

**Chike Ife**
8 Fidelity Lane
McCarthy, NE 96145
(909) 555–2777
CHI487@earthlink.com

## OBJECTIVE

Management position in retail sales, using skills in design, administration, and public contact.

## PROFESSIONAL EXPERIENCE AND SKILLS

*Management*  Coordinated operations, managed and assisted in sales at Peterson Stationery.

Managed small medical laboratory at Petri Laboratories.

Trained military personnel in hazardous-waste procedures at Reamsly Air Force Base.

*Administration*  Wrote and catalogued procedures for medical laboratory.

Designed record entry system, evaluated and carried out daily priorities.

Coordinated numerous experiments from inception through subsequent interpretation and reporting of findings.

*Technical Skills*  Highly proficient with most desktop publishing and spreadsheet programs.

## WORK HISTORY

2011        Research Assistant—Petrie Laboratories, McCarthy, NE
2009        Sales & Operations—Peterson Stationery, Campbell, KS
2007–2010   Hotline Volunteer—Women's Crisis Center, Mankato, KS
2004–2009   Family management and independent study.

## EDUCATION

B.S., Business Management, Mankato University, Mankato, KS

References available on request.

**Sample 5.7    Functional Résumé**

# Nathan Cellucci

22 Peppercorn Lane
St. George, Utah 82134
(508) 555–9898

## JOB OBJECTIVE

Bank teller in a large metropolitan bank.

## SKILLS AND EXPERIENCE

**Customer Service**   Handled customer inquiries and complaints at brokerage firm. Educated and advised customers on new insurance products.

Responded to questions and arranged conferences to address parents' curriculum questions.

**Sales**   Solicited donations for renovations of community gardens.

**Administrative**   Experienced data entry clerk.

Recently completed course work in Personal Computer Hardware and Software.

Recorded patients and insurance and medical data using a variety of medical software systems.

## EMPLOYMENT HISTORY

| | | |
|---|---|---|
| **Insurance Agent** | Jellison Insurance, Worley, UT | 2010 |
| **Office Assistant** | Harvey-Kennum Associates, St. George, UT | 2008 |
| **Medical Assistant** | Robin Fellbruck, M.D., St. George, UT | 2006–2008 |
| **Assistant Teacher** | Bright Beginnings Daycare, Hopkins, UT | 2006 |

## EDUCATION

| | |
|---|---|
| A.S., Business Studies, St. George College, St. George, UT | 2012 |
| Certificate & License, Medical Assisting, Holy Angels Medical Center, Hopkins, UT | 2006 |

References available upon request.

**Sample 5.8   FUNCTIONAL RÉSUMÉ**

## Samantha Bilodeau

2121 Wight Street
Oak Hill, CA 97078
(602) 555–0074
bilodeau555@gmail.com

**JOB OBJECTIVE:** Assistant Lead Teacher at a Child Care Center

### SKILLS

*Curriculum Development:* Independently implemented and developed appropriate and inclusionary activities for three preschool-aged children in my care. Planned curriculum units on Native Americans Studies, Forest Studies, and Dinosaurs for children aged 3–5 as part of practicum experience. Wrote three children's books (unpublished) as part of Children's Literature course.

*Music/Art/Drama/Storytelling:* Coordinated, and participated in creation of a full wall mural at Oak Hill YMCA. Accomplished musician, 10 years study of piano and guitar. Independently developed art activities, including innovative paint, bead, and cooking activities for children aged 2–5.

*Communications/Teamwork:* Completed observations of children at Adams Community College Early Childhood Center and prepared weekly reports to be shared with classmates and site supervisor. Discussed behavior and educational growth with parents. Worked as part of a team of five Youth Counselors and Program Director. Planned and conducted Information Night for parents of children attending YMCA After School Program.

### EDUCATION

Adams Community College, Trialto, CA. A.S., Early Childhood Education, 2013.
Course work included:

|  |  |
|---|---|
| Growth and Development of the Young Child | Exceptional and At-Risk Children |
| Child, Family, and Community | Children's Literature |

Completed 120 hours of observation and 150 hours of practical training.

### WORK HISTORY

*Youth Counselor,* Oak Hill YMCA, Oak Hill, CA, 2010–present
*Teacher's Aide* (practicum), Adams Community College Early Childhood Center, Trialto, CA, 2009
*Deli Clerk,* Shop 'N' Save, Vernon, CA, 2008
*Child Care Provider,* Mr. and Mrs. Donald and Deborah Howard, 2006–2008

### RELATED INTERESTS

Big Brother, Big Brothers of America, Inc., 2009–present

### REFERENCES

Available upon request.

**Sample 5.9    FUNCTIONAL RÉSUMÉ**

**EXERCISE**    ### Résumé Revision

The résumé on the following page contains at least a dozen errors. Look it over, and begin planning some corrections.

This résumé is clearly a first draft that is in need of revisions before it is ready to be presented to an employer. In its current condition, it makes a negative statement about the candidate.

Try your own revision of this résumé. Practice with chronological and functional formats, and experiment with the layout. See how you can improve Michael Nelson's chances of getting an interview and then compare your revisions with the two other versions that follow here. (You may have to be creative and fill in some of the details omitted in the original version.)

**RÉSUMÉ**                                            August 17, 2011

Mike Nelson
box 199
Goldfield, Nev,
Onehotbiker@yahoo.com


PERSONNEL DATA

Separated, 2 children
Excellant Health


EDUCATION

Charles Tucker H.S. 2006-7
GED '09
Attempted 5 courses at Mesa Comm. College


Experience

Schuylers' Dept. Store, 491 Wentworth Blvd. Biron, Nevada
(415) 555–6130
January–Nov. 2009


Part-time Assembly Line worker at Microtex Incorp. Allen Springs, Nevada 16 Industrial Drive September '10—now. I make printed circuit boards and do many p-50 forms I also help QC when needed.


HOBBIES

Painting, voleyball, suntanning, biking, poetry, basketball, and all sports, reading, guitar, etc. also a singer in the choir of Faith Christian Church.

**Sample 5.10    Poorly Done Résumé**

# MICHAEL NELSON

P.O. Box 199
Goldfield, NV 98965-0199
(305) 555-2323
Smoothpath@yahoo.com

**Job Objective:**    Position as a medical office assistant in a busy pediatric practice.

**Experience:**

2011–present    *Child-Care Provider.* Self-employed, Goldfield, NV. Care for three children aged six months to five years. Plan and supervise activities and meals. Confer with parents.

2010    *Medical Office Assistant* (internship). Red Rock Pediatric Group, Goldfield, NV. Greeted patients. Processed various health insurance forms. Filed and retrieved medical records. Made appointments.

2010    *Assembler* (part-time). Microtex, Inc., Allen Springs, NV. Assembled printed circuit boards. Cross-trained to assist quality control staff. Completed daily production reports.

2009    *Sales Associate.* Schuyler's Department Store, Biron, NV. Assisted customers with purchases and returns. Trained three junior associates. Operated cash register. Managed cosmetics department in manager's absence.

**Education:**

2009    Mesa Community College, Mesa, NV. Medical Secretary/ Transcriptionist Cerificate Program.

*Relevant Courses:* Medical Terminology, Medical Machine Transcription, Word/Information Processing, Office Systems Management.

**References:**    References provided on request.

Sample 5.11   REVISED RÉSUMÉ IN CHRONOLOGICAL FORMAT

# MICHAEL NELSON

P.O. Box 199
Goldfield, NV 98965-0199
(305) 555-2323
Smoothpath@longitude.com

| | |
|---|---|
| **Objective:** | Position as a medical office assistant in a busy pediatric practice. |
| **Skills:** | • <u>Administrative</u>—Keyboard 60 wpm. Experienced with general administrative support. Processed insurance forms. Filed and retrieved medical records. Made appointments. |
| | • <u>Technical Skills</u>—Knowledge of Appointment Book as well as various spreadsheet and word processing programs. |
| | • <u>Public Contact</u>—Assisted department store customers with purchases and returns. Confer with parents of young children on progress and behaviors. |
| | • <u>Teamwork</u>—Worked closely with seven other employees on circuit board assembly line. Cross-trained to assist with quality control staff. Assisted store manager with cosmetics department in department manager's absence. |
| **Employment History:** | Child Care Provider, self-employed. Goldfield, NV. 2011–present. |
| | Medical Office Assistant (Internship), Red Rock Pediatric Group. Goldfield, NV. 2010. |
| | Assembler (part time), Microtex, Inc, Allen Springs, NV. 2010. |
| | Sales Associate, Schuyler's Department Store, Biron, NV. 2009. |
| **Education:** | Mesa Community College, Mesa, NV. Certificate, Medical Secretary/Transcriptionist. 2009. |
| | <u>Relevant Courses:</u> Medical Terminology. Health Care Data Content and Delivery Systems. Word/Information Processing. Medical Transcription I and II. |
| **References:** | References provided on request. |

**Sample 5.12**    Revised Résumé in Functional Format

**EXERCISE**    **Résumé Revision Wrap-up**

Did you notice the misspellings, sloppy format, and lack of information about skills in the first résumé? Pertinent information is omitted, and irrelevant data are readily apparent. The applicant's name is not especially noticeable, and there is no phone number or mention of references. The date at the top of the page is unnecessary. Also note the inconsistencies in the presentation of dates and order of information.

By now, you may realize how much work is involved in résumé revision. Although Michael's first draft has many errors, it is not unusually bad for a first attempt. The act of diving in and committing information takes courage and, at the very least, provides a place to start.

Compare your first revision of this résumé with another person's draft revision. Do you agree with your classmate's revisions? What further changes could be made?

## Ways to Build Your Résumé While You're Still in College

Résumé building should begin well before you feel ready to search for your first full-time job.

- The college campus provides many opportunities to gain experience and improve your workplace skills—and to make the most of them on your résumé.

- **Get a job.** Most colleges and universities offer a wide variety of part-time positions on and around campus. Even when surrounding towns have limited opportunities, there are often many jobs available in academic and administrative offices, food service, tutoring, and facilities management areas. Some students may also qualify for federal Work Study jobs as part of their financial aid package. Working while balancing academics not only provides spending money, but it demonstrates a student's ambition, time management skills, and drive. These job postings can usually be found on the college's website or in the Career Services office, and the hours and schedule are often flexible.

- **Volunteer.** College towns look to the local college students as a source of free labor in exchange for providing the exposure and experience (not to mention personal fulfillment!) volunteer opportunities provide. Students can easily find invaluable experience while helping out in local schools, businesses, and social service agencies. Even if their college doesn't offer formal community service opportunities, most students find it fairly easy to create their own.

- **Participate.** Attending lectures, leadership seminars, plays, concerts, and sporting events all help students become more well rounded and to speak more intelligently on a wide variety of subjects. Meeting other student, faculty, and community members at these events also helps students increase the size of their contact network.

- **Join something.** Most colleges offer student chapters of professional organizations, allowing students exposure to their field as well as information on career information and job openings. Other student organizations, such as student government, interest clubs, and sports, provide invaluable leadership experience, improve students' communication skills, and show enthusiasm and well roundedness. Employers look for people who have done more than simply attend classes and get good grades; they want good communicators, team players, and leaders.

---

**EXERCISE**     ## Résumé Worksheet

This worksheet is for brainstorming. By completing it, you will be sure to remember all your education, skills, and experience, and you will be better able to organize your thoughts. Thinking through your skills should prove helpful not only for writing your résumé but also during the interview.

As in any brainstorming exercise, there are no wrong answers; include everything you can think of under each category. It is best to complete items 2 through 11 only after you've let the information in item 1 sit for a few days. This way, you'll be able to gain some distance from your work, and your revisions will be more effective. You may want to repeat this process as you revise your résumé further along in your job hunt.

**1.** Fill in the information requested in the six following sections.

  a. **Job Objective**

   Career fields in which you'd
   be interested                       _____

   Specific positions or types
   of positions                        _____

   Skills you'd like to use            _____

   Size or location (e.g., urban,
   rural) of desirable workplace       _____

  b. **Education.** List schooling in reverse chronological order (most recent first).

   College attended (name) _____ (city/state) _____

   Degree received/date _____

   Relevant or important courses _____

   Other college(s) attended (name) _____ (city/state) _____

   Degree received/date _____

   Relevant or important courses _____

Additional educational training (seminars, workshops, extracurricular activities)

_____

_____

c. **Experience.** List experience in reverse chronological order. Include volunteer work and internships (list in parentheses after job title). You may need additional sheets to fully describe your skills.

| *Employer (City/State)* | *Job Title/Dates Worked* | *Description of Skills (Use Action Verbs)* |
|---|---|---|
| _____ | _____ | _____ |
| _____ | _____ | _____ |
| _____ | _____ | _____ |
| _____ | _____ | _____ |
| _____ | _____ | _____ |

d. **Awards and Honors**

| *Award/Honor* | *Date Received* |
|---|---|
| _____ | _____ |
| _____ | _____ |
| _____ | _____ |

e. **Professional Affiliations**

| *Organization* | *Year Joined* | *Position Held* |
|---|---|---|
| _____ | _____ | _____ |
| _____ | _____ | _____ |
| _____ | _____ | _____ |

f. **Interests and Activities.** List all extracurricular activities, interests, hobbies, volunteer work, clubs to which you belong, etc.

_____

_____

_____

**2.** Referring back to item 1(c), revise your job duties here. Reorder your skills so that the most impressive appear first in the job description. Use strong verbs to begin each sentence.

**Position 1** _____

Description of skills _____

**Position 2** _____

Description of skills _____

**Position 3** _____

Description of skills _____

**3.** Using the ideas generated in item 1(a), write several one-sentence versions of your job objective here. Then, circle the one that is clearest and most concise.

a. _____

b. _____

c. _____

**4.** Review the previous sections. Cross out any mention of controversial, political, or religious activities.

**5.** Using the space to the left of each heading in item 1, number the headings in the order in which you'd like them to appear on your résumé. Remember to place your strongest sections close to the top of the page. If you have a strong career objective, it should appear second only to your name and address. References are usually mentioned last. The order of the rest of these elements is flexible. Mark an *X* by any sections you would not like to include.

**6.** Now try a draft of your résumé. Lay out the rough information you have here. Where will the headings be placed? How will you present the employment information? Where will you use capital letters, bold print, italics, white space, or underlining? By now, you should have a rough draft of your résumé.

**7.** Show your draft to at least one other person who has had experience working with résumés. A teacher, employer, or businessperson would be ideal. Have a brief conversation with him or her.

a. What does the person notice first? Is this what you had intended to highlight?

b. Is your career objective clear? Is it too vague or too narrow?

    c. Are all your strengths included?

    d. Are the descriptions of your skills thorough, and do they start with action verbs?

    e. Is the layout neat and eye catching?

    f. What other comments does this person have about your résumé? Would the person hire you?

8. Proofread carefully. Be sure there are no typos or misspellings. Make sure you have handled dates and punctuation in a consistent style.

9. Proofread again.

10. Print several copies of your résumé on good-quality résumé paper, sold in office supplies stores and print shops. Keep these hard copies, along with spare pages and envelopes, so you can send them through the postal mail if needed, and have them ready for the interview.

# What to Do about Gaps in Your Job History

For a variety of reasons, many people have unexplained gaps in their job histories. Some were not employed outside the home after they had children; some may have taken time off for travel, medical reasons, or soul searching. People who are re-entering the job market after retiring or after a long job search may also wonder how to express this time appropriately on a résumé. If you are concerned about how to explain the gaps in your job history, consider the following suggestions:

- **Create a functional résumé.** Emphasize your objective and then list three or four transferable skill areas. Describe all the ways in which you have demonstrated those skills. Place the dates of your employment in a section lower on the page.

- **Write a chronological résumé.** Place the dates of your employment at the end of each job description.

- **Minimize the gap.** Give only the years of employment instead of the month and the year.

- **Create a job title to explain the time gap.** Many people actually have done productive, albeit unpaid, work during their "gap time." Be honest but creative. Could you call yourself an independent consultant? Family manager? One woman who spent years entertaining her husband's international business clients for weeks at a time decided on a title of International Hostess/Party Planner. Be sure not to overlook volunteer work or internships. Create a job title and put the word *volunteer* or *intern* in parentheses following the title.

- **Create new headings on your résumé.** If your work experience is limited or spotty, stress other strengths. Create categories for "Special Skills," "Awards and Honors," "Interests and Activities," "Relevant Courses," or "Additional Training."
- **Don't lie.** In the interview, explain any time gaps briefly but honestly. Remember that even a great résumé does not get you the job. *You* get yourself the job during the interview. In minimizing time gaps in your résumé, your intention is not to deceive the employer but to prevent yourself from being eliminated before the interview. Plan ahead how to explain the time gap should the question arise.

# FAQs for Experienced Job Hunters

Experienced job hunters face questions unlike those that challenge someone new to the job market. When writing a résumé and preparing to search for a position in a new field, how is it best to document an extensive, unusual, or complicated work history? What about any unpaid positions? What training or education should be included? Although the general rules of résumé writing hold true for more experienced job hunters, consideration should be given to the special circumstances discussed below.

**Q:** *When writing my résumé, how far back should I go in listing the positions I've held?*

**A:** Remember that the résumé's purpose is not to provide detailed documentation of all the positions you've ever held. While it may be frustrating to omit experience and skills that have played a role in making you the strong candidate you are, you would be better served to carefully select the jobs and responsibilities that are most relevant to the reader.

Generally, go back ten years or your last three jobs. Jobs held in the more distant past may be too outdated to be of interest to a potential employer or might be better discussed in an interview. Use your judgment here.

If duties you performed on the job fifteen years ago are a perfect match for those required for the job you want now, note them on your résumé in a job description or summary of skills.

**Q:** *How long should my résumé be? I have a lot of ground to cover.*

**A:** Strive for brevity, even if that's difficult. If you have more than ten years' experience overall, it is perfectly acceptable to write a two-page résumé. It is not usually acceptable to write a résumé longer than two pages, but in certain fields, such as elementary or postsecondary education, long résumés are expected. Conduct informational interviews and other types of research to learn the standard in your field. Remember that prospective employers look at a résumé for only a few seconds and that the second page gets an even briefer glance than the first. Think carefully about the needs of your reader and what he or she will find relevant, and don't worry excessively about including every skill you have.

**Q:** *I have spent many years gaining experience in one field and now am making a switch to something entirely different. How can I write a résumé that still showcases my strengths?*

**A:** Career changers need to put extra thought into assessing and describing transferable skills. Which of the required skills of the new position do you already possess from some prior experience?

Consider using the functional format for your résumé, and list the broad skill areas at the top of the first page. Then, briefly list a work history toward the bottom of your résumé. Another alternative is to use font size or underlining to highlight the companies you've worked for, listing job titles in smaller print. You may also need to change your cover letter to make mention of your extensive experience, your career change, and your unique qualifications for the new position.

**Q:** *How do I effectively describe the various training sessions or workshops I've participated in?*

**A:** You have a couple of alternatives. One is that you could include this information in the "Education" section of your résumé. Using the same format in which you listed attendance at a college or university, note the sites, dates, and titles of the workshops or training sessions you've attended. Or you could mention these training sessions at the end of the description of each job. For example, after "Supervised 25 customer service representatives," you might add "Completed training seminars in Effective Management and Creating and Maximizing Work Teams."

**Q:** *How do I account for the years I was unemployed while raising a family, traveling, or attending school?*

**A:** Arrange your résumé so the reader has a moment to be impressed with your experience before wondering about the gaps in your job history. Don't be untruthful, but list your employment by the years instead of by months and years, and list the dates at the end of a job description or at the bottom of the page. Also, don't neglect to list time spent volunteering, working for yourself, or working as a consultant. Some job hunters mention their travel or unpaid work in their cover letters, but most address these topics during the interview.

**Q:** *I've held many positions within the same company. What's the correct way to include them all in a résumé?*

**A:** Rather than sticking with the convention of listing all employment by date, employer, and title, begin the "Experience" portion of the résumé with the name of the company displayed in a prominent way. Then, indent, listing your job titles and descriptions and dates in reverse chronological order. This technique effectively demonstrates the breadth of experience you've gained at a single workplace, and it shows that you've moved up in the company.

## GRAHAM M. ELIOT
*3108 Silver Lake Drive*
*Maitland, Florida 34701*
407–229–1182

### OBJECTIVE
Management position with company involved in emergency response activities.

### EMPLOYMENT

**VICE PRESIDENT FOR CORPORATE DEVELOPMENT**                    2009–PRESENT
*TOPP Information, Ltd.*                                        *Maitland, Florida*
Perform consultant duties for all clients, direct emergency outreach and public affairs activities, and facilitate focus groups. Serve as contractor for the U.S. Environmental Protection Agency's (EPA) Emergency Community Outreach Team. Develop and continually update pocket guide for emergency response. Participate as a team trainer for Crisis Communications course. Placed on 24-hour call to man incident command post for national emergency response per federal guidelines.

**PUBLIC INFORMATION MANAGER**                                 1999–2009
*Rural/Metro, Inc.*                                            *Orlando, Florida*
Served as media spokesperson with responsibility for governmental and public affairs. Managed the advertising and public relations budgets and community service programs, and coordinated internal and external community activities. Served on state-level Emergency Medical Services (EMS) committees while working closely with operations as a member of the Corporate Communications Strategic Planning Team.

**PARAMEDIC/SENIOR PARAMEDIC**                                 1998–2003
*Rural/Metro, Inc.*                                            *Orlando, Florida*
Emergency patient care and front-line supervision. Served regularly as County Operations Supervisor.

**FIREFIGHTER/PARAMEDIC**                                      1997–2002
*City of Oviedo*                                               *Oviedo, Florida*
Part-time firefighter/paramedic. Provided emergency patient care.

### EDUCATION

**BACHELOR OF ARTS**                                           2009
*Rollins College*                                             *Winter Park, Florida*
Major: Organizational Communication. Graduated cum laude.

### QUALIFICATIONS
- Florida Certified Paramedic
- Incident Command System level 100, 200 and 300—USCG
- Joint Information Center (JIC) training—USCG
- HazWOPER certificate—Hazardous Waste Operations and Emergency Response
- EMS Public Information, Education & Relations Instructor for National Highway Traffic Safety Administration (NHTSA)

### HONORS
- Multiple Public Safety Program Award for 2009—Rural/Metro Corporation
- 2007 Charles C. Hall Award—Orange County Department of EMS
- 2000 Internal EMS Week National Award—American Ambulance Association

**Sample 5.13    CHRONOLOGICAL RÉSUMÉ FOR AN EXPERIENCED WORKER**

# Ford Mason 38 Southland Drive, Seabrook, SC 27501    878–217–7577
Ford.mason@snco.net

## Summary

Over 15 years of technical and analytical software systems development experience. Involved with mission-critical projects from conception through analysis, design development, and implementation. Well-versed with web application open source technologies.

## Technical Summary

Languages: Java, JavScript, CSS, PHP, Python, Perl, SQL.

## Experience
2000–Present        SENIOR SYSTEMS CONSULTANT
Carolinian Financial
Charlotte, SC

Responsibilities: As a senior client/server architect and developer, lead teams that developed mission-critical applications as well as reusable components used by multiple development projects for field and home office applications. Researched emerging open source technologies for line of business development projects, and mentored application developers.

Designed secure web framework for access to multiple legacy systems with an integrated single sign-on security feature to roll and synchronize passwords on multiple tiers. Systems leveraging this framework were deployed on all field workstations across the country.

Designed and developed API services for web-based applications connected to corporate network.

Designed and developed data distribution for 3-tier web-based sales force automation system. Developed utility to analyze, deduplicate, and merge disparate customer contact databases.

Sample 5.14    Chronological Résumé for an Experienced Worker

**Ford Mason**

Migrated client teleservicing center applications in VB and PowerBuilder to web-based technologies.

Designed and developed a password provider service API and framework, reducing help desk password reset support costs by more than $300,000 per year.

Researched and recommended virtualization solution for software testing lab, saving $240,000 in hardware costs. Researched emerging open source component technologies for use in enterprise web-based applications.

1992–2000    CONSULTANT
C. R. Jameson Associates
Cambridge, MA

Provided software design and development services for user-customizable Personal Information Management product that was marketed internationally.

Provided contract computer programming and support services for the financial services industry.

1990–1992    CONSULTANT
Lily Corporation
Cambridge, MA

Designed database access library for proprietary language (LEAF) extending Lily A-B-C releases for Windows 3.

Automated and enhanced development process.

**Education**

Eastern College, Dalton, MA
B.A., Chemistry, 1990

Listed in *Who's Who in American Colleges and Universities*

President of Student Outreach Society

References available upon request.

Sample 5.14    Chronological Résumé for an Experienced Worker (*continued*)

# KHARI DANICEC

*83 Woodbine Drive*
*Howard, NH 04213*
*(765) 321–1962*
*KhariD83@aol.com*

## SUMMARY OF SKILLS

- *Nine years of experience in service assurance in a five-state district*
- *Experienced corporate troubleshooter*
- *Effective manager of team of 30 employees*
- *Extensive training in leadership, diversity, service assurance, workplace safety*

## EMPLOYMENT

*FedEx Corporation*

**Service Assurance Manager,** *Northeast District Office.*

*Improved service and quality within the Northeast District Domestic Ground Operations, which included ME, NH, VT, and portions of NY and MA. Collaborated with a network of agents, operations, and senior management to improve tracking, scanning, and delivering packages on time. Developed and implemented a system of root cause analysis of failed deliveries. Traveled to various hub, metroplex, and ramp facilities to ensure efficient and timely loading and departure of aircraft. Responsible for troubleshooting and designing remediation for any issue affecting service. Compiled, submitted, and presented data to local, regional, and corporate levels for analysis. 2003–2012.*

**Operations Manager,** *Wilmington, MA; Londonderry, NH.*

*Supervised team of 15–30 customer-service agents, trailer drivers, couriers, and package handlers on day, night, and weekend shifts. Balanced daily workload of packages to ensure 100% on-time delivery. Monitored hours to meet budgets. Supervised sorts and reload operations. Monitored compliance with all DOT and FedEx road requirements. Investigated incidents and accidents involving FedEx vehicles. Interviewed, hired, and trained all couriers, agents, and handlers. 1996–2030.*

**Sample 5.15   CHRONOLOGICAL RÉSUMÉ FOR AN EXPERIENCED WORKER**

# *Khari Danicec*

**Customer Service Agent,** *Londonderry, NH.*

*Dispatched calls to drivers, processed packages over the station counter, handled customer complaints, entered payroll, and compiled daily revenue paperwork. 1991–1996.*

## EDUCATION

**B.S., Office Administration,** *minors in French and Psychology, Falmouth State College, Falmouth, NH, 1994.*

**FedEx training courses:** *Service Agent training, International Freight Handling, Dangerous Goods Handling, Defensive Driving, Driver Instructor training, Containerized Vehicle Management Leadership, Safety Management, Diversity, Courier Best Practices, Point-of-Sale Device, Service Assurance. 1987–2006.*

**Intensive Leadership Training,** *Eckerd College, St. Petersburg, FL, 1991.*

*Microsoft Office Intensive Review, Women in Leadership Seminar Series, Workplace Diversity Seminar 2003–2011.*

## AWARDS AND HONORS

*Received 33 Bravo Zulu commendation letters for performance above and beyond, 2010.*

*Member of the Year, Portland Power Squadron, 2009.*

*FedEx Star Award, 2008.*

*FedEx Staff Award, 2005.*

*FedEx Delegate, Maine Quality Forum, 2003.*

## REFERENCES

*Available upon request.*

**Sample 5.15   Chronological Résumé for an Experienced Worker (*continued*)**

# Résumé Alternatives

Although chronological and functional résumés are the most common formats for presenting experience, they are not the only options. Using an alternative format can help you stand out in a crowd. It can also be seen as a fresh way to organize information that transcends job descriptions and dates of employment.

Sometimes, an alternative résumé can be used in conjunction with your traditional résumé. You'll have to decide what is most appropriate for your individual situation. Here are some alternatives to consider.

- **Video Résumés.** A short (one to four minute) video describing your education, skills, and experiences can effectively supplement your résumé. It doesn't have to be a broadcast-caliber production, but the production quality shouldn't detract or distract from your presentation. View other video résumés before creating your own, and be sure to dress and speak professionally. You can upload the video to YouTube.com, Viddler.com, or other video hosting website. Then, include a link to it in your résumé and cover letter. The benefit of using video is that it can help you be memorable as an applicant and also allows you to show off your personality.

- **Narrative Résumés.** These are conversational in tone, telling a story about the candidate's career progression while integrating relevant personal data. Stick to one page, and break up long blocks of text with headlines and subheads. You may also want to use bullets to present information. The narrative résumé may be combined with a letter starting with a personal greeting, such as "Dear Ms. Smith: I am pleased to send you further information about my work experience, as you requested."

- **Biographies.** In this context, a biography presents a concise, interesting story about your background and most impressive accomplishments. Keep this summary to about five or six paragraphs. Lay out the information on a single page, using an easy-to-read typeface and possibly some graphic elements, like a border or even a head-and-shoulders photo of yourself.

- **Addenda.** An **addendum** (*addenda* is the plural form of the word) is a single page that accompanies your résumé and describes a particular skill or position in more detail. It gives you the opportunity to elaborate on your most impressive or relevant experience. Good topics for an addendum include key volunteer, internship, or life experiences; computer skills, including hardware, software, and networking systems used; training experiences, including classes taught or attended; and project leadership, including the number of staff, budget, and goals accomplished.

- **Curriculum Vitae (C.V.).** Although occasionally used by people in the medical community, curriculum vitae are most often use when applying for work with a firm outside the United States. A curriculum vitae tends to be much more detailed than a traditional résumé—as long as four or five pages. In addition to information about work background and education, it may note international travel experience and language skills; list references and their contact information; and provide personal data, such as nationality, passport number, birthdate, and marital status.

- **Job Search Business Cards.** If your job hunt is well targeted, the key points of the search will fit on a business card printed on one or both sides or in a fold-over tent format. These points would include one to three areas of expertise, your job search goal, and your name and contact information. Distribute your business cards at networking meetings, social events, business open houses, job fairs, and interviews.

- **Work Samples.** If you have been previously employed or have taken courses directly related to the job for which you're applying, consider sending samples of your work to potential employers. These should be truly reflective of the quality of work you do and accompanied by an explanatory cover letter and a traditional résumé. Keep in mind that your work samples may not be returned to you, so you may want to send photocopies.

## Résumé Software

One of the job hunting tools you might want to consider adding to your repertoire is a résumé software package. Although some packages can be a bit simplistic and generic in terms of the types of résumés they can help you to create, others include thousands of fonts, prewritten phrases, and writing wizards help you compose.

Most packages offer the option of creating a functional or chronological résumé. You'll probably be able to choose from many different templates of each. Depending on the sophistication of the package, you'll have varying degrees of flexibility from there. Most packages offer you choices of fonts, graphic elements, colors, and layouts. Just make sure that the package you choose is easy to use, install, and edit.

Perhaps the best reason for investing in résumé software is if you intend to customize your résumé for different employers. Some software simplifies that task while creating crisp, professional layouts.

You can purchase résumé software packages online, at any office supplies store, or at any store that sells electronics. Packages cost from $25 to $75, depending on their capabilities. Read the software reviews and the product information carefully, and decide whether you need all the features.

Another option is to search online for résumé programs. Some career websites offer résumé building tools either for free or as part of their paid services.

No matter which type of program you use to help craft your résumé, it will never be a substitute for your own creative thinking and your knowledge of the job market for your field. If you rigidly follow the résumé format that comes with your computer and its word processing software, be assured that your résumé will look exactly like the résumés of the thousands of other people who also use that software. To create an effective résumé, you and only you must take the time to determine how to present your skills and experience in the best light for the type of position you seek. Customize your résumé, and be sure to continue to follow all the basic résumé do's and don'ts. Take extra care to ensure that the final layout is pleasing and not too busy.

# How to E-mail Your Résumé

Ninety percent of the time, you will be e-mailing your résumé, and very few companies expect you to use regular mail. If you are introducing yourself to a company that has not advertised a position, using regular mail may help you stand out. However, unless you're only mailing to a handful of companies, it is probably not worth the added expense (postage/paper/envelope). Because sending résumés electronically has become standard and preferred practice, be sure to remember the following:

- Use MS Word. While some companies will accept PDF documents, Word is the safest option.

  E-mail your résumé as an attachment. Most companies will accept attachments; however, you must use a good subject line and post a cover letter in the body of the e-mail so the recipient knows that the attachment is your résumé. Some employers offer you the option to upload your résumé along with your application.

- Don't paste your résumé into the text of your e-mail, as you will lose the formatting. Instead, only put your cover letter into the body of the e-mail.

- Use an appropriate but attention-getting subject line to let the employer know your résumé is not spam. "Résumé of Keith Smith" is acceptable. Also, name your attachment in a way that makes sense to the recipient. *Myrésumé51884* is not as helpful to the employer as *NicoleSmithRésumé.doc*.

- Write an effective cover letter. Merely sending a résumé as an attachment is not enough to get an employer's attention. Remember that in order to guard against computer viruses, most businesses will not open an unexpected, unexplained attachment. Your cover letter must be doubly convincing.

- Run your word processor's spell-check, but don't rely too heavily on it because it can miss many errors. Sending your résumé electronically does not allow you to neglect the important steps of revising, editing, and proofreading.

## Using Keywords

When résumés and cover letters are downloaded, the data from them are placed in a database for retrieval when a need arises. Employers and recruiters search résumé databases by using keywords, which are nouns and phrases that highlight areas of expertise, industry-related jargon, achievements, and other distinctive features of an applicant's work history.

Wording your résumé for the computer means that verbs—the hallmarks of a good paper résumé—are less useful than nouns because recruiters more often search for nouns. You should even consider the form of the nouns you're using. For example, *management* can be a dangerous choice because a recruiter who typed in *manager* would miss it. Your best bet is to find a way to incorporate both words. You may even want to have a "Keywords" section that unabashedly plays to the computer, seeking to pop up in as many employer searches as possible.

The job seeker with the most keywords, plus required experience, rises to the top of the candidate heap. Cover your bases by lacing your résumé and cover letter with career-specific keywords.

Choosing the best keywords largely depends on your career objective and the type of position you're hoping to obtain. Keywords are unique to each field and to each position within a field, and there is no master list that works for all job hunters. Research the words used to describe your field or the position for which you're applying by scouring job descriptions, reading the *Occupational Outlook Handbook* (**www.bls.gov**), visiting company websites, and reading employers' mission statements and annual reports. Notice which nouns are used most frequently, and develop a list to use in your own résumé. There are also websites that list keywords by career field, such as **www.careers.ucr.edu/ Students/JobSearch/nouns.html**.

Here is a brief list of some keywords that could help a candidate for a teaching position land on an employer's "hit list":

| | |
|---|---|
| private and public school | master's degree |
| special education | guidance counselor |
| detail oriented | budget planning |
| school board | textbook author |
| extracurricular activities | computer literate |
| gifted students | Microsoft Office |
| inner-city schools | spreadsheet development |
| teacher-of-the-year award | |

---

**EXERCISE**    **Keyword Review**

Review your résumé. Make a list of keywords you've used. Then, look for opportunities to insert additional keywords. Revise your résumé accordingly.

*Keywords Used*                          *New Keywords to Use*

_____          _____

_____          _____

_____          _____

_____          _____

_____          _____

_____          _____

## Posting Your Résumé on the Internet

Now that your résumé is created, you're ready to post it on the Internet. Posting sites and services offer different ways for employers to access their résumé databases. Use a search engine to find these sites and then read the home page and the Frequently Asked Questions (FAQ) sections to get a sense of the focus and scope of the site. Some allow employers and even job candidates direct access. Others require that employers tell the service what kind of job they want to fill and what qualifications they seek. The database service then searches the database and provides the employer with résumés from suitable applicants. When deciding whether to post your résumé, you must weigh questions of résumé placement and privacy. Be sure to ask the following questions:

- Does the database post the kinds of jobs that interest you?
- Would your ideal employer be likely to search this database? In other words, is it general enough that an average employer would easily find it?
- How long does a résumé stay on the system?
- What are the site's privacy policies? Can your information be shared or sold?
- What are the posting requirements?
- Are there any costs associated with posting?
- Can access to your résumé be restricted in any way—for example, to avoid having your current employer see it?

## Hints for Posting Your Résumé Online

- **Post your résumé strategically.** Use one or two of the large popular job sites as well as one or two smaller job sites unique to your specific field.
- **Limit access to your personal contact information.** Be sure you understand your options and proofread the registration and instruction forms carefully.
- **Limit the contact information on your résumé.** Only list an e-mail account created specifically for your job search, and delete all other standard contact information.
- **Monitor the site routinely.** Renew your résumé every thirty days, and if you don't get any response within forty-five, remove it and post elsewhere. Once you are hired, delete your résumé so you don't continue to get inquiries and so your current employer doesn't see it and believe you are still job hunting.

## Online Résumé Tools and Services

Online résumé services offer help with building and disseminating your résumé—usually for a fee. Some, such as www.ResumeSocial.com and www.Razume.com allow you to post your résumé and get feedback from other job hunters or professionals. Others, such as www.VisualCV.com, allow you to create a digital résumé that can include audio, video and photos. Other sites to explore include www.Emurse.com, which allows you to create, share, and store your résumé, and www.Gigtide.com, where you can create, publish, manage, and track your résumé. These sites can be another helpful tool at any stage of résumé writing—from drafting to distributing.

## SUCCESS STORIES

Often, the greatest inspiration comes from those who have succeeded. Consider the following success stories from job hunters who were once like you!

I began creating résumé drafts six months before I gave notice at my former job. I showed drafts to friends with business experience and a career counselor. I tried to implement every worthwhile suggestion and notice the comments that were most often repeated. My final version looked nothing like the one I started with, but at almost every interview, I received genuine compliments on my outstanding résumé. What a great way to start an interview.

Fabio
*Physician's Assistant*

I had hurriedly created a résumé, mailed out dozens, and received few responses. I was mystified because I had been a strong student in college and I had several years of experience. Frustrated, I began to call the human resources departments of several local health insurance companies until I found a few who agreed to give me an informational interview about insurance sales. One HR manager was particularly helpful and offered to look over my résumé. When I showed her what I'd been mailing out, she was shocked at the difference between the professionalism I'd displayed in person and the lackluster résumé I'd mailed out. She made several suggestions, including that I change the order of the sections of my résumé and shorten the whole thing. I took her advice and mailed her a revised copy. She not only called to offer me an interview for a position, but I also got appointments for three other interviews. I will never again underestimate the importance of the résumé as a sales tool.

Rochelle
*Insurance Sales*

# Chapter Follow-Up

Your résumé is the most important tool when hunting for a job:

- Write your résumé with care and precision, choosing the wording and format that make the most of your education and skills.

- Learn the different formats and basic elements of the résumé and then rearrange those building blocks to your best advantage while paying careful attention to the rules and specialized language of résumé writing.

- Begin building your résumé while still in college, seeking out employment and volunteer opportunities as well as participating fully in campus life.

- E-mail your résumé as an MS Word attachment, paying special attention to subject line and cover letter.

- Résumé software and online résumé services are additional helpful tools that can help you better customize and distribute your résumé.

### Multiple Choice Answers to Check Your Résumé Savvy

1. The correct answer is *d.* Some novice job hunters become so enamored with new job hunting technology that they forget that creating a résumé that is unique to their own skills, education, and objectives still takes work.

2. The correct answer is *b,* chronological résumé. Be sure to examine many different résumé formats to decide if and how to highlight the dates of your employment experience.

3. The correct answer is *d.* As a rule, do not list your high school unless you are a recent graduate who has not yet matriculated into a degree program. If you had special work experience during high school or demonstrated leadership skills or athletic or academic talent, you may want to include these facts on your résumé. Weigh the decision to list your high school skills against the fact that they may flag an employer to examine your youth or lack of experience.

4. The correct answer is *a.* A well-written one-page résumé is almost always the best choice for those with limited employment experience.

5. The correct answer is *d.* Any schooling or training provided by an employer, any honors or achievements you earned in high school or college, and an expected graduation date from college are all important items to include in the education section of your résumé.

# Chapter 6

# Writing Cover Letters

## What Do You Know?

### True or False

_____ 1. You should always send a cover letter with every résumé.

_____ 2. Don't include a "call to action" in your cover letter because you'll come across as being pushy.

_____ 3. You should personalize the cover letter if possible, addressing a specific individual, as opposed to a generic approach, such as "To Whom It May Concern."

_____ 4. Your cover letter should be two or more pages and include much of the same information as your résumé.

_____ 5. It's perfectly acceptable to send your cover letter by e-mail, unless the employer has specifically requested that applicants use postal mail.

_____ 6. A referral cover letter mentions a mutual contact as a means to persuade the employer to give you consideration.

_____ 7. The main purpose of the cover letter is to get you an interview.

## Chapter Focus

In this chapter, you'll learn to:

- Identify the three parts of a cover letter.
- Target a cover letter to a specific person, mentioning a specific position.
- Expand and elaborate on your education and skills listed on your résumé.
- Request an interview, and explain your plans for follow-up.

## Real-Life Relevance

If you want to stand out from the crowd of job seekers vying for your dream job, a well-written cover letter is your best tactic. It's your first opportunity to make a good impression, so be sure to make it count. Don't just ramble on about your experience and education. Instead, use your cover letter to explain, as specifically as possible, how hiring you would benefit the company you are targeting and to request an interview.

# Elements of the Cover Letter

When most people think about job hunting, they tend to focus on preparing a résumé. In fact, the cover letter deserves as much—if not more—attention. The cover letter is your chance to introduce yourself, describe your strengths and skills, and express your interest in a particular job in narrative form.

Think of the cover letter as a marketing tool used to move your customer one step closer to buying your product. Be sure you've provided the answers to these questions:

- How will the employer benefit from hiring you?
- How will adding you to the team give the company a competitive advantage in the marketplace?
- What do you bring to the table?
- What differentiates you from all the other job hunters hoping to be recruited?

Recognize that many employers will look at your cover letter as an indicator of your writing skills. A well-written cover letter can help you stand out. It encourages the potential employer to give consideration to your résumé and, ultimately, interview you for the position.

Because a cover letter is also a way to indicate formal application for a specific position, it can be called a *letter of application* and is usually accompanied by a résumé. A cover letter has three main elements:

1. **Introductory paragraph.** The first paragraph mentions the position you're interested in and how you learned of the job opening (if indeed you have learned of a job opening). If a friend or business contact told you about the position, mention his or her name, and be sure to send him or her a copy of your letter. In this paragraph, you may also want to specify why you're applying to this particular company (for example, because of its outstanding reputation in the field). This paragraph is normally two to four sentences long.

   Introduce some of your abilities that could be of interest to an employer—in addition to emphasizing the type of position you are seeking. If you are sending a cover letter to a specific company and don't know whether there is a current job opening, begin by explaining the type of position you want.

2. **Body.** In the middle two paragraphs, "toot your own horn"—honestly, of course. In essence, this is your opportunity to sell yourself. Tell the employer why you're the perfect candidate for the job, and mention at least three of your strong points. One good technique is to use the first paragraph of the body to explain your educational background and the second to describe your work experience. Give specifics when you can. Also, mention personal qualities that suggest you're a highly desirable employee. Are you energetic, enthusiastic, detail oriented, and a fast learner? Choose adjectives that are applicable to the position you want. Use the body of your cover letter to make a connection to the employer.

    If you didn't already mention in your introduction why you want to work for this particular employer, this is the place to do it. Focus on the company's needs and how you meet them. Make a crystal-clear correlation between your skills and the needs and character of the company. Explain why you think you would be an asset. Your knowledge about the company based on research you've done should be apparent to the reader.

    For example, if you're applying for a health care position, you might mention the company's reputation for excellent patient care and then cite specific instances in which you've worked one-on-one with patients to ensure their needs were met or exceeded. If you're applying for a high school teaching position, you might comment on the school's impressive graduation rate and then give examples of your experience in working with high school–age students to bring up their grades and standardized test scores. It's not enough to give general statements. Support your claims with specific cases to illustrate your point.

3. **Closing.** Don't forget the overall purpose of your cover letter and résumé: to obtain an interview. That's your call to action. In other words, this is where you "ask for the sale." Be sure to indicate specifically and assertively what you want the employer to do next—for example, "I'd like to arrange an interview at your earliest convenience" is a clear statement. Mention how and where you can be reached or, better yet, use a more proactive approach and state that you'll call the employer on a specific day. The tone of this section should be polite yet explicit.

# The Write Stuff

Keep these tips in mind regarding cover letters:

1. **The best cover letters reveal your enthusiasm for a particular job and the employer, and tell the employer why you are worthy of consideration.** Your letter should reflect your understanding of the company and how you may be able to meet its needs. Think of the cover letter as your initial knock on the door—your chance to make that all-important first impression. In today's highly competitive job market, your cover letter has to be as dynamic and impressive as your résumé and your personality.

2. **Don't send a résumé without a cover letter.** A résumé sent by itself is usually ignored. Besides, why pass up an opportunity to present your best qualities? Your cover letter puts your résumé in context, drawing attention to your strengths and best attributes. It gives you a chance to reveal your personality in a way that a strictly formatted résumé does not. At a basic level, it allows you to demonstrate your writing skills. But most important, it serves as an introduction to your résumé—a teaser that encourages the reader to take the time to learn more about you.

3. **Personalize your cover letter.** If you address your letter to a specific individual rather than "Dear Sir or Madam," "To Whom It May Concern," or "Human Resources Department," it has a much better chance of being read. To get the name of the appropriate individual, call the company for information, check trade publications and reference materials that list company officers, search the Internet for company information, or find out from a personal contact. Invest your energy in doing solid research so you can aim your cover letter at a target person who makes hiring decisions.

4. **Make sure your letter looks professional.** It should be typed, spell-checked, and error-free. Typos, misspellings, grammatical errors, and cross-outs immediately communicate that you lack written communication skills and don't pay attention to detail. If you are unsure of your writing abilities, ask a professor, coworker, or friend to proofread your work. Even the best writers have editors; enlist several of your own. If you are sending your letter by regular mail as opposed to e-mail, consider using quality paper—white or off-white—and of reasonable thickness. You can find professional-quality paper as well as matching envelopes at most office supplies stores. Plain white, lightweight, or recycled copier paper will detract from the impression your letter will make.

5. **Keep your letter to one page.** Your cover letter should be concise but thorough. The length will depend on how much you have to convey, but three to six paragraphs should allow you to cover the most important points. If your letter is too long, the reader may find it overwhelming and simply push it aside to be dealt with later or never. Devote one paragraph to each key thought. Keep paragraphs to three or four sentences each. This is especially true if you are sending your letter via e-mail; long paragraphs are difficult to read on a computer.

6. **Familiarize yourself with standard letter formats.** The sample letters in this chapter follow standard rules for spacing and punctuation. Demonstrate your written communication skills by creating professional-looking and -sounding letters. If you are unsure of proper letter format, copy one of the samples in this chapter. Many people find the full-block format easiest to follow. For a letter sent via postal mail, you can use the format of the sample letter written to Mindy Karsten. For a sample of a letter to be sent via e-mail, see the letter sent to Tyler Steed, which is in a standard format.

7. **Make your cover letter scannable.** Today's cover letters are often read by computers as well as by humans. They are scanned into applicant databases, along with résumés. To ensure proper scanning of your letter, use black type on white

or off-white paper. Choose an easy-to-read typeface, such as Helvetica, Times New Roman, or Arial, in a point size between 10 and 14. If you're sending your letter via e-mail, include your résumé as an attachment. If you use regular mail, then paper-clip your résumé to the cover letter; don't use a staple because staples can't be put through a scanner.

**EXERCISE**

### Preparing to Write Your Cover Letter

A good cover letter takes into account the following questions. Think of the type of position and employer you are seeking and then answer the questions accordingly.

1. Who is most likely to read this letter? What type of person is she? List at least five descriptive phrases. Of course, if you've never met this person, you'll be forced to make some assumptions. The point is that if you're writing a letter to a banker, you should probably phrase your letter more formally than if you were writing a letter to the creative director of an advertising agency.

2. Why will your letter be interesting and important to the reader? What's in it for him or her? Give specific examples of what you can do for the company or how the employer will benefit from hiring you.

3. What do you think is important for the reader to know about you? What special talents, skills, experience, or educational background make you a better choice than other applicants?

4. Why would you like to work for the reader's company?

5. Write a call to action—a sentence or two that either tells the employer what you'd like her to do after reading this letter or clearly states your intentions for following up on this initial inquiry.

## Alternative Letter-Writing Strategies

Because no two prospective employers are alike, there's no one way to write cover letters. When seeking an especially competitive position or when stressing unusual skills or abilities, you might consider an alternative to the standard cover letter format.

## What Not to Write in Your Cover Letter

Here's a humorous collection of sentences that were used in actual cover letters. (They were submitted by various human resources departments.)

- I demand a salary commiserate with my extensive experience.
- Wholly responsible for two (2) failed financial institutions.
- Reason for leaving last job: maturity leave.
- It's best for employers that I not work with people.
- Let's meet so you can "ooh" and "aah" over my experience.
- You will want me to be Head Honcho in no time.
- I am a perfectionist and rarely if ever forget details.
- I was working for my mom until she decided to move.
- I have an excellent track record, although I am not a horse.
- I am loyal to my employer at all costs. . . . Please feel free to respond to my résumé on my office voice mail.
- I have become completely paranoid, trusting completely no one and absolutely nothing.
- My goal is to be a meteorologist. But since I possess no training in meteorology, I suppose I should try stock brokerage.
- I procrastinate, especially when the task is unpleasant.
- Instrumental in ruining entire operation for a Midwest chain store.
- Reason for leaving last job: They insisted that all employees get to work by 8:45 a.m. every morning. I couldn't work under those conditions.
- The company made me a scapegoat, just like my three previous employers.

Your best bet is to take the information you have about the job opening (from a classified ad, personal contact, library or Internet research, or some other source) and use it to craft a letter that fits the needs of the prospective employer. The more you can customize your cover letter, the better. Here are some suggested styles:

- **Problem/solution.** Identify the employer's need and then describe in your letter how you would be the perfect answer to that need. For example, if the employer has mentioned accurate keyboarding skills as a requirement, cite your ability to proofread text and your attention to detail.

- **Inverted pyramid.** Read any newspaper, and you'll see that most news stories are written in inverted pyramid style, which begins with the most important information. Put your most important, broad, and relevant information first. Begin with a statement of your career goal and the reasons for your interest in the position. Then, move into the specifics of why you're the best candidate.

- **Deductive order.** Begin your letter with a generalization—almost a thesis statement. Then, support that thesis with examples in the body of the letter. For example, name a specific ability you have. Then, give examples of how you demonstrated that skill in a previous job or at school.

- **Inductive order.** This is the reverse of deductive order. Begin your letter by describing a specific situation in which you've been involved, and from that example, draw the general conclusion that you have a particular skill—one that is necessary for success in the job you're applying for.

- **List.** Extremely popular, this is one of the most effective formats because of its readability. Insert a bulleted list in the body of your letter. It may be a list of relevant job experiences, related skills, or reasons that you think you're a good candidate for the position.

## An Old Marketing Trick: Use a P.S. to Make Your Case

Do you know what is the most-read part of a letter? The P.S. That's right: the postscript. That separate little paragraph that looks like a casual afterthought has a special way of grabbing the eye. Direct marketers have known this for years. That's why if you examine a letter that's trying to sell you something, you'll almost always see a P.S. included. Sometimes, you'll even see a P.P.S., as the copywriter makes the very most of this effective marketing technique.

Don't be afraid to also try this method in your cover letters. If you truly want maximum impact, handwrite your P.S. It will stand out next to your typed letter. Use your P.S. to restate your most marketable asset and give your best "sales pitch." Here are two examples:

> *P.S. When I worked at Avril Associates, I was the youngest employee ever to sell more than 100 units in just one month. My sales exceeded the quota by 12%. I know I can bring that same level of commitment and success to Hastings!*

> *P.S. At WKMR, my college's radio station, my weekly program consistently had the station's largest audience. I look forward to bringing my enthusiasm, creativity, and unique style to your show.*

**EXERCISE**    **Construct a Compelling P.S. Statement**

Write a P.S. statement that you can use in your cover letters. Be sure it gives a specific example of why you're a great candidate for the job.

_____

# E-mail Versus Postal Mail

Anyone applying for a job today must consider whether to e-mail their cover letter and résumé or use regular mail. E-mail has become increasingly accepted, and in many cases, it is preferred. The only time e-mail is not a good option is if the employer has specifically requested that candidates apply via postal mail.

One of the key benefits to e-mail is that if you are able to obtain the e-mail address of the hiring person, you can write to him or her directly, thereby evading such gatekeepers as those who work in the human resources department and secretaries.

**A résumé should always be accompanied by a cover letter that expresses your enthusiasm for a specific job and clearly states why you are a worthy candidate.**
(© WP Simon / Digital Vision / Royalty-Free / Getty Images)

If you decide to go the e-mail route, here are some guidelines to follow:

**Put Your Cover Letter in the Body of the E-mail, Not as an Attachment.**   In today's world of e-mail viruses and spam mail, many people will not open attachments unless they know what they are and who they're from. Therefore, your cover letter should make it clear to the reader that yours is a legitimate e-mail and that the attachment is simply a résumé.

**Type in Upper- and Lowercase Letters.**   Just as you would type a letter on paper using capital and small letters, do the same for an e-mail. All caps look like you're YELLING, and nobody likes to be yelled at. E-mails in all lowercase are difficult to read. Choose a familiar font, such as Arial, Times New Roman, or Verdana, in 10- or 12-point size, black type.

**Avoid Lingo, Emoticons, and Jargon.**    While you may know e-mail and texting lingo, such as BTW (by the way), or be proficient in using emoticons, such as:) (smile), they don't look professional in a cover letter. Also, avoid using industry jargon, acronyms, and abbreviations that the recipient may not understand. Readers should never have to guess what you mean.

**Keep Paragraphs Short.**    Big blocks of text are hard to read, especially on a monitor. Paragraphs should be no more than five lines in length. Consider whether any of your paragraphs lend themselves to bullets, which can help break up copy chunks and add visual impact.

**Give Your Full Name and Contact Information in Your Sign-Off.**    A signature isn't necessary. Beneath your name, type your e-mail address, phone number, and website URL, if you have one. Include a mailing address only if you think it will work in your favor to show your proximity to the employer.

**Use a Good, Specific Subject Line.**    Because the recipient probably doesn't know you and won't recognize your e-mail address, your subject line is your only chance to convince him to open your e-mail and not delete it for fear it could be junk mail or spam. Your subject line can be something like: "Application for Secretarial Position," or "Karen Johnson said to contact you," or "John, regarding your Technology Team."

**Send Your E-mail to One Person at a Time.**    Nobody likes to receive an impersonal e-mail that has been blasted to others. It borders on spam. Don't put anything in the "cc" box. Instead, for best results, send each employer a personalized, customized letter that she is likely to feel obligated to read and reply to.

**Don't Mark Your E-mail Urgent.**    Urgent to you is not urgent to the recipient.

**Be Sure to Use a Respectable E-Mail Address.**    sexslave@gmail.com, sweetiepie@hotmail.com, or drunkbynoon@aol.com is not the type of address to impress an employer. It's probably best to choose something that incorporates your real name.

**Reply Promptly to E-mails.**    If you choose to use e-mail as your means of communicating with an employer, be sure to regularly check your e-mail for a response. Always reply within twenty-four hours and preferably sooner or the employer will simply move on to the next candidate.

# Types of Cover Letters

Cover letters can be a highly effective means of communicating with a potential employer. Seek out opportunities to send them. Because you compose them at your leisure and can therefore give them careful thought, letters often get better results than telephone calls.

The three most common types of cover letters are: (1) the letter to generate a lead; (2) the referral letter (also called a *networking letter* because it uses one contact to make another); and (3) the response to a help wanted ad. Here's how to use each type:

- **Lead-generating letter.** Use this type of letter when you've identified a company you'd like to work for but you don't know if any positions are open. You may send out five to ten of these letters or many more depending on the type of job you want and the breadth of your search. The good news is that if you obtain an interview from a lead-generating letter, you'll probably be one of a few (or even the only one) being considered for a position. The bad news is that of the many letters you send, only a small percentage—and maybe none at all—will receive a response. You'll have a much better chance of success if you do some research so as to be able to customize each letter to the company. A generic letter that you broadcast en masse is unlikely to be effective in today's competitive employment market.

- **Referral letter.** Referral letters often bring good results. The mere mention of a mutual contact can get your letter past the secretary to the decision-maker. If you are networking effectively, you'll have many opportunities to send out this type of letter.

- **Response to a help wanted ad.** The best thing about responding to an ad is that you know that a position exists. Unfortunately, a help wanted ad posted online or published in a major newspaper or trade journal can generate hundreds of responses, so your cover letter had better be exceptional.

## Sample Cover Letters

Once you've written one or two cover letters, you'll find it's easy to write more. In fact, you'll probably be able to use much of the same wording with minor modifications in future letters.

**EXERCISE**    **Creating Cover Letter Templates**

Read the sample cover letters on the following pages. They are written in several formats—all equally acceptable. Then create your own. Compose three cover letters: (1) a lead-generating letter, (2) a referral letter, and (3) a response to a help wanted ad found online or clipped from a newspaper or trade publication.

This assignment may take some time, but it is a worthwhile endeavor. Although this is a practice exercise, you may still want to use the name, address, and title of a person you wish to contact later in your job search. Show your letter to instructors, employers you know, and friends. Use their feedback to hone your work.

Once you have revised these three letters, consider them as templates. You can use them or modified versions of them in your actual job search. When you've finished this exercise, give yourself a hearty pat on the back. You've just completed one of the most arduous tasks of job hunting: writing your first cover letters.

14 Hill Street
Middletown, SD 61604
February 24, 2011


Ms. Mindy Karsten
Vice President
Salespro, Inc.
672 Charles Avenue
Bedford, SD 61604

Dear Ms. Karsten:

Is your company looking for an experienced, detail-oriented bookkeeper? If so, I would like to be considered for the position.

In June, I will receive an associate's degree in business from Middletown College and will be seeking full-time employment. I have been attending school in the evenings while working days as an assistant bookkeeper at Molly's Chinese Restaurant. That experience has enabled me to gain valuable knowledge in bookkeeping while learning the basics of operating a small business. I believe I could effectively bring these skills along with my high level of productivity to work in Salespro's accounting department.

I would be interested in arranging an interview at your convenience. I will call you next Tuesday to see if you can set aside just 20 minutes to meet with me. If you do not have an opening at this time, please feel free to pass my résumé along to your colleagues. Thank you for your consideration. I can be reached at 385-555-8888 or chrisgeorge@comcast.net.

Sincerely,

*Tina Kaplan*

Tina Kaplan

Enc.

**Sample 6.1    Lead-Generating Letter Formatted for Postal Mail**

Subject Line — Proven Salesperson for Horace Chemicals

Mr. Tyler Steed
V. P. Sales
Horace Chemicals, Inc.
111 Orange Street
Clarence, NM 60689

Dear Mr. Steed:

I was the kid on the block with the lemonade stand, the student who won the digital camera because I sold the most candy bars, the Girl Scout who went to Disney World for free because I moved the most cookies. Sales has always been my forté.

Now, however, my sales expertise has progressed from cookies and candy to medical technology, specifically pharmaceutical products. I'm writing to see if you might have a need for my skills. Briefly, here's what I would bring to the job:

• Five years with CapCom Pharmaceuticals as sales representative
• CapCom Salesperson of the Year, 2002, 2003
• Instrumental in the launch of three new pharmaceutical products
• Specialized knowledge of cancer treatments
• M.S. degree in chemistry from Purdue University; B.S. in biology from the University of Notre Dame

My clients and coworkers would describe me as highly energetic, pleasant to work with, and extremely detail oriented. I would welcome the opportunity to meet with you and discuss how I might fit in as a part of the Horace Chemicals sales team.

Attached is my résumé. I will contact you next week to set up an appointment. By the way, I'll bring the lemonade and cookies when we meet. Old habits are tough to break.

Sincerely,

Liana Michaels
3499 West Oak Lane
Clarence, NM 60689 (601) 555–7147
lmichaels@gmail.com

Sample 6.2    Lead-Generating Letter, Formatted for E-mail

Subject Line — Maureen Hudson Referred Me to You

Mr. Glenn Severance
Director of Human Resources
Almeda Corporation
802 Maple Street
Allston, WY 70011

Dear Mr. Severance:

Maureen Hudson of your Marketing Department recently informed me of the opening for an administrative assistant. I believe that my educational background and my experience in business qualify me for the position. Please consider this letter as my formal application.

On May 24, I will graduate from the University of New England with an associate's degree in Business Administration. I have up-to-date knowledge of the field, having completed courses in everything from marketing to managerial finance. I have maintained a 3.6 cumulative average while financing my education myself by working at part- and full-time jobs.

As you will note on the enclosed résumé, I have several years' background in business. As a secretary at Wallace's, Inc., I've experienced the day-to-day operation of a large manufacturing company such as yours. I've also demonstrated my managerial skills by supervising and training other employees at ComputerMart.

I look forward to discussing my capabilities and potential with you. You can contact me at (307) 555–4242 or Kenny220@earthlink.net.

Sincerely,

*Langdon Kenney*

Langdon Kenney
220 Boulder Drive
Manchester, WY 73104
(307) 555-4242
Kenny220@earthlink.net

Enc.
c: M. Hudson

P.S. At ComputerMart, I won the Employee of the Month award twice. I look forward to bringing my good work ethic and enthusiasm to Almeda Corporation.

**Sample 6.3    Referral Letter, Following Up on a Lead, Formatted for E-mail**

Subject: Your controller position (referred by Marisol Playa)

Mr. John Zofchack
Vice President
Manley Accounting Services
2220 Conway Ave.
Charleston, VA 44999

Dear Mr. Zofchack:

As an accountant with more than five years in the field, I was excited to learn of your need for an experienced controller. Marisol Playa, a former colleague, suggested I contact you. She thought my experience closely matched your job requirements.

**Your Needs and My Qualifications**
- Four-year degree—I have a BS in accounting.
- CPA credential—I have a CPA plus additional course work in financial management.
- Experience in report generation—have experience compiling data for quarterly and annual reports.
- Accounting software proficiency—I am proficient in Excel, Peachtree, and Lotus.
- Five years' experience with major accounting firm—I have two years with Whitney Marcel Ltd. as an accountant; three years with Kosmos Corp. as senior accountant/controller.

This abbreviated list represents only some of my relevant experience, so I am attaching my résumé. I am currently employed with Kosmos Corp. but am seeking new and exciting challenges. I will contact you next week in hopes that we can further discuss the requirements of the position. Thank you for your interest.

Sincerely yours,

Frank Nagle
6688 Glen Haven Circle
Orley Park, VA 44989
(505) 555–3338
Nagle99@mediaone.com

**Sample 6.4   Referral Letter, Following Up on a Lead, Formatted for E-mail**

127 D.W. Highway
Kensington, IL 64333
(405) 555–6784
kbartlett@aol.com

June 1, 2011


Mr. Kyle Cooke
Office Manager
Midtown Software, Inc.
575 Island Rd.
Kensington, IL 64333

Dear Mr. Cooke:

I am writing to apply for the position of Administrative Assistant as advertised on monster.
com on May 25, 2011.

For the past year, I have worked as a secretary at Royer's Hospital in downtown Kensington.
My responsibilities are diverse and include receptionist duties, bookkeeping, word
processing, and file management.

At the end of this month, I will graduate from Kensington Community College with an
associate degree in liberal arts. I would like to use the skills I've acquired at Royer's,
combined with my degree from Kensington, in an interesting, challenging position.

Enclosed is my résumé. It details the skills I could bring to Midtown Software in the position
of administrative assistant. I will contact you next week to discuss how we can explore this
possibility further. Thank you for your consideration.

Sincerely,

*Kimba Bartlett*

Kimba Bartlett

**Sample 6.5    Response to Help Wanted Ad, Formatted for Postal Mail**

Subject: Collections Agent Position

Castor Credit Union
Opportunity Plaza
Burbank, CA 99877

To Whom It May Concern:

Please consider me for the position of collections agent as advertised on your website.

In the past three years, I have had much experience in collections. Frequently, in my position as a customer service representative at Village Bank, I assisted collections clerks with their telephone and written inquiries, as well as answered many customer questions regarding past-due accounts. My employers have often complimented me on my attention to detail and my perseverance in solving difficult problems.

I have attached my résumé for your review. However, I would greatly appreciate the opportunity to meet with you and further discuss this position and my qualifications. I can be contacted at (443) 565-1121 or sbourke@gmail.com.

Sincerely,

Shannon Bourke

P. S. Working with customers is my specialty. My previous bosses have always noted my outstanding people skills. I look forward to applying those same qualities to my work as your collections agent.

1654 Daige Street
Burbank, CA 99877
443-565-1121
sbourke@gmail.com

Enclosure: Résumé Sample 6.6    RESPONSE TO ONLINE AD, FORMATTED FOR E-MAIL

6 Cumberland Ave
Boseman, MD 10365
(312) 874–9065
hdranton@attbi.com

July 17, 2011

Donald O'Neil
Principal
Westbrook High School
7568 Mammoth Road
Westbrook, MD 10357

Dear Mr. O'Neil:

I am applying for a full-time position as a science teacher at Westbrook High School beginning September 2011. Having the opportunity to join the quality team of educators at Westbrook High would be a welcome experience.

Enclosed is my résumé for your review. I have completed a bachelor's degree in secondary education at Boseman College and am currently pursuing a master's degree from Olivian University in Lee, Delaware. By the completion of the summer semester, I will have earned 36 of the required 62 credits.

During my student teaching at George Washington Middle School, I collaborated with the science faculty and administrators to develop an earth science curriculum targeting at-risk children in the district. I was able to implement and instruct the first three units of the curriculum, including field trips to study coastal ecosystems. My students and coteachers especially enjoyed an online dialogue with middle school students studying similar coastal ecosystems in a small town in southern California.

This experience, as well as my work on community projects and with the Girl Scouts of America, demonstrates my commitment to teamwork, my passion for education, and my innovation in the classroom.

My résumé gives a brief overview of my professional abilities, but I'd welcome the opportunity to meet with you for an interview and provide a clearer picture of the type of person I am. I will call you next week to see what time is best for you. Thank you in advance for your time and consideration.

Sincerely,

*Holly Antonnucci*

Holly Antonnucci
Enc.

**Sample 6.7    Lead-Generating Letter Formatted for Postal Mail**

Ms. Caroline DeNauw
New Day Dynamics Associates
99 Farbush St.
Hastings, AL 20534

Dear Ms. DeNauw:

I have learned from our mutual friend, Tyler Phillipian, that you may have a need for an additional counselor at New Day Dynamics Associates. I would very much welcome the opportunity to be considered for the position, in which I could implement my relevant skills as a member of your practice.

My credentials include:
• M.Ed., Agency and Rehabilitative Counseling, Roget College
• Certified Alcohol and Drug Rehabilitation Counselor
• Seven years' experience, counselor at Greater Montgomery Mental Health
• Extensive counseling experience with multicultural and socioeconomically diverse clients
• Program and seminar development experience
• Member, Committee for Ethical Review, Alabama Mental Health Professional Association

I would greatly appreciate the chance to learn more about the needs of your practice and to explore how my qualifications might meet those needs. I will call early next week to discuss the possibility of an interview. In the meantime, I've attached my résumé for your review.

Sincerely,

Thomas R. Moser
93 S. Maple Ave
Montgomery, AL 20534
(256) 223–6768
TRMoser@yahoo.com

**Sample 6.8   Referral Letter, Following Up on a Lead, Formatted for E-mail**

# A Few Techniques to Make Your Letter Stand Out

By now you should know how to write a basic cover letter, and you've reviewed a variety of examples to help you draft your own. Now let's take cover letter writing to the next level.

Assume there are dozens of other qualified candidates applying for the same position. While your cover letter may be well written, that may not be enough to stand out. Think about using some imaginative techniques to help get your cover letter noticed.

However, a word of caution: Always keep your recipient in mind. Not all companies and individuals are receptive to creative approaches. And not all professions lend themselves to a nontraditional strategy. Use your best judgment when considering the ideas below.

**Try a Headline.**   Employ a marketing technique that you often see in ads: Write a benefit-oriented headline.

Just after the salutation (Dear Ms. Jensen:), center in bold type, upper- and lower case, a statement that lets the employer know why you're writing or, even better, what you can do for the company. Consider these examples:

1. Three Reasons Why I'm the Best Candidate for the [Job Title] Position
   (Remember to list those three reasons in the body of your cover letter.)

2. If [Company Name] Wants to Generate More Sales, I'm Your Man [or Woman]

3. I Increased Productivity 17% at My Last Job. I Can Do the Same for [Company Name]

4. Creativity, Great Work Ethic, and a Can-Do Attitude Are What I'll Bring to the [Job Title] Position

**Add a List.**   Using three to ten bullets, create a list for the body of your letter. It can be a list of your best assets, skills, job experiences, or even reasons why you believe you are a good fit for the open position.

**Use a Quotation.**   Is there a quote that epitomizes your personal beliefs or has given you motivation to succeed? You can find quotes online or in a book of quotes at your library.

Place the quote at the top of your cover letter after the salutation (Dear Mr. Ross:) and above the first paragraph. Center it and use italics to make it stand out. Give the full name of the person quoted. In your first paragraph, refer to the quote and explain how it relates to you or your beliefs.

**Include a Testimonial.**   Instead of using a famous quote, use the words of a previous employer or customer commenting on the quality of your work. Be sure that you give credit to the person who made the comment and obtain permission to use it if you think it's necessary.

Place the quote at the top of the letter after the salutation and above the first paragraph. Or insert it in the body of the cover letter where you think it best fits with your content. Follow the testimonial with an explanation as to why you've included it in your cover letter as a means to help the employer get to know you.

**Describe a Problem and Solution.**   Create two paragraphs. Label one "Problem" and the other one "Solution." In "Problem," identify the employer's needs. In "Solution," explain how you would meet those needs. For example, if the employer needs a legal assistant, discuss your expertise in working with court documents.

If "Problem" seems too negative, then substitute the word "Challenge" or "Needs."

**Ask a Question.**   Pose a question and then present yourself as the answer. For example, ask: "Would you like to see a 17% increase in productivity in just one year?" Answer by explaining how you accomplished that result at your previous job and that you are confident you can do the same for this employer.

**Provide a Notable Example.**   Begin your letter with a brief anecdote. Describe an actual situation in which you were involved. From that example, lead into an explanation of your particular talent or skill—one that makes you a superior candidate for the job opening.

**Be Bold.**   If you have one or two particular phrases or sentences in your cover letter that best describe you, put them in bold type. That way, the reader can't miss them. Just don't overdo it. Only use this technique for your most compelling statements.

**Stamp the Envelope "Confidential."**   You can pick up a rubber stamp at any office supplies store for about $5.00. A bright red "Confidential" notation on the envelope containing your résumé and cover letter is sure to get noticed by the recipient.

## Follow-Up Cover Letters

You've sent a cover letter along with your résumé and you have yet to get a reply from the company. You've even called and left a message. Now what?

After seven to ten days, you can send a follow-up cover letter. Your persistence will nudge the employer to consider you and prove your enthusiasm for the job. Here are some options you can try:

Send the same person the exact same cover letter and résumé you originally sent but with one small addition. This time, stick a Post-It note on your cover letter and handwrite the following: "Second submission. I know I'm a fit for this position!"

Or write: "Just following up to let you know I'm still very interested in this position. Hope we can meet soon!"

Sign the sticky note with only your first name, which will come across as informal and friendly.

Another option is to use the same cover letter you originally sent but rewrite the first paragraph to explain why you're writing again.

Here are two sample paragraphs that you can use in starting your follow-up cover letter:

1. You've probably received letters from dozens of applicants seeking the position of [insert job title here]—mine included. I'm writing again because I know I have the skills and great attitude you seek. So, I'm sending you this second letter to demonstrate my genuine enthusiasm and to again request an interview. [Now continue with the text from your original cover letter.]

2. I applied for the position of [insert job title] about 10 days ago. I'm following up because I know I have the ability and experience that the position requires. I hope you don't mind if I introduce myself again and respectfully ask to be considered for an interview. [Now continue with some of the paragraphs from your original cover letter.]

One more option is to write a completely new cover letter. This time, highlight a specific skill or provide more detail about your prior work experience.

The purpose of this follow-up letter is to provide the employer a second opportunity to notice you and consider offering you an interview.

## SUCCESS STORIES

Often, the greatest inspiration comes from those who have succeeded. Consider the following success stories from job hunters who were once just like you!

When I first started job hunting, I sent out dozens of cover letters via e-mail to employers each day. I literally got no replies. It was very discouraging. Then, a friend pointed out to me some of the things I was doing wrong: I was sending the cover letters to employers in a mass mailing in which each recipient could see all the other people who had received copies of the same letter; I was using a very generic letter that was not addressed to a particular person and didn't reference a specific company or position; and my cover letter didn't include any specific reasons that I would be an excellent candidate worthy of consideration for a job.

My friend helped me focus the letter and add compelling reasons for the recipient to open my attached résumé. He also taught me that it was far better to send out a few highly personalized, targeted letters to potential employers where my skills would be a good fit than to blast a "broadcast e-mail" to dozens of companies whose names I'd found on the Internet. My new cover letters generated replies—some of which resulted in interviews and eventually job offers.

Karen
*Project Manager for Textiles Manufacturer*

I had little success answering classified ads with a traditional cover letter and résumé. I decided to try a unique approach. I created what essentially was a one-page flyer about me—complete with compelling headline and eye-catching graphics. I used that flyer with my résumé to apply for a position as a research technician. It helped me stand out from the other applicants, and I did end up getting interviews and eventually a job offer.

Paulina
*Research Technician*

I sent what I thought was a well-written, creative cover letter and my résumé to a major advertising agency in my area asking if it had any openings for a copywriter. They sent me a form rejection letter. I figured that was the end of it. But about two weeks later, I got a call from that agency's largest client—a major cruise line—seeking an in-house promotions writer. The agency had been impressed with my cover letter and résumé and had passed along my information. I had a brief interview with the manager, who hired me on the spot, saying the referral from the ad agency helped her make her decision.

Jennifer
*Promotions Writer*

## Chapter Follow-Up

- Always include a cover letter with your résumé.
- Targeted, personalized letters that explain specifically what you can do for the employer will generate better results than mass mailing generic-sounding letters.
- Your cover letter should highlight your most impressive strengths and experience but leave the detailed chronological listing of your prior employment to your résumé.
- E-mailing your cover letter and résumé is acceptable and often preferred over regular mail.
- When e-mailing your cover letter, paste it into the body of the e-mail, not as an attachment, or the recipient is likely to delete it without opening.
- Keep your letter to one page—a total of three to six paragraphs.
- Make sure your letter looks and sounds professional.
- Remember, a cover letter won't get you a job. Its function, along with your résumé, is to help you to get an interview.

# Chapter 7

## Obtaining References

## What Do You Know?

### Short Answers

1. Can you obtain any references if you've never held a job in your field before?

   _____

   _____

2. What purpose do letters of recommendation and references serve?

   _____

   _____

3. Why is it important to let people whom you list as references know that you're providing their name and contact information to your prospective employers?

   _____

   _____

4. Why should you never provide your originals when giving an employer letters of recommendation?

   _____

   _____

## Chapter Focus

In this chapter, you'll learn to:

- Gather and present information that complements your résumé.
- Lay the groundwork for solid telephone references.
- Obtain letters of recommendation.

## Real-Life Relevance

In today's highly competitive marketplace, employers welcome proof of a candidate's strengths and capabilities. Letters of reference serve as persuasive examples of your employment successes. When you prepare former employers, neighbors, or teachers to receive a reference-checking phone call, you increase the chances that they will give you a good employment or character reference.

# References Available Upon Request

You have a winning résumé and a dynamic cover letter. You have assembled many of the tools you'll need for a successful job hunt, but your explanation of your education, your experience, and your skills isn't enough. The final step is to line up good references.

There are two routes to presenting good references. One is to generate a list of names for the employer to call. Some employers make the effort to follow up; some don't. The other—and more certain—approach is to provide the employer with positive letters of recommendation (also called letters of reference) written in advance by your references. These letters can be your ultimate sales tool in getting an employer to choose you.

Whether you opt to take one route or both, the important thing is that you not wait until you're on the verge of getting a job offer before you take care of this important step.

## Phone References

Employers want to be as confident as possible in their hiring decisions because it's costly and time consuming to hire and train the wrong individual. One of the ways employers try to back up the impressions they form of you during an interview is to talk to a few references whose names you provide. Usually, they do this by phone. These references are people not related to you who can give informed assessments of your job performance and character. Good people to ask include former employers, coaches, teachers, supervisors from internships or volunteer sites and even neighbors you have worked for informally.

Because glowing references can set you apart from other candidates, it's important to choose these people carefully. To generate your list of phone references, follow these steps:

1. **Begin to form good references your first day of any job.** Your supervisors and coworkers make note of your punctuality, thoroughness, ability to take on responsibility, and ability to work well with others from your first day on the job. Develop good work habits and a positive rapport with supervisors and coworkers, and you'll foster good references for future jobs.

2. **Make a list of people you think might serve as references.** Former bosses and coworkers are possible candidates. If you have not held many paying positions, brainstorm a list of people who can serve as character references—people such as neighbors, teachers, or guidance counselors who can speak about your willingness to be helpful or other positive character traits.

3. **Contact the people on your list.** Ask them if they would be willing to serve as a reference. Remind them of the work you did with them and mention qualities you would like them to tell prospective employers about you. Establish an honest, open line of communication. Make sure the individual is comfortable providing a strong reference. If you sense any hesitation, you may want to cross that person off your list of references; remember, you want only enthusiastic recommendations.

4. **Tell your references about the jobs you're seeking.** Explain the position you're seeking and the name of the company or companies they can expect will contact them. This will help your references prepare for the call and enable them to provide the most relevant information to the employer regarding your experience and qualifications. Make mention of the skills you demonstrated while working with them that would be valuable with your prospective employer.

5. **Keep in touch with your references.** Reconnect with your references every few months to be sure the contact information you have on file for them is up to date. Let them know by phone, letter, or e-mail that you're still job hunting and you appreciate being able to keep them on your reference list.

6. **Be selective in giving your references' names to employers.** You don't want your references barraged by too many phone calls, which could be annoying and could also make them wonder if you're having trouble landing a job. If a prospective employer asks for your references before you've even had an interview, explain that your references are very important to you and should be called only if the employer is relatively serious about hiring you.

7. **Ask your references to let you know when they've been called by prospective employers.** This will help you keep tabs on the hiring process. A call to a reference usually suggests that you're a leading candidate for the job. Conversely, if you've given out four names and none have been called within approximately a two-week period, then you're probably not a strong contender for the position.

8. **Thank your references.** When you are successful in getting a job, it's important to thank your references for their willingness to help and let them know about your new position—whether or not they played a part in the process. Showing your appreciation is not only the right thing to do; it also makes it easier to ask them to serve as a reference again in the future should the need arise.

## Letters of Recommendation

In an effort to select the absolute best employees, prospective employers are increasingly relying on letters of recommendation. These letters can be provided in addition to or instead of phone references.

The strongest references come from previous employers who can vouch for your knowledge, integrity, and enthusiasm toward work. A letter of recommendation should include your relationship to the writer, the time frame of your employment, your association with that person, and also several strengths you demonstrated while working. If the writer can also provide specific examples to support those examples of your strengths, the reference will be even stronger. The reference writer must be familiar with who you are and what you did as a former employee. Your best bet is to get a reference from an immediate supervisor, manager, or coworker. The higher the professional status of the person providing reference, the more weight that reference will carry. If you think it would be helpful, you may even want to get references from several people at the company.

Keep in mind that you don't have to have worked full time to get a letter of recommendation. Requesting references at places where you were employed part-time, interned, volunteered, or freelanced is entirely appropriate. Ideally, you should begin gathering letters of recommendation either just before you leave a position or soon after while the quality of your work is still fresh in the mind of the letter writer. As with phone references, request letters only from people who think positively of you. If you believe that your manager is unlikely to give you a good reference, consider asking your immediate supervisor or even a coworker.

Other potential writers of reference letters may include teachers, guidance counselors, leaders of organizations or clubs, or other people familiar with your work. They should all be professional contacts. Personal references from friends, neighbors, or relatives should be used rarely and then only when the employer needs a character reference.

---

**EXERCISE**    ## Who Knows You?

When lining up references, even more important than whom you know is who knows you. Make a list of people whom you think would be willing to either act as a positive phone reference or write a letter of recommendation for you. Your list should include their names, how they know you, and their contact information. You'll soon put this list to use.

---

## How Do You Get a Letter of Recommendation?

The easiest way to get a letter of recommendation is to ask your supervisor or manager. Tell that person about the type of position you're seeking so the letter can be focused toward your objective. Also, give the writer a deadline—politely, of course—to ensure that your letter is treated as a priority. Provide supporting documentation that might help the writer draft an effective letter. For example, give the writer a copy of your résumé and a description of the position you're applying for.

Whereas some people are quite adept at letter writing, others may find the task challenging or may be so busy they can't comply within your time frame. You can help speed the process along and ensure the content of the letter by following these steps:

1. **Prepare a draft of your letter of recommendation.** You'll learn in the next section exactly what that letter should include. Remember to write your letter about yourself as if you were the employer and stick to the facts, supporting your points with specific examples of your accomplishments at work.

2. **Hand-deliver or e-mail to your reference person a copy of your draft recommendation letter.** No matter how you choose to submit your materials, be sure to explain that it's only a draft, and the person is certainly welcome to either edit the text or provide his or her own version. He or she can send it to you via e-mail or create a hard copy signed and on company letterhead and either send it to you through regular mail or you'll personally pick it up.

3. **If the letter of recommendation he or she provides is a hard copy, make copies of it.** Never send an original to a prospective employer. You may not get it back.

4. **Send a thank-you note or e-mail to the person who wrote your letter.** A note will help ensure a positive referral should the individual be personally contacted by a potential employer seeking additional information.

## What Should a Letter of Recommendation Say?

If you are drafting your own letter, be sure to do the following:

1. Identify your reference—his or her position and how the two of you are acquainted.

2. State who is being recommended (namely you) and for what type of position.

3. Describe the reference's relationship to you—how long you worked together, in what capacity, and specific projects that you worked on together.

4. List your top skills, qualities, work habits, attributes, and achievements.

5. Mention that the reference can be contacted for additional information.

If your reference person prefers to write his or her own letter, provide this checklist and ask him or her to be sure to include this information to ensure the effectiveness of the letter. A letter of recommendation lacking these points of information won't help your case.

## How Many Recommendations Are Enough?

Six references should be the maximum, but even one or two can help sway a prospective employer. Focus on quality rather than quantity. If you have limited work experience, add to your collection of recommendations by obtaining character references. Be sure the letters present you in the best light and are consistent with how you describe yourself in your résumé and during interviews.

## When Should You Submit Your Letters of Recommendation?

There is no hard-and-fast rule about when to give a prospective employer your letters of recommendation. Because letters of reference are not routinely requested in the way that a résumé or job application is, you'll have to use your judgment. If you think your résumé and cover letter are strong enough to stand on their own, wait until the interview or until you are requested to present them. If your letters are relevant to the job you're applying for and are extremely positive, you may want to include them with your résumé and cover letter. Treat your letters as another tool of persuasion in convincing the prospective employer you are the best candidate for the job.

Beginning on the following page are examples of a cover letter requesting a recommendation from a former employer, a proposed letter of recommendation, and a sample character reference letter. You can use these as ideas to help begin the process of getting your own letters of recommendation.

# LORETTA BRYAN

42 Celtic Way
Trenton, NY 10921
(404) 555–7534
VRyan625@bny.com

March 12, 2011

Ms. Naomi Sands
Vice President, Human Resources
Sapphire Corporation
338 Orleans Lane
Trenton, NY 10921

Dear Ms. Sands:

As you know, I will be graduating in June and am seeking full-time employment as a human resources representative back in my hometown of Charlotte, South Carolina. I would greatly appreciate it if you could write a letter of recommendation for me regarding my work in your department as a human resources coordinator during the past two years.

I have taken the liberty of drafting a letter to help expedite the process. Feel free to edit the letter or write one of your own. Then please return the final draft to me on company letterhead by March 25, 2011, if at all possible.

Thank you in advance. I will stay in touch and keep you apprised of my job search.

Sincerely,

*Loretta Bryan*

Loretta Bryan

Enclosure

**Sample 7.1    Cover Letter to Request a Letter of Recommendation**

# Sapphire Corporation

338 Orleans Lane
Trenton, NY 10921
(404) 555–1121

March 20, 2011

To Whom It May Concern:

Loretta Bryan worked as a human resources coordinator for two years in my department at Sapphire Corporation. During that time, Loretta had diverse responsibilities. She reviewed résumés to identify qualified employment candidates, conducted preliminary applicant interviews, documented hiring and firing policy, and coordinated supervisors' guideline handbooks for distribution to Sapphire's department supervisors.

Loretta is bright, articulate, and hard working. Her enthusiasm for the job comes through in all she does. She has a positive attitude that makes her a pleasure to work with and is one of the reasons she was so well liked by her coworkers.

I highly recommend Loretta for any job she is considering in the human resources field. She would be an asset to any employer. If you have further questions about Loretta, please do not hesitate to contact me at (404) 555–1121, ext. 200.

Sincerely,

*Naomi Sands*

Naomi Sands
Vice President, Human Resources

**Sample 7.2   Letter of Recommendation Proposed by the Job Hunter**

168 Tallon Street
Rochester, IN 43721
March 25, 2011

To Whom It May Concern:

I have known Chet Minton since his family moved to my neighborhood seven years ago.
Since that time, Chet has become a helpful, dependable assistant to many of us who live
nearby.

Chet first began working for me as a landscaper. He mowed my lawn each week every
summer, and shovelled the drive each winter. His work is always meticulous, and he cleans
up after yard projects quickly and thoroughly. Chet has also been a house sitter when I travel
and has provided excellent care for my pets and property. Often, when Chet sees me working
on a landscaping project, he pitches in to help, and without being asked.

Chet is a prompt and dependable young man who reports to work early, stays until the job
is finished, and has taken on increasingly complex projects in the past several years. In my
many years operating a small business of my own, I have found out what a rare and valuable
trait this is.

Chet's cheerful and professional disposition make working with him a pleasure, and his hard
work and dependability make relying on him easy. I will truly miss having Chet around the
neighborhood when he takes on work more related to his field. I would be happy to provide
additional information about this fine young man. Please do not hesitate to contact me at the
address above or at (523) 212-9879.

Sincerely,

*Walter P. Grassle*

Walter P. Grassle

**Sample 7.3   Sample Character Reference for a Person with Limited Work Experience**

# Background Checks

In addition to requesting references, it has become increasingly common for prospective employers to require job candidates to submit to criminal background checks and credit checks. It's just another way to get a third-party view of the candidate.

A criminal background check is required by law in certain fields—for example, child care and law enforcement—to ensure that employees have no criminal record. Many employers also request a credit history to be sure the applicant has no history of financial fraud.

As a job hunter, you need to be aware that you may be asked to provide permission for these types of checks. It pays to obtain your own credit report to be sure it is correct and to be forthcoming with employers if you feel any incidents in your past will become an issue during the hiring process.

## SUCCESS STORIES

Often, the greatest inspiration comes from those who have succeeded. Consider the following success stories from job hunters who were once just like you!

When I was 16, I applied to be a locker room assistant at the local health club. The job involved checking membership cards and handing out towels during the late afternoon rush hours at the gym. Many kids from my high school applied, but I was one of the few interviewed. I later learned I was the only applicant who submitted letters of reference from people I'd babysat for. I got the job over many others, along with a free membership. And it was this job that eventually led me to my career as a personal trainer.

**Emily**
*Personal Trainer*

I took a work-study job with the buildings and grounds department at the college I attended. I loved the work because I got a chance to solve all sorts of maintenance problems at the school. My supervisor was impressed and wrote me a great letter of recommendation. When I got my degree in architectural design, I used that letter to help get a job as a CAD manager for the campus.

**Chris**
*CAD Manager*

## Chapter Follow-Up

- You can provide prospective employers with a list of people they can contact for references about you or provide written letters of recommendation.

- You should always let your referrals know that you are providing their name and contact information to employers and that you'd appreciate their assistance in recommending you for the job.

- The best references are previous employers; however, you can also include favorable recommendations from teachers, guidance counselors, athletic coaches, and even neighbors.

- Four to six references are ideal.

- Always thank the people who write letters or recommendation or agree to be phone references for you. Keep them posted on the status of your job search.

# Chapter 8

## Building a Portfolio or Personal Website

Résumé Banks
Career Guidance
Company Research

## What Do You Know?

### Short Answers

1. List at least four items that you think are appropriate for inclusion in a portfolio.

   _____

   _____

2. When should you present your portfolio to an employer?

   _____

   _____

3. What are some of the benefits of creating an e-portfolio or personal website as opposed to a more traditional portfolio containing hard copies of your documents?

   _____

   _____

## Chapter Focus

In this chapter, you'll learn to:

- Create a portfolio or personal website.
- Include materials that provide evidence of your abilities.
- Make the portfolio or website well organized and easy to navigate.
- Introduce your e-portfolio or personal website to an employer prior to the interview.
- Present your portfolio in an interview.

## Real-Life Relevance

Although an employer may only require a résumé to consider a candidate, the job seeker may benefit from offering additional evidence of his or her capabilities. A portfolio or personal website that includes such items as actual work samples and letters of recommendation will help you stand out and give the employer a better understanding of who you are.

## Assemble a Portfolio

Although artists and architects have traditionally used portfolios as part of their job application process, professionals in other fields have only begun to see their value as a means of differentiating themselves from other applicants. Even if you're not in a visual type of profession, consider assembling a work portfolio of your own to add to your job search tools.

A portfolio or personal website (also sometimes called an electronic or e-portfolio) is a collection of items that demonstrate your skills as they relate to a particular field. It will serve as evidence that you succeeded in the past and therefore are likely to have the same types of achievements in the future at your next job.

Your goal in creating a portfolio or website is to present your credentials and personal information in a manner that is well organized, interesting, and aesthetically pleasing.

**Consider assembling a portfolio. It allows you to present samples of your work and additional evidence that you are the best candidate for the job.**
(© David Barber / PhotoEdit)

# What Should a Portfolio Contain?

Consider your portfolio or personal website as a work in progress. You don't need to assemble everything at once. Take time to create a professional-looking presentation. Sloppy work won't reflect well on your candidacy for employment.

In the case of a portfolio, you can and should modify its contents to fit the needs of the employer, including those items that are most relevant to the specific job opening. It's not quantity that will impress the employer but rather the substance and relevance of the items. For a personal website, you won't be able to customize its contents for every employer, so make sure the navigation is clear, enabling visitors to easily find the sections that interest them.

Although the contents of your individual portfolio or website will, of course, depend on your field and the type of position you're seeking, you can consider including some of these items:

- **Résumé.** Even though the employer may already have your résumé, place a copy in your portfolio or on your website so the package is complete, with all your information in one place and easily accessible.

- **References.** Include copies of your letters of recommendation as well as a list of references whose contact information you can supply upon request. (Be sure you don't post their contact information on your site, as they may not want it published online.)

- **Licenses.** Photocopies of any professional certifications related to your field demonstrate that you have met the requirements and passed the necessary skills tests for work in a specific area.

- **Letters of commendation.** Like letters of recommendation, these statements from credible sources serve as third-party endorsements, testifying to your skills and accomplishments. They are usually unsolicited letters that praise an employee to their superior or organization for outstanding work.

- **Awards.** Include documentation of any awards or special recognition you've received that relate to your profession.

- **Work samples.** Showcase any items of your work that demonstrate your capabilities. These can be reports, project write-ups, examples of your writing, PowerPoint presentations, computer programs, drawings, photographs, manuals, blueprints, business plans, and so on. If you are a recent graduate, these work samples may have been generated in courses you took. As you gather experience in your career, you'll want to replace schoolwork with professional work.

- **Performance reviews.** Excellent reviews from previous employers illustrate your work ethic and skills. If you're a recent graduate, you can include copies of your transcripts, highlighting courses related to your field.

- **Case studies.** Provide a detailed description of a problem, the solution you proposed, and the result that you achieved. Include up to five case studies, each one demonstrating your ability to handle challenging situations.

- **Accomplishments.** A detailed list highlighting your major career achievements to date can be persuasive.

- **Certificates.** If you've completed certain courses or attended a professional conference or workshop, you may have received certificates of completion. These certificates demonstrate that your skills are current and that you are committed to ongoing professional growth.

- **Conferences.** Create a list of any relevant conferences, seminars, or workshops that you've participated in or attended.

- **Transcripts.** If this is your first job out of school, you may want to include a copy of your transcripts to show the courses you've taken and the grades you received.

- **Publicity.** Perhaps you've received some publicity for your work, such as through articles you've published in trade journals or mentions you've received in press releases. If so, include copies of this media attention or links to the online references. If possible, highlight the places where you are mentioned so the reader can go directly to the relevant material.

- **Volunteer work/community service.** Write a description of any community service activities, volunteer, or pro bono work you've done, especially if related to your career. If possible, include photos of yourself "in action."

- **Military records, awards, and badges.** Provide an account of your military service if applicable.

- **Hobbies.** If your pastimes reveal an interesting side of your personality or are at all relevant to your line of work, you can include something about them in your portfolio. Use good judgment as to whether they can help or might hurt your presentation to an employer. If you're not sure, err on the side of caution and leave them out.

- **Business cards.** As part of your portfolio, you may want to include a professional business card, which you can give to your interviewers. A business card includes your name, a brief tagline under your name where you'd otherwise see a job title (e.g., "corporate trainer with Fortune 500 experience"), your contact information, and, on the back, four to five bullet points summarizing your skills or professional accomplishments. If you have a personal website, be sure to note the URL.

**EXERCISE**   **Planning Your Portfolio or Personal Website**

Make a list of the items that could go in your own portfolio or on your personal website. Most should have some relevance to the type of employment you're seeking, and all should present you as a competent professional worthy of serious consideration. Be specific. For example, if you plan to include letters of recommendation, note who those letters are from.

Once you've composed your list, consider how you would organize these items if you were placing them on a personal website. What menu buttons would you have on your navigation? Which items would go with each button?

Of course, the next step will be to assemble your portfolio or begin building your personal website. Read on for additional ideas on how to present your portfolio.

## How Do You Present Your Portfolio?

If you've created an e-portfolio or personal website, you can include a link to it in your cover letter and on your résumé.

At an interview, you can present your portfolio of hard copies in a binder, a folder, a file, or a portfolio case (available in most office supplies and art supplies stores). Choose a method of display that is professional plus easy to carry and maneuver through.

Consider bringing copies of key items to leave behind for further review if the interviewer should display a keen interest. Never offer your originals because—despite the interviewer's best intentions—there's no way to guarantee when or even if they'll be returned.

Another option is to put a copy of the items in your portfolio on a CD or DVD. They can be arranged into a short PowerPoint presentation or into PDF files. CDs and DVDs are cheap enough that you won't have to hesitate in giving them out to potential employers. Organize your materials into topics, each with its own folder, to make it easy for the employer to navigate. Label the CD or DVD with your full name and contact information.

What's great is that with today's technology, you have plenty of acceptable and affordable options for presenting your materials to give the employer a more complete picture of who you are.

## SUCCESS STORIES

Often, the greatest inspiration comes from those who have succeeded. Consider the following success stories from job hunters who were once just like you!

Melissa was seeking a position as a paralegal in a law firm. She knew competition would be stiff, so she wanted to find a way to stand out. With a few years experience under her belt, she had some excellent letters of recommendation, certificates from workshops she'd attended, and examples of her writing on legal issues.

Although Melissa lacked the technical ability to build her own website, she searched for some online platforms that would allow her to create an e-portfolio or digital portfolio. She found some that were free and easy to use.

Once she'd created her e-portfolio, she was able to include a link to it in her résumé and cover letter to employers. The items she'd posted helped persuade employers that she was worthy of an interview and also serious consideration for the job.

Melissa
*Paralegal*

Rajiv was an oncology nurse who had worked in a hospital setting for many years. When a new cancer treatment facility opened in his city, he decided to apply for a job there. He created a portfolio that included his professional license, some performance reviews he'd received at the hospital, thank-you notes from some of his patients, and letters of commendation from the American Cancer Society for his volunteer efforts.

The portfolio was contained in an easy-to-carry binder. Rajiv took it with him when interviewed. He had also made a CD that included copies of all the items in it. He would quickly go through the portfolio page by page with his interviewer but then offer to leave the CD behind for the interviewer to keep and review at her leisure.

Rajiv
*Oncology Nurse*

## Chapter Follow-Up

- A portfolio can be a useful job hunting tool, even if you're not in a visual profession, such as photography or graphic design.

- Your portfolio can consist of hard copies that you show to an employer in an interview situation or it can be an e-portfolio or personal website that has electronic versions of your documents. You can provide the employer with the URL on your résumé and in your cover letters.

- Your portfolio can contain items ranging from work samples and letters of recommendation to photos and descriptions of your volunteer work if relevant.

- The main purpose of a portfolio—whether in hard-copy form or posted online—is to help give the employer a more comprehensive understanding of your capabilities and your personality.

# Part Three

# Hunting for an Employer

## Chapter 9

# Finding Potential Employers

## What Do You Know?

### Short Answers

1. What is networking?
   _____
   _____

2. Why is networking an important part of job hunting?
   _____
   _____

3. What are some different ways to find out about job openings?
   _____
   _____

4. What is a job fair?
   _____
   _____

5. Where can you search online to find job openings?
   _____
   _____

6. What are some ways you can research employers?
   _____
   _____

## Chapter Focus

In this chapter, you'll learn to:

- Network effectively.
- Track your contacts.
- Generate job leads.
- Search online for job openings.
- Make contacts at job fairs.
- Research companies.
- Search for a job outside your geographical area.

## Real-Life Relevance

The best-written résumé and cover letter don't amount too much if you have no one to send them to. Similarly, polished interview skills are useless if no one wants to interview you. Therefore, the crux of the job hunting process hinges on finding potential employers. The point this chapter makes is that there is no single right way to go about this task. Instead, you need to have a multifaceted strategy to increase your chances of success.

# Start by Networking

You've probably heard the saying "It's not what you know but who you know." The reality is that most people get jobs through personal contacts—also called *networking*.

Therefore, the first place you look for job leads is through your network. Get in touch with your friends, former classmates, former work associates, suppliers, vendors, relatives, neighbors, fellow professionals, organization members, and anyone else you can think of to see if they can offer any job leads. Don't forget to ask them for the names and contact information of any people they know who might be able to help you in your job search networking. Initially, you may feel uncomfortable asking others for help in locating employment, but remember that most people are flattered to be considered a resource. Making the series of contacts necessary to find the ideal position isn't easy. You need to be friendly, persistent, and sure of the type of job you seek.

Take a look at the chart on page 138. You may want to photocopy this chart for future use. Or if you prefer, create a spreadsheet on your computer with the same information. Begin by completing the left-hand tier. Tell as many people as you can about the type of job you're seeking. If necessary, fill them in on your background and skills. Ask if they know of anyone who might be interviewing or who you should contact. As you learn of more people who could help you, add their names on the appropriate lines of the chart.

**Names/Phone Numbers/**
**E-Mail Addresses**
**of Initial Contacts**
**(friends/family)**                    **Names They Provide**                    **Names They Provide**

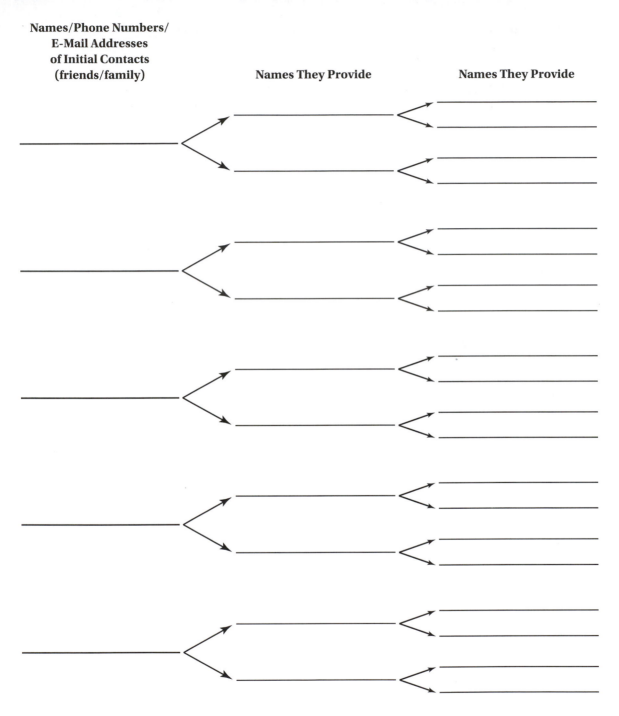

## KEEPING TRACK OF YOUR CONTACTS

In generating leads, you'll develop a list of contacts. Photocopy the chart in Figure 9.2 for future use or create a spreadsheet on your computer. Keep track of your contacts by filling in the necessary information. It will help you stay organized and be on top of any potential job leads. Continue to add to the list as you make additional contacts.

| Contact Person Name/Phone Number or E-Mail | Relationship/ Recommended by | Occupation/ Where Employed | Last Date of Contact | Suggested Next Date of Contact | Additional Action Required | Contacts He/ She Provided |
|---|---|---|---|---|---|---|
| Example: Mark Bergen (617) 555-9919 | Coworker at last job | Accountant, Hyde Accounting | 9/12/02 | 9/30/02 | Send copy of résumé to him | Mary Smith, Telco (617) 555-1234 |
| | | | | | | |
| | | | | | | |
| | | | | | | |
| | | | | | | |
| | | | | | | |
| | | | | | | |
| | | | | | | |

Be sure to thank everyone who provides you with even the tiniest hint. If you are gracious and appreciative, your contacts are more likely to keep their eyes open for leads to steer your way in the future.

## Generate Job Leads

Once you've made contact with everyone in your network, you'll need to progress to other proactive methods of finding a potential employer. Consider these ideas for generating job leads:

1. **Career Websites.** Although reading classified ads, cold-calling, letter writing, and networking have traditionally been the most widely used means of finding a job, the Internet has emerged as one of the most important tools in the job search process. With its extensive, easily accessible information, its powerful searching capabilities, and its instant channels of communication, it has revolutionized the way people look for jobs and the way companies recruit.

   You can find thousands of job listings on such general career websites as Monster.com and CareerBuilder.com. There may even be niche employment sites for your field. Search for openings by profession and, if desired, by location. You can also post your résumé with career sites, and employers who are interested may contact you. You can even sign up to have job opportunities that meet your preferences e-mailed to you or sent to your smartphone via an app.

2. **Classified Ads.** The classifieds in local newspapers and in trade journals were once the primary source of job leads. Today, the printed classifieds offer slim pickings, although they're still worth checking. Many publications now post their classifieds online and allow you to search for positions by using keywords. The biggest benefit of using newspaper classified ads is that most of the jobs being advertised are local to the area.

3. **Blogs.** Search online for bloggers who are writing about your industry. Subscribe to their blogs and read their posts, looking for job leads and ideas. Some blogs even have job boards. Once you've become familiar with a blog, you may feel comfortable contacting the blog owner and asking him or her for any contacts or suggestions.

4. **Alumni placement offices.** Keep in touch with your college placement office, even years after you've graduated. Placement offices often learn of jobs that require more experience than that of the average graduating senior. Also, the staff may have industry contacts that they can refer you to for networking purposes.

5. **Trade and professional organizations.** Join these associations or at least attend a few meetings as an opportunity to network with people in your field. This is a great way to make contacts. Some trade organizations post job openings in their industry on their websites.

6. **Managers who just got promoted or hired.** You can find the names of these people in your local newspaper's promotions section, which is usually a weekly

column on the business pages, or in trade journals. These people may be building new staffs. Write a cover letter to one of these managers—first congratulating him or her on the recent promotion or new job and then explaining why you would be a terrific addition to the team.

7. **Growth companies.** Look for companies that appear to be expanding and hiring new people. Perhaps they're continually placing ads for job openings or maybe you heard that they're establishing new departments or targeting new markets. It could be worth a letter or phone call to the company's human resources department to investigate further.

8. **Newsletter editors.** Most industries have newsletters, e-newsletters, or trade journals. The editors of these publications are often aware of jobs in their markets. Look for editors of printed newsletters as well as online publications. Send them an e-mail or call to explain the type of position you're seeking and to ask for their recommendations. Even if they can't tell you about specific job openings, they may be able to give you some employer names or steer you toward some good information sources.

9. **Position wanted ads.** Some newspapers, trade publications, and blogs have sections in which you can advertise for the position you're seeking. For example, if you're looking for work in the editorial field, you might publish a position wanted ad in *Editor & Publisher* or *Publishers Weekly*. In the ad, briefly state your accomplishments and experience. If you have a personal website or e-portfolio, be sure to include its URL.

10. **Employment agencies.** Call employment agencies in your area to see if any fill positions in your field. Many specialize in particular professions. For example, there are employment agencies that fill technical positions, such as computer software engineers, and others that mostly handle such clerical positions as secretaries and data entry clerks. There may not be an employment agency that fills jobs in your field, but it's worth checking, as agencies can be a great source of job leads.

    In most cases, the hiring employer pays the agency fee, not the employee. So, be cautious if you come across any employment agencies requesting money up front from you. Check out these companies with the Better Business Bureau, and search their name online to see if any negative information has been posted. Ask a lot of questions, and carefully read any contracts you're asked to sign *before* handing over your cash.

11. **Executive search firms.** Contact these firms if you have experience in your field and you're seeking a management-level position. Write a letter that describes your job requirements, lists your salary needs, and details your experience. Then, follow up to see if they have any positions for which you could be considered.

12. **State job services.** Most state job services have a professional employee placement division. They can tell you what government jobs are available in your city, county, and state.

13. **Use the Yellow Pages.** Even the phone book can yield leads. Brainstorm words associated with your field and then let your fingers do the walking. Once you find some companies that could be a match for you, do some research online to learn more about them. Then, craft a letter of introduction, and follow up with a phone call a few days later.

Finding a job is often a numbers game. The key to winning is having as many irons in the fire as possible. The more tactics you use, the sooner you are likely to find that perfect job.

**EXERCISE**    Because the Internet will likely play a significant role in your search, get familiar with career websites. Visit the site of your choice or find one using a search engine and then answer the following questions:

1. What kinds of information can you find on this website?

    _____

2. How would this information be helpful to you in your job search?

    _____

3. What services are offered for free on this website, and what services require payment of a fee?

    _____

4. Do you plan to use a job website such as this in your search? Why or why not?

    _____

# Make Contacts at Job Fairs

With the right preparation and plan, job fairs can be a great way to get in the door of companies you might otherwise never get to know. Companies usually participate in job fairs for one of two reasons: to fill current positions or collect résumés for anticipated future openings. Because they commonly spend hundreds or thousands of dollars to participate, the companies' presence alone says they are serious about hiring.

A job fair can be a great way to get in the door of companies that you might otherwise be unable to access.
(Jeff Greenberg/Photo Edit)

If you've never been to a job fair, here's what to expect. Each participating company sets up a table staffed by representatives. The representatives are there to greet you, tell you something about the company, and, most importantly, assess whether you might be a potential candidate for employment. Companies with the most urgent staffing needs often rent an interview room in addition to the table space, where they can do on-the-spot qualifying of candidates.

To find out when and where job fairs are being held, check with your college career office, keep an eye on your local newspaper, and visit the major career websites—some of which maintain career fair calendars or post notices about upcoming fairs.

To gain the most benefit from a job fair, consider these tips:

- **Find out in advance which companies plan to be present.** Often, the show's promoters print a list and post it online. Ads promoting the job fair also often list participants.

- **Determine which companies are your primary targets.** Do a little advance research about these companies, and you'll make a solid impression when you talk to their representatives. Look up the companies on the Internet or at your campus career office. Search for their corporate website and also for any mentions of them in the media.

- **Dress for a job, not a fair.** Conservative, professional attire is the way to go. Think of a job fair in the same way you would think of a job interview and dress accordingly.

- **Practice your delivery.** First, go to the booths of a few companies you're not interested in. Hone your presentation with the representatives of those companies, and get comfortable in the job fair environment before moving on to your primary targets.

- **Give yourself enough time to be thorough.** Job fairs may last several hours or even several days, so you should have plenty of time to accomplish your goals. Take the time to evaluate each company and meet the representatives of your key targets. At the booths of the most heavily visited companies, you may have to wait in line. Consider getting to the fair early to avoid the crowds, and you'll also have the best chance of meeting with employers when they're fresh.

- **Bring many copies of your résumé.** Carry them in a folder, portfolio cover, or notebook, and don't be embarrassed to pass them out. That's what companies are there for: to collect résumés.

- **Be professional when you meet representatives.** Treat your meeting like a brief job interview. Shake hands, state your name, and be prepared to give a two-minute introduction of yourself.

- **Ask questions.** In addition to putting out information about yourself, job fairs are a great place to get information. When meeting with representatives, try to learn about their companies and obtain names of contacts to whom you can personally send your résumé. Ask the representatives for business cards so you can reference them in writing cover letters to the contacts—for example, "I met Sarah Jones at a recent job fair, and she suggested I contact you."

- **Make notes.** Bring a notebook or write notes on the back of business cards you receive to help you remember useful tidbits of information about the company or the representative. Use that information when writing follow-up thank-you notes or future cover letters to the company.

- **Collect company materials.** Most companies display corporate literature at their booths. Take advantage of this literature to learn about the company—its capabilities, corporate philosophy, and operations. If you get an interview, you'll be able to speak knowledgeably about the company.

- **Shoot for an interview, not a job.** Your goal at a job fair is to obtain a follow-up interview. Rarely do companies hire for professional positions on the spot. Instead, they contact their best candidates within a few weeks (sometimes months) of the job fair to schedule appointments for interviews at their company.

- **Look, listen, and learn.** Use a job fair to gain insight about employers, practice your interviewing skills, and get a sense of the competition by checking out other job hunters.

## Research Potential Employers

Even if a company is not advertising any openings, you can still send a letter of introduction and your résumé. Perhaps that company will have a need for your talents in the near future or knows someone who does. If your skills are unique, the company might be willing to create a position for you. There could be any number of reasons why your letter and résumé could be well received even though no job opening has been posted.

Before contacting a potential employer, you'll want to do your research. The more you know about a company, the more specific you can be in your cover letter. Your research will also help you decide whether a particular company is a good fit for your skills and career goals.

The following list describes some of the ways to conduct research on potential employers. The first two—checking the Internet and setting up Google Alerts—are the easiest to do and may be sufficient for your purposes. You'll have to decide whether it's necessary to take additional steps.

1. **Check the Internet.** The Web is an excellent tool for researching companies and industries. Most companies today—big and small—have a website you can locate by using a major search engine or by calling the company directly and asking for its website address. Typically, such websites contain information about the company, its products or services, its key personnel, and any newsworthy advances or changes that are taking place. They may list current job openings as well and offer you the option of applying online for available positions.

   In addition to looking at the company's own website, search for any mentions of it in the media. You may find press releases and articles that give you additional insights into the company.

2. **Set up Google Alerts for specific companies or industries.** Google Alerts are e-mail updates of the latest relevant Google results (web, news, etc.) for your choice of query or topic. They're based on keywords. So, for example, if you set up a Google Alert for ABC Company, you'd get an e-mail notification with links to any information newly posted online that mentions ABC Company. Google Alerts are free, although there is a charge for Google Alerts' premium services. To set up an account, go to http://www.google.com/alerts to register.

3. **Read your local newspaper.** Keep your eyes open for any stories on companies you are interested in. Many newspapers also have cataloged archives in which you can find relevant articles. You may be able to access those archives online.

4. **Read trade literature.** Many firms regularly distribute information on their new products, services, and employees to business-to-business magazines and industry trade journals. You'll also be learning about the industry in general, which will come in handy in job interviews and in your career.

5. **Learn about the company's competitors.** Search for potential competitors on the Web. Review their websites, using this information to learn about not only the competition but also the field. And as mentioned earlier, you can also set up Google Alerts to track those competitor companies.

6. **Check Hoover's.** Hoover's (**www.hoovers.com**) is a first-rate resource. If a company is listed on Hoover's, its competitors and hyperlinks to their websites will be also often referenced. Some of the information is free; however, there may be fees for more in-depth reports.

7. **Research individuals.** Just as you can research a company, you can also research an individual. It's always a good idea to see if any information exists on the key players at the employer you're considering. If they've received awards, written any books or articles, spoken at a conference, or been involved with a political or volunteer organization, there's a good chance you'll find that information on the Web by typing their name into a major search engine, such as Google or Bing. They may also have a public profile set up on a social networking site, such as LinkedIn (www.linkedin.com) or Facebook (www.facebook.com). And the more you know about them, the more targeted you can make your cover letter to introduce yourself and request an interview.

8. **Attend trade shows.** Many companies participate in local and national trade shows relevant to their industry. Visit their booths, and ask about their products, markets, achievements, and future plans. You may also be able to obtain the names of the appropriate people to contact regarding employment.

9. **Go to meetings of clubs or trade organizations in your field.** Through these meetings, you'll be able to learn about the industry and potential employers. To find out about relevant associations, try the *Encyclopedia of Associations,* available in most large libraries. Some libraries allow you to access this reference publication online. Once you have the association names, see if they have websites that can provide you with ideas for additional industry resources as well as potential employers and specific contact names.

10. **Obtain financial data.** If the company is a public corporation, you can solicit an annual report as a potential investor. This document provides a wealth of information—from sales volume and product distribution to its plans for the future. Much of that information may also be available online. (If the company is privately owned, this information may be difficult to acquire.)

11. **Visit the local chamber of commerce.** Local chambers often keep information on the businesses in their communities. Chamber employees might even be able to give you some personal insights if they have had an opportunity to interact with the company.

12. **Speak to former employees.** If you can find people who have worked for the company in the past, they can be excellent sources of information.

13. **Call or visit your local library.** Ask at the reference desk how to go about researching a particular company. Librarians can often steer you toward a wealth of resources.

14. **Be resourceful.** Try to come up with additional ideas or contacts for getting information about the companies you are interested in.

## Effective Networking

Good networking is about building relationships. The more people you know and who know you, the more connected you will be in your field. Connected people learn about job openings earlier, meet more people at a high level, and generally know more about their industries. Furthermore, connected people are more valuable to their future employers because they keep current on the developments and players in their field. Here's how to approach networking:

- Choose a goal or identify a target industry or employer. People won't be able to help you if you can't tell them specifically what you need.

- Develop a long-term, career-building approach. Who is it important for you to get to know in furthering your career?

- Keep track of the people you meet, and make an effort to stay in touch with them through occasional phone calls, notes, e-mails, and even holiday cards.

- Think of others without being asked. That's part of the give-and-take of networking. For example, is there a project someone may want to know about or a relevant newspaper article he or she may not have seen? Or could you help someone else with his or her career networking by making an introduction or lending your name as a contact?

- Always thank others for their help.

---

**EXERCISE**

## Company Research

Identify a company in your area that you could be interested in working for. Perhaps it's a company you know of personally or one you've found through some mention in your local newspaper.

Using a search engine, such as Google, locate the company's website and then answer these questions:

1. What is the company's main product or service?

2. How long has the company been in business?

3. Does the company post job openings on its website? If so, are there any that you might like to apply for? If not, does it list a contact for its human resources department?

**4.** If you were to send this company a cover letter and résumé, what type of job would you say you want?

**5.** What qualifications would you mention in your cover letter so the company is more likely to give you serious consideration?

**6.** Finally, go back to the search engine to research whether any news or information exists about the company other than its own website. Seek out news stories, press releases, directory listings, and even consumer reviews. Is there anything you can reference in your cover letter to demonstrate your knowledge of the company?

## Long-Distance Job Hunting

Depending on where you live, there may or may not be opportunities appropriate to your field in your geographical area. Many of the best professional positions continue to be concentrated in such major metropolitan areas as New York, Chicago, Boston, Atlanta, and Los Angeles.

The first decision you'll have to make is whether to job hunt first and then move once you've found a position or to move first and then job hunt. While the better option is usually to get a job first, it can be extremely difficult to job hunt from a distance. Most companies have a sufficient supply of good candidates in their local area. They can easily interview and hire local candidates and avoid the problems and expenses associated with relocating an out-of-the-area employee.

To find job listings outside your area, use the Internet. Many career sites allow you to search want ads by location. Also, many newspapers from around the country post their classified ads on the Web. Of course, libraries can also be a resource for out-of-town newspapers and trade publications with classified ad sections.

If you must have a job before you can relocate, try to spend weekends and vacations in the new city. Do as much research as you can before you make these trips, and if possible, line up interviews. Be sure to explain to potential employers that you plan to move to the city once you are hired. It can take a long time to obtain a job this way, so be prepared for a lengthy job search.

If you relocate first, begin job hunting as soon as you can. It takes awhile to learn the ropes in a new city, and you'll want to land a position before your finances run out. Consider taking a temporary or contract position to help you buy time; you may even meet a potential employer through such jobs. Then, follow the usual steps in job hunting.

## SUCCESS STORIES

Often, the greatest inspiration comes from those who've succeeded. Consider the following success stories from job hunters who were once just like you!

I was right out of school with a degree in advertising, but I had no contacts in the field. The first thing I did was to contact the local professional association for advertising executives. I let the director know I was job hunting and sent her a few copies of my résumé. Less than a week later, I received a call from an ad agency. Apparently, the ad agency had called the association requesting referrals for a production assistant.

Joan
*Production Coordinator*

Many months after I was hired at the accounting firm, I had an opportunity to speak casually with the person who'd interviewed me. I asked why she had chosen me when I knew there had been several other highly qualified candidates. She said it was because in the interview, I proved I already knew quite a lot about the company. She felt that anyone who had done that much research really wanted the position and would therefore make a great employee.

Daniel
*Tax Accountant*

I studied to become a teacher, but when I graduated, no jobs were available at local schools. Reading the classified ads one day, I saw several positions advertised for corporate training associates. I found I had most of the required skills and decided to apply. Now I work for a large computer company "teaching" new hires our policies and procedures.

Stephen
*Corporate Training Associate*

I moved to Orlando, Florida, because that was where I wanted to live. Finding a job can be hard when you don't know anyone in the area and aren't familiar with local employers. One of the best things I did was attend every job fair I could. I learned about companies and positions available and made contacts as well. Even though I often found myself talking to employers about jobs I knew I might not want, I tried to view it as an opportunity to practice my interviewing skills. I did eventually land a hospitality management job with a major hotel resort. Although I didn't learn about the job at a trade fair, it was a contact that I made at one of the fairs who passed my résumé along to another manager whose department had an opening.

Carlene
*Front Desk Agent*

As an art history major, I had always dreamed of working in a museum. I frequented our local art museum and became friends with one of the researchers. When she mentioned she was leaving to take another position, I told her I was interested in her job. She gave me the name of her supervisor and helped me to get an interview. With her recommendation, I was hired.

Phillip
*Museum Researcher*

I found my job as a computer programmer by posting my résumé on a career website. I had several employers contact me for interviews, and I chose the one that felt like the best fit for me.

Krystal
*Computer Programmer/Analyst*

I moved out to Los Angeles hoping to become a scriptwriter for a TV show. I was not having a lot of success getting interviews, let alone getting a job. One night, I was on a career website chatting with other job hunters. I mentioned the type of job I was seeking, and one of the people in the chat room said she had a cousin who worked in TV in Los Angeles. She provided me with a name and phone number. I followed up, and we immediately hit it off. He was able to give me the names of some people in the industry to contact. Using his referral, I was able to obtain several interviews with various TV executives and finally landed a position as a scriptwriter for a sitcom.

Carey
*TV Scriptwriter*

I signed up with several career websites. By searching each one daily, I was able to find numerous positions that fit my career objectives. I probably applied to over 100 companies, but in the end, after numerous interviews, I had a few offers and was able to choose where I wanted to work.

Tara
*Administrative Assistant*

## Chapter Follow-Up

- One of the best ways to learn about job openings is through personal contacts—also called *networking*.

- Don't use just one method to generate job leads. Working multiple angles will accelerate your search and improve your chances of success.

- Career websites post help wanted ads. You can search by job type as well as geographically.

- Job fairs can be useful as a means to meet employers, network, and practice your interviewing skills.

- Even if a company is not advertising any openings, you can still send a letter of introduction and your résumé. Research the company to better target your letter.

- Long-distance job hunting poses challenges—some of which can be overcome by using online resources.

# Chapter 10

## Social Networking and Your Online Reputation

## What Do You Know?

### Short Answers

1. What is online social networking?
   _____
   _____

2. Can you name at least two online social networks?
   _____
   _____

3. How might social networks be useful in your job hunt?
   _____
   _____

4. Can you think of a way to combine online social networking with offline networking?
   _____
   _____

5. What is your online reputation, and why is it important?
   _____
   _____

## Chapter Focus

In this chapter, you'll learn to:

- Make new contacts using online social networks.
- Join business networking sites like LinkedIn.
- Build online relationships.
- Create your personal brand.
- Publish online so employers will find you.
- Use sites like YouTube to stand out to employers.
- Ensure your online reputation is favorable.

## Real-Life Relevance

The Internet has changed everything, including how to find a job. Beyond job boards and websites where you can post your résumé are online social networks that allow you to greatly expand your circle of contacts. Blogs and website articles provide a platform for you to self-publish and provide employers with a broader view of your capabilities. All these tools represent opportunities for you to build an online image that accelerates your job search.

## Who Knows You?

By now you realize that networking is an important component of the job search. Today, however, because of the Internet, who you know isn't limited to friends, family, and business associates. Now it includes virtual friends and contacts. And even more important than who you know is who knows you!

Social networking online is the practice of expanding your business and social contacts by making connections through individuals via the Internet. It's a way to meet more people, which increases your chances of finding a potential employer or someone who can refer you to one.

It provides you the ability to easily access someone you don't know personally. And it mobilizes an army of other people to keep their eyes open for possible opportunities for you. Incorporate online social networking into your job search, and you'll greatly increase your chances for employment.

## Get Connected with LinkedIn

LinkedIn (www.linkedin.com) has become one of the most successful business networking websites. It's an interconnected network of experienced professionals from around the world. You can easily find, be introduced to, and collaborate with others.

When you join LinkedIn, you create a profile that summarizes your professional expertise and accomplishments. You can then connect with people you know who are already on LinkedIn or invite trusted contacts to join. Your network consists of your connections and also your connections' connections, thus linking you to a vast number of people.

LinkedIn is free to join, although a premium version is available that gives you more tools for reaching out to people.

Every Fortune 500 company is on LinkedIn and using it to add connections, answer questions about their products, and promote their brand. The companies also use it to engage in conversations with potential customers and employees. Recruiters use LinkedIn as a source for finding candidates.

Some of the ways you can network on LinkedIn are to:

- Check out LinkedIn Job (www.linkedin.com/jobs) for postings.
- Be active on LinkedIn Answers (www.linkedin.com/answers) by responding to questions and drawing other LinkedIn users to connect to you.
- Look for someone local to you or who has similar interests or perhaps is an alumnus of your high school or college. Find something in common to make a connection.
- Don't only single out contacts you want for a job or job advice. Do it for your hobbies too.
- Identify people in positions that interest you. Ask them to tell you about their work or pose specific questions about how they ended up where they are. They're likely to be flattered by your interest. Most people are happy to share their story and provide advice, especially if you are appreciative of their time.
- Join some LinkedIn groups that interest you or are related to your field. Then, be an active participant, not just a lurker. Get to know the others in the group. Join in discussions. Message people you'd like to meet.

Some other ways you can promote yourself on LinkedIn are:

- Update your status regularly to keep your contacts aware of your job search efforts.
- Ask colleagues and friends to give you LinkedIn recommendations.
- Find out where people with your background are working.
- Find where people in a company came from by using the LinkedIn "Company Profiles" feature.
- Find and connect with the hiring manager of companies you like.
- Seek out start-up companies that might be hiring.
- Search for recruiters who place people in your field.
- Check "LinkedIn Event" listings to network with other professionals.

Step out of your comfort zone, and you'll be able to take networking to the next level. You have absolutely nothing to lose and everything to gain from connecting with like-minded people.

Because your LinkedIn profile will contain background information on your work experience and education, consider including a link to it on your résumé. You always want to make it easy for employers who are interested to learn more about you.

## Get Face Time on Facebook

Most networking sites are not as business-focused as LinkedIn, but at least one has transitioned from its original emphasis on socializing to also become a useful business tool.

Facebook began in 2004 as a site for college students to mingle online. It quickly soared in popularity and was opened to the general public in 2006.

To use Facebook in your job search, first create a profile. Include information that will help others get to know you. Also be sure to upload a photo. People want to see you; after all, it is *Face*book.

If you're already on Facebook interacting with friends and family, start looking for ways to use it to network with other professionals and get job leads. Search for career-related applications and groups. Some have daily job postings.

Consider using Facebook to do a little behind-the-scenes research. Your real-life friends may not know anything about a company that's hiring but how about your Facebook friends? It doesn't hurt to ask. Tap their collective knowledge. Most people are happy to share their knowledge and offer advice.

Facebook is ideal for bringing together groups of people to discuss, debate, and share information online. Search for existing groups that match your interests. Join them and become active in the discussions. Or create your own group.

One of the best uses of Facebook is catching up with old friends and colleagues. Track down old associates already on Facebook by using the site's search engine.

You can also have Facebook comb through your e-mail address book and send invitations to your contacts to become your friends on Facebook.

Another strategy to grow your friends list is to search Facebook profiles for people who went to your high school or college or who you once worked with. Even better, you can look through your friends' list of friends to see if there's anyone you know or would like to know.

Keep expanding your network and then make it a point to continually update your status (a short statement at the top of your profile page) and to maintain contact with your online friends.

Facebook is a versatile tool with new applications continually being added, so its potential usefulness keeps growing. With a little time and effort, you'll quickly become comfortable on this social network and be able to adapt its capabilities to your job hunt.

A word of caution though. Facebook offers many such nonbusiness-related applications as games, quizzes, and social forums—all of which are fun but can also be time-burning distractions if you're not disciplined.

## Use Twitter in Your Job Search

Twitter is an increasingly popular tool that can be used to leverage your job hunt.

It's a cross between an online social network and a micro-blogging service. Twitter allows you to send and read other users' updates.

Think of it as a giant virtual watercooler—a place where people can make friends, get to know each other, network, and, most importantly, converse.

But here's what makes Twitter so unique. Posts, known as *tweets,* can only contain up to 140 characters in length. These brief updates are displayed on the user's profile page and delivered to other users who have signed up to receive them.

With millions of users and growing daily, Twitter can help you rapidly build your network of contacts. You can use it to access other professionals in your field, share information, and get tips about jobs.

## Other Business Networking Sites

While LinkedIn, Facebook, and Twitter are among the most popular business networking sites, they're certainly not the only ones. Check out other networks, such as XING (www.xing.com), Plaxo (www.plaxo.com), Ziggs (www.ziggs.com), Ecademy (www.ecademy.com), and ZoomInfo (www.zoominfo.com).

Use the one whose features you like. Or use several if you're able to manage their various demands.

Some social sites cater to job hunters such as ResumeSocial (www.resumesocial.com), Ziggs (www.ziggs.com), and Emurse (www.emurse.com).

You can also join industry-specific social networks—many of which are created on the Ning (www.ning.com) platform. Use Ning's search engine to find relevant networks or start a Ning network yourself.

Most of these business networking sites offer a basic service for free or more advanced functionality for a modest monthly fee. Eventually, using the resources of these sites, you will have a large pool of people who are pulling for you.

## How to Use Social Networks

Social networking online is not a replacement for your other job hunting tasks. Instead, it should complement them. Use social networks to:

- **Access other professionals in your field.** Find and follow the leaders in your profession. Take note of the conferences they attend, the books they read, and the issues on which they feel strongly. Learn from these experts, and incorporate some of their success strategies into your own repertoire. Eventually, you may even be able to befriend them and have them assist you in your job search.

- **Get exposure.** Develop relationships by connecting with other professionals— particularly those in your industry. You'll gain visibility and credibility as you network.

- **Share information.** Look for opportunities to demonstrate your expertise. That doesn't mean you should act like a know-it-all, but if you can answer someone's question or provide helpful advice, you'll be establishing yourself as an authority.

- **Get leads about jobs.** You'll find that the majority of people participating in social networking make an effort to be cordial and to reach out whenever they can. Your online friends can become an extended family of helpful people keeping their eyes open for opportunities to send your way—particularly jobs that haven't been advertised.

## Why Social Networks Are So Effective

One of the best reasons to jump into the social networking pool is that it's so easy. Think about it: You can meet people whose path you'd otherwise never cross, and you don't even have to put on shoes!

Social networks really do work. They offer a relaxed atmosphere that makes it easy for you to meet and talk with others without coming across as pushy. You can even gain access to people you otherwise wouldn't get to know: CEOs, top executives, industry leaders, hiring managers, recruiters, and everyone in between.

By joining online groups and connecting with others through friends and colleagues, you can expand your network on a daily basis in a comfortable, non-intimidating way. As you socialize with others, you'll get practice and feedback that enables you to refine your pitch as a job hunter.

## How to Get Started on Social Networks

Follow these ten steps to get off on the right foot:

1. **Create an account.** On most social networks, you can and should use your real name. On some, such as Twitter, you can strive for something clever, such as a combination of your name and profession that is easy to remember. Extra points if it's particularly catchy. For example, JoseNuruMarketingGuru.

2. **Craft a professional profile.** Your profile is essentially a bio—a brief summary of who you are. Include the salient information, and try to present it in an interesting way. If you have a personal website or blog, include the URL. You can also link to your online résumé and to your profiles on other social networking sites.

3. **Use a professional-looking avatar (picture) of yourself.** You want people to begin to recognize you, so add a photo to your profile. It will help people to feel they know you. Choose a photo that is both professional and personable. A close-up shot of your face is best because in many cases, the picture will display as a thumbnail (small format).

4. **Start with people you know.** Connect with friends, colleagues, and schoolmates. By watching how they participate on the social network, you'll quickly get up to speed on what's acceptable and most effective.

5. **Search for power networkers.** As you begin to network online, you'll find some people who are exceptional at socializing. They're highly visible and seem to know or be known by everyone. They speak with authority. They're tapped into relevant news sources and readily share information. Their opinions are valued, and others in the social community treat them with respect.

    You can watch how these power players work. Get to know them, and connect with the people they know. You'll be gaining an education in online networking while growing your own professional network.

6. **Become active.** Lurking isn't cool. You have to jump into the game and participate. You can talk about your job search, industry trends, or your opinion on relevant issues. You can even discuss nonwork-related topics, such as tidbits about your family. That will help people feel they know you. Just be careful not to share anything you wouldn't want an employer to find out.

    Don't waste others' time by sharing such boring details as what you ate for lunch or that you've misplaced a file. You can be clever and funny but also be sure to add useful information. For example, mention an interesting article you've just read or share a useful link. Soon, you will develop a following.

7. **Use the social network's tools.** Most social networks have applications or tools to help you find and connect with others who share like interests. Use them to build your network. Some sites even have tools specifically for job hunters that help you connect with recruiters and employers who are hiring.

   Every social network is different, so you'll have to find your way around each one individually. Don't be intimidated; most are extremely user-friendly, and you can always ask other members for assistance on specific issues.

8. **Be selective.** Don't connect with everybody just because you can. You'll end up spending all your time reading their updates. You're better off getting to know a relatively small group of people well rather than connecting to thousands of people with whom you never interact.

9. **Don't just take—give!** As in all networking, shameless self-promotion is a no-no. That's a surefire way to offend others. Instead, look for ways to help others. Pass along useful information and contacts when you can. Be supportive of others, and they'll do the same for you.

10. **Let your personality shine through.** Allow people to get to know the real you. Nobody likes a phony online any more than they do in real life.

---

**EXERCISE**   ## Join a Social Network

Pick one social network on which to get started. If you're not already on LinkedIn, that would be a good choice.

You'll need to register, which usually entails providing your e-mail address and a password. Then, fill out the application to join.

Next, upload a photo of yourself. If you don't have one handy, make a note to get one soon—even it if means just asking a friend to do a quick snapshot of your head and shoulders.

Then, seek out at least two other people with whom you'd like to connect. These can be people you already know through work, school, or social life. Send them invitations to connect.

If you're on LinkedIn, look in the Groups Directory. Find at least two groups that you'd like to join. If you're on a different social network, you'll have to locate where they list their groups.

Next, edit your Public Profile Settings and Contact Settings. On sites other than LinkedIn, these may be known as Privacy Settings or just Settings.

Lastly, click around to begin to familiarize yourself with the network. Make it a point to visit the site at least once a day for a week. Participate in the groups you've joined by reading updates and adding comments. Add more contacts as you become more comfortable. You may also be able to add more to your profile over time. Become an active member.

Once you've become comfortable on one social network, tackling another should be no big deal. They're user friendly, and they're fun! So, go ahead, get your feet wet, and start making the most of these exciting online tools.

## Build Online Relationships

While it's easy enough to meet people online, building relationships is what it's all about. As you grow your contact network, use some of the following ideas to help enhance your interactions:

- **Post frequently.** Depending on the social network, you may want to update your status daily or every few days. Keep it fresh. Stay active and visible on your social network sites, but don't spend so much time that it detracts from other important job searching tasks.

- **Establish yourself as an expert.** Write about things that will interest others in your field. When employers are considering you for a position, you'll have more than your résumé to back up your expertise.

- **Pursue, engage, reach out.** Make a sincere effort to get to know the person behind the screen name. Use the same techniques you might use if you were trying to meet the members of a club that you just joined.

- **Don't just talk—listen!** As in real conversations, you should show interest in what others are saying. So, read other people's updates and posts. Comment on them—particularly if you have something interesting to add.

- **Share information.** Pass on links to good articles or relevant blog posts you discover. This will position you as an expert and a conversation starter. Along the same lines, you can help others to promote. If someone you know is trying to get the word out about their new product or a seminar they're hosting, spread the information to your circles.

- **Introduce topics of mutual interest and get people talking.** These topics don't all have to be business related. They can be about news of the day, sports, hobbies, whatever. The goal is to forge a connection with others.

- **Make virtual introductions.** When you see people who would benefit from knowing each other, be the conduit to bring them together.

- **Remember things about others.** Show people that you're a good listener, and remember where they're going on vacation or when they're giving a big presentation. After the event, ask them how it went. They'll appreciate your interest.

- **Assist with causes and nonprofit ventures.** Volunteerism builds character and shows you're not self-centered.

- **Reply promptly to anyone who contacts you.** Engage them in conversations. Add them to your social networks, such as Facebook and Twitter.

- **Be appreciative of people who are helpful.** A simple "thank you" goes a long way.

- **Broaden your reach.** Keep adding to your network. Continually seek out additional people who share your interests.

- **Be honest about your situation.** It's okay to let others know that you are job hunting. When appropriate, you can ask others for advice or encourage them to send job leads your way. You might be pleasantly surprised to see how helpful people can be.

Social networking sites are growing exponentially. As more people join, you'll have additional opportunities to network in your job search. Start today, and you'll be well positioned to capitalize on the industry's rapid expansion. Your next job could be just a social connection away.

## Integrate Social Media with Traditional Networking

Most of your interaction on social networking sites will be via posts and messaging (a form of e-mail through the networking website). However, that doesn't mean you can't reach out when you find someone you can help or who can help you.

Bring your virtual world into your real world by combining online networking with offline socializing. Pick up the phone if that's an easier way to discuss a situation. If your contact happens to be in your particular neck of the woods, then arrange to meet for coffee or lunch.

Look for social events being held in your area. For example, Twitter has what they call Tweet ups. They're essentially meet ups that take place in a casual environment, such as a bar or restaurant, and attract local professionals who met on Twitter and are interested in networking. Most cities now have Tweet ups. Just start asking around on Twitter, and you'll soon find one that's close to you.

Also check www.meetup.com, which lists thousands of group get-togethers with specialty interests around the country. There's probably one that interests you in your area. Some other up-and-coming websites that mix online networking with offline social events are www.networkingforprofessionals.com and www.netparty.com.

## Create Your Personal Brand

When you use online social networking, you give others an insight into your personality, your interests, and your goals. Be sure that the image you create is one that will help you in your job search.

Think of the companies Apple, Coca-Cola, Walmart, and Google. Did a picture immediately form in your mind of their logo or products? These companies have been successful in building their brands.

When job hunting, you are the brand. You have to promote and differentiate yourself among job seekers who may have similar skills and levels of experience. Your brand should encompass everything you are as a person, including your strengths, experiences, abilities, perspectives, appearance, and character. It's what makes you special. Building a personal brand will help you gain a competitive edge—a necessity in a tough economy when jobs are scarce. Think of it as a means to enhance your recognition in your field, establish your reputation and credibility, and ultimately advance your career.

Realize, though, that you can't expect your brand to gain traction in social media by simply setting up a Facebook page or posting your résumé online. Network in the virtual world just as you would in the real world—"working it" on multiple levels. You have to engage your audience by participating in the conversation, providing value and reaching out to potential contacts.

## Publish So Employers Will Find You

One of the best ways to build your personal brand is to get published online. Today's employers search the Web for prospective employees and to check out candidates they're considering.

Posting your writing online will give you added visibility and credibility. Become a content producer, and your network will flourish, positioning your brand for career success.

You can start by reading blogs, forums, and news sites that are relevant to your industry or simply are of interest to you. But don't just be an observer; participate. Demonstrate strong thought leadership in your field. Add your two cents to blog posts, news stories, and forum discussions. Share your expertise. Your brilliant response to an item in the news or your insightful advice to a newbie could steer an employer in your direction.

Use an avatar (also called a gravatar, or globally recognized avatar)—a small picture of yourself that accompanies your comments—so people will begin to associate a face with your name.

Consider starting your own blog. A blog is one of the best ways to let people get to know you. You can share your ideas on issues, giving potential employers insight into what you might add to their company.

Blogging software such as WordPress is free and can be readily downloaded online from www.wordpress.org. Blogs can be hosted for free on www.wordpress.com or for a small fee for added functionality on such sites as Host Gator (www.hostgator.com) and Go Daddy (www.godaddy.com). Of course, you'll want to include links to your blog on all your social networking profiles, on your résumé, and in your cover letters.

If a blog is more of a challenge than you can handle, how about writing a few articles and posting them on such article directory sites as Ezine Articles (www.ezinearticles.com), Go Articles (www.goarticles.com), or iSnare (www.isnare.com)? Submission is free and can help position you as an expert on a topic.

Some other sites that offer the option of self-publishing are:

- Google Knol (http://knol.google.com/k)
- Squidoo (www.squidoo.com)
- Hubpages (www.hubpages.com)
- Scribd (www.scribd.com)
- Wet Paint (www.wetpaint.com)
- eHow (www.ehow.com)

By creating content, you'll be using the power of the Web to advance your career. Your writing will supplement what's on your résumé. You'll be establishing a Web presence and building your personal brand.

**EXERCISE**   **Become an Online Author**

Getting published used to be nearly impossible unless you were already an established expert in your field or your writing was extraordinary. The Internet now offers many opportunities to publish your work, and the requirements aren't as stringent.

Anyone can become an online author. And because being published can help you in your job hunt, it's certainly worth exploring the process.

Begin by familiarizing yourself with the different publishing formats available. Visit each of the following sites to see the works they publish:

- Ezine Articles (www.ezinearticles.com)
- Google Knol (http://knol.google.com/k)
- Squidoo (www.squidoo.com)
- Hubpages (www.hubpages.com)
- Scribd (www.scribd.com)
- Wet Paint (www.wetpaint.com)
- eHow (www.ehow.com)

As you can tell, each of these sites has a different style for its submissions. For example, a Squidoo Web page is called a *lens* and is markedly different than a how-to article on eHow or a mini-website on Wet Paint. Pick one site that you might feel comfortable producing content for. Now carefully review its submission guidelines and examples of other authors' contributions.

Next, choose your topic. What do you feel qualified to write about? Keep in mind that it should be related to your chosen field. Be sure your theme isn't too broad. A more specific, well-defined topic will work best. For the purposes of this exercise, you don't need to actually write your submission, but do take the time to come up with a working title and at least three main points that you could include.

By now, you should feel confident that if you were to complete your write-up, you'd know where and how to submit it. It's not so scary, right? So, keep the publishing option in mind as you proceed with your job hunt.

## Use Video to Build Your Brand Too

If you're a better speaker than you are writer, consider making videos to build your brand. Do a video of yourself talking about your capabilities and the type of job you're seeking. You can also use the video to show tangible samples of your work.

Another option is to create multiple videos on specific topics that put you in the expert's role. For example, if you're a marketing professional, you can do short informational videos on print advertising, public relations, direct mail, and e-mail marketing.

Consider developing a vlog. That's the video equivalent of a blog. Simply create videos (production quality need not be broadcast-caliber) on issues of interest in your field. Use them to showcase your ideas and to build your credibility.

Think of your videos as opportunities to show and tell. You're giving employers a better feel for your personality, knowledge base, and work ethic.

Your videos don't have to be major motion pictures. They can be short—just a minute or two—or longer if you have adequate material. Production should be clean and devoid of any annoying distractions, such as a TV in the background or the hum of an air conditioner. You can use your home video camera, but take the time to evaluate the lighting and setting.

Upload your videos to YouTube (www.youtube.com) or Viddler (www.viddler.com). If you have a personal website or online portfolio, include hyperlinks to them. You can also include links to your videos in your cover letters and résumés sent to potential employers. Further promote your videos on any social networks you belong to, such as LinkedIn, Facebook, and Twitter.

## Manage Your Online Image

Just as online marketing can help you to get a job, it can also work against you. You may have an outstanding résumé  and say all the right things in your interview, but if your online reputation isn't golden, it could be the obstacle that prevents you from being hired. Your online image can make or break you.

Many employers search the Internet to see if the picture you've painted for them in your résumé and interview matches the person displayed on social networks and other online sources. Recruiters and HR professionals routinely use online reputational information in their candidate review processes.

For better or for worse, the search engines find content you produce or that mention you and index it. And the search engines don't forget. Ever.

As you participate in social media, be authentic, be yourself, but use common sense. Don't put yourself in a position that could have a detrimental effect on your career later.

Check your Facebook profile and MySpace page for political correctness. Remove anything an employer might view as inappropriate or immature. Explicit photos, comments about drinking binges, or descriptions of your latest sexual exploits won't create a favorable picture.

Don't assume that just because you've set up privacy settings that employers can't see what you post. There are often ways to get around those settings. Some employers will even come right out and ask you to grant them access to your social networking profiles.

Dig deep. Have friends posted any potentially damaging information that includes your name? Have you been tagged in any questionable photos posted by others? Are you a member of any Facebook groups whose names and activities could be considered controversial? Have you chosen any applications that are posted on your wall and might not reflect well on you? Publishing the results of "What is your stripper name?" might not be the best idea. When in doubt, take it out. Eliminate all potential red flags that might cause an employer to hesitate in hiring you.

Do you keep a personal blog? If there's anything you wouldn't want your grandmother to read, then you probably wouldn't want your prospective employer reading it either. Delete it, and in the future, keep the private stuff offline.

Do you post comments on other's blogs? Employers can easily track down those statements, so choose your words carefully.

Go a step further and Google yourself. Check other search engines, such as Yahoo and Bing. Take action to get rid of any information that might make you look unprofessional or reveal a strong viewpoint that could be seen as objectionable.

Information that has influenced rejections of candidates includes:

- Lifestyle
- Poor communication skills displayed in comments or posts
- Remarks criticizing previous employers
- Photos, videos, and information considered inappropriate or immature
- Membership in certain groups
- Concerns about finances
- Negative comments or text written about the candidate by friends, relatives, colleagues, or work acquaintances

Your online reputation is as important as the picture you've painted in your résumé  and job interview. Expect that employers will Google your name and search for you on social networks. Consider these stories that recently surfaced in the news:

- A chemical engineering student at a prestigious university in the Northeast was eliminated from consideration for a job opening after a company recruiter Googled the student's name and discovered the following remark: "I like to blow things up."

- A recent graduate of a small Midwestern university was only a few weeks into her first job when the boss called her into his office. He had discovered the young woman's personal blog, where she had written in detail about how miserable she was in her new position. She soon became a former employee.

- A student at a school in the southeastern United States was interviewed by a small business owner for a key position. She was the leading candidate—that is, until the owner saw the student's Facebook profile, which featured explicit photos and stories about her drinking and pot smoking.

- A successful account executive at an advertising agency was fired after the firm's president learned that the employee was the writer behind a racy blog that described her deviant sexual exploits, including some with a coworker.

- A recent graduate had difficulty getting hired. At a friend's suggestion, he researched himself on search engines. He found a link to a satirical essay, titled "Lying Your Way to the Top," that he had published the previous year on a website for college students. Realizing that potential employers were likely seeing the essay, he asked that it be removed, but by then, he'd already been passed over for several desirable jobs.

- A woman applied for a clerical position. A Google search turned up her personal blog. One of the entries said "I am applying for menial jobs that are beneath me. It's degrading. I'll quit the minute I find anything better."

- A small, privately owned engineering firm was considering several candidates for an entry-level engineering position. When the owner searched online for information about the candidates, he came across a photo of one of them with cigarette in hand. Because the owner was staunchly against smoking and was also aware of how smokers can cost companies more for health insurance, that candidate was eliminated from the running.

With few exceptions, whatever you put on the Internet is public and available indefinitely. Potential employers are a mouse click away from learning everything about you.

You need to make sure your online presence is working for you, not against you. Leave out anything questionable in blog posts, comments, photos, profiles, tweets, etc., that could damage your reputation and adversely affect an employer's decision on whether to hire you.

Instead, use social networks and blogs to enhance your online reputation by stacking the Web with good information about you. Take a proactive approach to getting your name out there. Post articles, profiles, and status updates that you would want an employer to find. Use your full name whenever possible to maximize your exposure. Make your online reputation just one more reason an employer should choose you for the job!

# SUCCESS STORIES

Often, the greatest inspiration comes from those who have succeeded. Consider the following success stories from job hunters who were once just like you!

I had been active on LinkedIn for more than a year. I spent the most time in a LinkedIn group for marketing professionals and often provided helpful tips to other members. When I was laid off from my job as a marketing associate, I wrote about the situation on my LinkedIn page.

One of my contacts in the marketing group saw my post and referred me for a job that was open at his company. I got the interview and the job all within one week of being laid off. Without actively participating in that LinkedIn marketing group, I never would have heard about the job and certainly wouldn't have had the advantage of being referred by someone who already worked there.

Barbara
*Marketing Representative*

I was right out of school and actively seeking employment as a Web developer when I saw a tweet from one of the people I follow on Twitter. It said: "Looking for HTML developer and PSD slicer. Know anyone? Send them my way." I immediately responded with my own contact information. That led to an inteview and then a full-time job. The most amazing thing is that the position was never advertised anywhere other than that 75-character tweet on Twitter.

**George**
*Web Developer*

While I was job hunting, I began writing a blog about nutrition. In it, I posted everything from recipes to commentary on the latest diets. I also wrote about my personal journey from junk food addict to health food advocate.

When I applied for jobs, I made sure to include a link to my blog on my résumé and in my cover letter. The employer who hired me said that the blog made me stand out from all the other candidates who applied. It was clear after reading it that I not only knew my stuff but practiced what I preached.

**Charlotte**
*Registered Dietician*

## Chapter Follow-Up

- Social networking online is the practice of expanding your business and social contacts by making connections through individuals via the Internet. It's a way to meet more people, which increases your chances of finding a potential employer or someone who can refer you to one.

- To be effective on social networks, you can't just be an observer; you need to participate.

- The Internet offers opportunities for you to publish your views in the form of blogs and articles you write and even videos you produce. Use online media to give employers a better understanding of all you have to offer their company.

- Actively manage your online reputation so employers doing their due diligence before offering you a job find only positive information about you.

# Chapter 11

## Have You Considered . . . ?

## What Do You Know?

### True or False

_____ 1. Government jobs are only for politicians.

_____ 2. If you want to work for the government, you need to move to Washington, D.C.

_____ 3. Nonprofits don't have paid employees; they only hire volunteers.

_____ 4. Working for a small company versus a larger company could be a great learning experience in that you may get to wear many hats and have diverse responsibilities.

_____ 5. Starting your own business is a viable alternative if you have a good idea, the means to implement the idea, and the desire to "give it your all."

_____ 6. If you can't find a job in your field, you should go back to college for a more advanced degree or a degree in a different field.

## Chapter Focus

In this chapter, you'll learn to explore:

- Federal and local government jobs.
- Positions with nonprofit organizations.
- Opportunities with small companies.
- Entrepreneurship and self-employment.
- Working in an alternative field.
- Further education.

## Real-Life Relevance

Finding a job is often not an easy task, and finding the perfect job is even more challenging, particularly when you're just starting out in your career. Therefore, your best chance for success is to consider all potential opportunities. Although your dream job may be to one day operate a large multinational corporation, you don't want to limit your search to these types of employers—at least not in the early stages of your career. Keeping an open mind to a variety of employment opportunities could help to open more doors during your job search.

# Federal Jobs

Should you consider a federal job? Absolutely. To leave out the federal government in your job search is to eliminate the nation's largest employer. Furthermore, about three out of four federal workers are employed in managerial, business, financial, or professional positions.

## Types of Federal Jobs

Among the ranks of federal employees, you'll find statisticians, accountants, engineers, pharmacists, lawyers, law enforcement officers, social workers, economists, artists, researchers, bus drivers, teachers, and morticians. In all, the federal government employs people in more than 1,000 occupations. Entire new departments have been created in recent years, such as the Department of Homeland Security, requiring people with specialized skills.

Don't think that you need to move to Washington, D.C., to get a job with the federal government. Actually, fewer than 15 percent of federal employees work there. Federal employees work in every state, and about 3 percent are assigned overseas—mostly in embassies or defense installations.

## Why Consider a Federal Job?

Job security is a primary reason to consider government work. Federal employment is generally not affected by cyclical fluctuations in the economy. Layoffs have occurred in the past, but they are uncommon and generally affect relatively few workers. Excellent pay and benefits—as good as or better than in the private sector—are another reason many people seek federal employment.

## Finding Federal Jobs

Discovering what federal jobs are available can be done online. The U.S. Office of Personnel Management maintains a website (www.usajobs.opm.gov) where you can search and apply for openings.

Keep in mind that more than half of all government workers are employed in local government positions. Some of the segments within local government are county government, school districts, fire and police districts, and park districts. Call your local state employment office or search on the Internet to learn about available positions.

## Working for a Nonprofit Organization

Because more than 10 percent of the U.S. workforce is employed in the nonprofit sector, you may want to give serious consideration to nonprofit organizations in your job search. Why work for a nonprofit company? Employees in nonprofit organizations often report a high degree of job satisfaction and personal fulfillment. They also say they enjoy the diversity of their work: Because budgets are often constrained in nonprofit organizations, one individual may be responsible for many different tasks.

On the downside, most employees in nonprofit organizations earn less than their counterparts in for-profit companies.

Working for a nonprofit organization can be an end in itself or it can serve as a stepping-stone to other types of work. However, because of limited recruiting budgets, nonprofits often rely on contacts and referrals when hiring. The implication is clear: If you are looking for a job in the nonprofit sector, you'll have to do more than read the help wanted ads.

**Consider working for the U.S. government. There are numerous professional positions at the federal, state, and local government levels.** (© David Ball / Stock Market / Corbis)

Begin by clarifying your goals. What issues interest you? Here are just a few examples of general issues addressed by nonprofits:

- Homelessness
- Religion
- Hunger
- Education
- Health care
- Poverty
- Arts and culture
- Disaster relief

On behalf of what group of people would you like to work? Again, here are a few examples:

- Children
- The disabled
- The elderly
- Homeless families
- Refugees
- The mentally ill
- Abuse victims
- Catastrophe survivors
- War veterans
- Single mothers

Next, learn which organizations focus on your issues of interest. Search online or seek out directories of nonprofit organizations at your library. You might also contact your local United Way chapter. Because the United Way disperses money to numerous nonprofit organizations, it often keeps a comprehensive list of such groups in its area. Your local chamber of commerce may also be familiar with nonprofit organizations in your area.

Use trade publications creatively. Don't review only current postings for a job; check out old job listings in order to identify organizations rather than specific positions. Consider consulting articles in trade publications to identify organizations that have just received funding or are working on a new initiative. Look for stories about changes in leadership. New leaders often make staffing changes and add new positions.

Ultimately, you'll want to examine the issues, missions, and methods of specific organizations, asking yourself how your interests and skills might fit into their goals. Because most organizations have their own website, you can conduct most of your initial research online. Then, apply the traditional job seeking tactics discussed throughout this text. Set up some informational interviews, begin networking, send out cover letters, and make cold calls.

If you find an organization you think would be a perfect fit but no openings exist, consider volunteering your time. It is an excellent way to prove your commitment, verify your career choice, and make the contacts that could lead to a paying job.

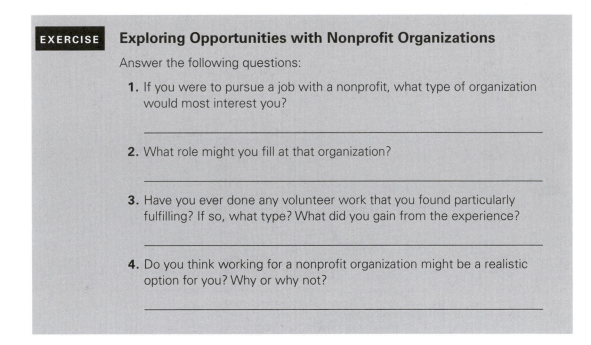

**EXERCISE**    **Exploring Opportunities with Nonprofit Organizations**

Answer the following questions:

**1.** If you were to pursue a job with a nonprofit, what type of organization would most interest you?

_____

**2.** What role might you fill at that organization?

_____

**3.** Have you ever done any volunteer work that you found particularly fulfilling? If so, what type? What did you gain from the experience?

_____

**4.** Do you think working for a nonprofit organization might be a realistic option for you? Why or why not?

_____

# Working for a Small Company

Although it may look better on your résumé and be more impressive to your friends and relatives to say you have a job at a large, well-known company, there are many benefits of working for a small business.

First, you'll likely have more responsibilities than you would at a larger company. You'll wear many hats, which makes the job challenging, interesting, and a great learning opportunity.

Second, you'll probably have more control over your areas of responsibility. There is typically less hierarchy with which to contend as well as fewer formal means of authorization. You'll be able to develop an idea and see it through to completion—probably without interference from people in numerous departments and superiors.

Third, it's easier to get hired at a small company when you have limited experience. Presumably, there are fewer candidates applying for positions in small companies than in prestigious, big companies. Also, a small company may not be able to afford employees with significant experience. They'll accept entry-level employees, knowing that those employees will need to do some of their learning on the job.

When you search for a small-company employer, don't forget to consider start-up companies, which are just getting off the ground. Although they may not offer job security (many new businesses eventually fail), they can provide an unsurpassed learning experience, not to mention a sense of pride in helping to create something new and different.

# Starting Your Own Business

Many people dream of being their own boss. Although the failure rate for new businesses is high, that doesn't mean you can't succeed. Such mega-companies as Microsoft and Apple were once start-ups too. So, don't rule out your potential for entrepreneurship. Consider the positives:

1. You're in charge of your own destiny. You make the decisions and don't have to deal with corporate politics and red tape.

2. You control the time you work—how many hours and which hours of the day or night. (This can be a terrific perk if you tend to do your best work at odd hours or if you have young children.)

3. You have the opportunity for great diversity. As an entrepreneur, you may find yourself doing everything from sales, to production, to accounting—tasks that might otherwise be split among specialized employees in an established company.

4. To some degree, you have control over your salary.

   Now consider the negatives:

1. You get to make the decisions, but you also suffer the consequences of those decisions.

2. Self-employment often means long hours because you are ultimately responsible for everything.

3. You have to be a jack-of-all-trades, overseeing every aspect of the business—at least during the start-up phase.

4. Because you are on your own, you do not have the support system of coworkers and an established organization.

5. Cash flow can be a serious problem for small businesses. In tough times, your own salary is often the first expense to go.

6. You shoulder the stress over the business's success.

7. Because of the risks, job security is low, and the potential for failure is high.

Now take a look at the personality traits you'll need to be an entrepreneur:

- High energy level
- Self-motivation
- Comfort taking risks
- Ability to make a long-range commitment
- Creativity
- Ability to spot or create opportunities
- Enjoyment of problem solving
- Ability to set high goals
- Optimism
- Ability to cope with setbacks
- Self-confidence
- Common sense

Do you think you have what it takes to make it as an entrepreneur? You just might, if you have a marketable skill or product and the sales savvy to get customers. Although the types of businesses change with the economy and technology, the fundamentals of entrepreneurship stay the same. If you'd like to pursue starting your own business, begin by doing market research. This will help you verify that the product or service you have in mind is likely in demand. You might even consider working for a company in the field before striking out on your own. For example, before starting your own restaurant, try working in one, and if possible, take on a variety of responsibilities to maximize what you learn.

Consider starting an Internet-based business. The start-up costs are often minimal. You can even begin your business as a side venture while you continue to seek or work at full-time employment. Grow your business, and it may one day be able to support you.

Develop a business plan and thoroughly investigate the feasibility of its implementation. You can find plenty of resources online to assist you with your business plan and any other hurdle you run into.

Contact the local office of the Small Business Administration. This group offers information and also mentoring for entrepreneurs. Be prepared to work long hours and not to take a salary in the beginning. Start modestly, keep an eye on your expenses, and plan your growth.

In the United States, 70 percent of all new businesses fail within the first years. But don't let that deter you. The more you prepare yourself and understand the challenges ahead, the more likely you are to be part of the 30 percent that succeed.

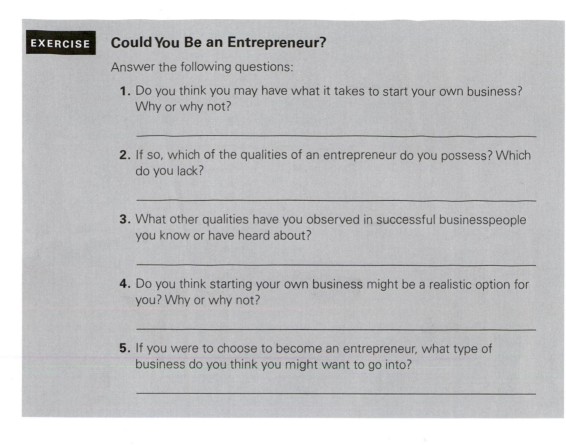

**EXERCISE**   **Could You Be an Entrepreneur?**

Answer the following questions:

1. Do you think you may have what it takes to start your own business? Why or why not?

   _____

2. If so, which of the qualities of an entrepreneur do you possess? Which do you lack?

   _____

3. What other qualities have you observed in successful businesspeople you know or have heard about?

   _____

4. Do you think starting your own business might be a realistic option for you? Why or why not?

   _____

5. If you were to choose to become an entrepreneur, what type of business do you think you might want to go into?

   _____

# Taking a Different Job Path

Having trouble finding a job that's in line with your chosen career? How about changing direction? Perhaps you have a secondary career interest or a hobby you could pursue in the job market—at least on a short-term basis. These days, it's not unusual for people to pursue several different careers or job types throughout the course of their working life, so don't feel that going in one direction means you'll never have the chance to go in another in the future.

Although taking a direct route up the corporate ladder to one's dream job may be everyone's first choice, that sometimes isn't possible. A job isn't necessarily a career. And a job that isn't quite the right fit doesn't have to be a waste of time. You can learn from your surroundings, make contacts, and gain valuable work experience in every position you hold. Furthermore, employers are more likely to hire someone who already has a job than someone who doesn't.

Don't become stressed if it takes you awhile to figure out exactly what you want to do or to obtain the perfect job. You may have several jobs before you find one that is your passion, and you'll quickly discover what you don't want to do. Talk with anyone who has been in the working world for more than a few years, and ask them about their first jobs. Although they may recount some horror stories, most will also acknowledge the value of those early experiences.

Sometimes, you can find a job that has an indirect connection to your chosen career—like the grade school teacher who works in a day care center, the landscape architect who works for a florist, the physical therapist who works as a personal trainer in a gym, or the chef who works in a grocery store. Other times, your first job may be a major departure from your career choice—like the actor who waits tables in a restaurant, the dental hygienist who works in a real estate office, or the paralegal who works for a stock brokerage firm.

Remember that first jobs are not likely to be where you will spend the rest of your career. During the time you're working in your less-than-perfect job, you can always continue to search for a position in your field—all while earning an income and learning something new.

**EXERCISE**

1. Briefly describe your dream job.

   _____

   _____

2. List at least two directions outside your primary career choice that you would consider for employment—at least on a short-term basis. To develop this answer, think of your minor in college, favorite elective classes, summer jobs you've held, hobbies, clubs you belong to, and any special talents you have.

   _____

   _____

3. Look online at one of the big career websites and then identify at least two positions outside your chosen career that sound interesting to you.

   _____

   _____

Now you can decide whether the time is right for you to apply for those jobs you selected or to employ some of the other job hunting techniques described in this book to help you find a position outside your primary career choice.

# Further Education

One of the most valuable assets to today's employers is an employee who has demonstrated the ability to learn and to continue learning. Perhaps your immediate future will have you sitting in a classroom instead of a boardroom!

Although many recent graduates shudder at the thought of spending another minute doing homework, further education or training could be an essential element of your job search. Just be certain you're not choosing to continue your education simply to avoid the potential rejection that comes with job hunting. Here are some questions to ask yourself:

1. Are you undereducated in comparison to others in your field? In some specialties, a master's or doctoral degree is necessary to stay truly competitive. Ask people who already work in your field, read help wanted ads to see what's required, and network with others to determine if more education would be beneficial to you.

2. Are your skills rusty? Have you been out of the job market for a while and feel like you're out of touch? Are you stranded in the breakdown lane of the information superhighway? Perhaps now is the time to invest in yourself and your career potential. Many local colleges have refresher courses ranging in length from an afternoon to weeks or years. Start with a simple goal, such as taking a computer course at a local community college or adult education center, and see how quickly you can regain your skills and self-confidence.

3. Do you have a burning desire to know more about widgets? Or topiary? Or Shakespeare? Some of the most exciting and profitable learning begins with a unique personal interest. Quenching your curiosities through a seminar, course, certificate program, or degree may be the beginning of a satisfying new career direction.

4. Will another degree or certificate make you more valuable to current or potential employers? Could you go even further in your current position if you signed up for a few classes? Would additional education or training enable you to apply for new positions within the company? Could you make more money if you obtained some training for the purpose of eventually switching careers? Sometimes, the only thing preventing an escape from a dead-end job is a few new skills. Research what training or education you need to secure positions that appeal to you.

5. Do you need to pass an exam, get a license, or be certified? Many professions separate the professionals from the amateurs by means of professional licensing exams or certifications. But many in those fields remain in lower-paying jobs—despite having all or most of the skills to move ahead—because they are intimidated by the rigors of passing a test or taking a course. It might be time to muster your courage and study for the big test. Take a refresher course or study with a colleague if that will help you take the next step. Ask yourself what you have to lose. If the answer is *nothing*, then get started today.

## SUCCESS STORIES

Often, the greatest inspiration comes from those who have succeeded. Consider the following success stories from job hunters who were once just like you!

During my college summer vacations, I volunteered at a local animal shelter. In addition to some great experience, I got to know all the local veterinarians. When I graduated, a veterinarian who remembered me from the shelter offered me a job.

Ken
*Veterinary Assistant*

I majored in law enforcement in college. Originally, I had planned to become a police officer, but when I graduated, the federal government was just forming the Department of Homeland Security. I had lost a friend in the attacks on 9/11, so the idea of helping to protect our country held a great deal of meaning to me. I applied and was able to obtain an entry-level position. After a year, I was promoted into a higher-level job in Homeland Security.

Steven
*U.S. Immigration and Customs Enforcement*

I grew up in a family of realtors. My father and my brother were realtors and owned a real estate firm. It was pretty much assumed I would join them one day. I obtained my B.S. in business and then joined the firm. But I wanted to create something unique—pursue a new niche—instead of just piggybacking on my dad and brother's success. Whereas they sold houses and apartment buildings, I focused my energy on selling condo vacation homes. I researched properties, met with developers, and eventually built a detailed website to promote my listings. Within about two years, the business became so successful that we created a separate division for it, with its own staff and budget. Today, I own and manage that vacation condo division, and I take great pride from what I've been able to accomplish and the growth that I was able to bring to my family's existing business.

Joel
*Real Estate Broker*

I am a stay-at-home mom. One day, when my kids were napping, I painted a floral design on a watering can I had in my garage. My mother-in-law happened to see it when visiting and asked if I could make some more for her upcoming garden club crafts fair. I painted seventeen watering cans, and they all sold. Then, I began painting on all kinds of objects—from glass vases to ceramic planters. I now sell my work to about a dozen retail establishments in my area and also on eBay. The painting gives me a creative outlet and an income while allowing me to be a stay-at-home mom.

Sophie
*Artist*

While I was a senior in college, I did volunteer work at the local chapter of the United Way. I got to know many of the staff people. When I graduated, they used their contacts to help me get a full-time position as an accountant with one of the agencies the United Way supports.

Mandy
*Accountant*

## Chapter Follow-Up

- Because it can often be difficult to find the perfect job, especially when you're just beginning your career, you may have to open your mind to some alternatives you previously hadn't considered.

- The government offers many job opportunities beyond politics, and most of those jobs are not in Washington, D.C. They can be right in your local community.

- A position with a nonprofit organization can be a smart career move as well as a personally fulfilling job.

- Small companies and start-ups are often more willing than large companies to hire an employee who has minimal experience but is enthusiastic and shows a willingness to take on multiple responsibilities.

- Starting your own business may be something you can do while you continue to search for full-time employment or it can be the career path you choose to follow.

- If you can't find a job in your field, perhaps you can find one that is loosely related for starters, such as a landscape architect who finds work in a plant nursery or a teacher who spends a summer as a camp counselor.

- Consider whether further education will make you more employable. If so, investigate what classes and programs are available, but don't return to school simply to avoid job hunting.

# Chapter 12

# Job Hunting in Tough Times

## What Do You Know?

### True or False

_____ 1. You shouldn't consider taking an entry-level job if you have a college degree.

_____ 2. A part-time job is worthy of your consideration if it gives you entry into your field and you can afford to live on the salary you'd earn—at least temporarily.

_____ 3. Freelancing is only an option for people in the graphic arts field.

_____ 4. Temporary work can give you income, put you in the workforce, and expose you to potential job opportunities.

_____ 5. Most internships are unpaid or include only a small stipend, but they can give you college credit toward your degree and valuable on-the-job experience.

_____ 6. Volunteer work is a waste of your time when you are looking for paid employment.

_____ 7. When the economy is down, you should be open to any and all potential sources of employment, and you may have to think creatively to generate your own opportunities.

## Chapter Focus

In this chapter, you'll learn to:

- Find an entry-level position.
- Seek a part-time job.
- Obtain freelance work.
- Try temp work.
- Work in a related position.
- Get an internship.
- Volunteer.

## Real-Life Relevance

Although you may have had good grades in school and used your summer vacations to get valuable work experience, unfortunately, that's still no guarantee you'll be able to land a full-time job in your chosen career as soon as you graduate, especially when times are tough. Depending on your field, geographical area, and the economy, you may find opportunities are limited and competition is fierce. Don't give up. Instead, think of some creative ways to get your foot in the door.

# Entry-Level Positions

It would be great if before you graduated that you had employers begging you to come work for them. You could name your salary and your terms, and you'd be doing the job you always dreamed of. Unfortunately, that's not the case for most of us.

Secretarial or mail-room work may not be your idea of the perfect job, but it can be a way to land your first career position. While it can be discouraging to have worked hard to obtain a degree in your field and then to be hired to do work that is beneath you, it may get you in the door and in sight of a more meaningful position.

Entry-level jobs won't provide the salary or prestige you had hoped for, but they're part of paying your dues—doing low-level work to prove yourself. There are many stories of famous businesspeople and celebrities who started this way—at the so-called bottom.

So, let's see how we can practically apply the concept of underemployment. If you've studied advertising, you might seek a job as an administrative assistant or account coordinator at an ad agency. You'll get to know the firm's clients, its methods of doing business, and the specific types of accounts it handles. Most importantly, you'll learn how an ad agency functions.

If you've studied television production and aspire to be a director one day, you may be able to get a job as a "gofer," or assistant—doing whatever extra tasks need to be done—from photocopying scripts to taking phone messages. If you're a beginning attorney, you might find yourself saddled with paralegal tasks. If you've studied physical therapy, you may get a job making appointments or greeting patients.

By now, you've realized that you're not going to start out as the president or chief executive officer of a firm. The first stage of your career development is more likely to be an entry-level position, for which you are somewhat overqualified and underpaid, but it could be a springboard to great things. Swallow your pride, work hard, and keep your eyes open for the next exciting opportunity.

# Part-Time Jobs

If finding your dream job isn't as easy as you thought, you might consider another tactic: getting a part-time job in your field, even if it's in addition to another full-time job outside your field that you hold simply to earn an adequate income.

Second jobs can be a way to supplement your income, explore a career, get some experience, or prepare to segue to something more fulfilling. Even if it isn't a position you'd want on a permanent basis, it can flesh out your résumé and help you gain contacts.

For example, if you're hoping to become a teacher but full-time teaching positions are few and far between, consider signing on as a substitute teacher. Chances are that the income from substitute teaching won't be enough for you to live on, but when combined with another job, it could help you get by. Best of all, you would  be gaining experience in your field and making contacts. When a full-time teaching position becomes available, you will be an obvious contender. As an aspiring teacher, you can also consider private tutoring. Or think about working part-time in a day care center, after school program, or recreational center.

If you'd like to be a reporter or photographer for a daily newspaper but are having trouble finding that first job, approach a small weekly or monthly publication as a part-timer. Once again, the income would be small, but the rewards in terms of potential opportunity and experience would be great.

If you're hoping to become a veterinarian, apply at the local animal shelter. If you'd like to be a corporate manager one day, start your own small business on the side. Maybe you do landscaping, data entry, disc jockeying at parties, or sales for such companies as Tupperware or Mary Kay. The scheduling, organizational, and money management skills you would develop can be transferred to any job.

Having two jobs simultaneously isn't for everyone. It requires abundant energy, extraordinary time management skills, and lots of "self" skills: self-discipline, self-sacrifice, self-marketing, and enough self-awareness to know your limits. To succeed, try not to think of your part-time work as just another job. Don't compete with or compromise any of your employers. And don't try to do too much at once.

---

**EXERCISE**    Answer the following questions:

**1.** What type of part-time job would you consider?

_____

**2.** What might you learn that could benefit you in your career?

_____

**3.** How could you find this type of part-time job?

_____

# Freelancing

Many full-time employees started out as freelancers or contractors. A freelancer is an individual who is self-employed and sells his or her unique services to multiple companies.

The word *freelance* comes from the Middle Ages, when a knight would offer his lance and, with it, his allegiance to the lord with the most money. Today's freelancers offer their special skills to companies that pay for their services.

Companies hire freelancers when they need individuals with a specific talent, when they have a temporary work overload, or simply don't want to incur the expenses and responsibilities of full-time employees.

Typically, freelancing has been associated with such fields as publishing and the arts. However, in today's ever-dynamic marketplace, freelance opportunities exist in many fields. Architects, writers, artists, secretaries, photographers, computer programmers, software engineers, nurses, and television producers are among the many types of professionals who freelance.

To be successful as a freelancer, you need a marketable skill and the persistence to develop a stable group of clients. Sales is a major component of successful freelancing. As a freelancer, you essentially run your own business, and you are solely responsible for the bottom line. On the plus side, you have independence, scheduling flexibility, and the financial rewards of being your own boss.

Freelancing can be a full-time undertaking or a means to an end. It's a great way to backdoor your way into a full-time job. As a freelancer, you have an opportunity to prove your value to an employer. And you have a chance to get to know the people who can recommend or hire you when a full-time position becomes available.

**Photographers are among the many types of professionals who can do freelance or contract work.**
(EdinEdin/istockphoto.com)

# Temping

One of the best ways to obtain a full-time job is to start off as a temporary employee, known as "temping." This opportunity gets your foot in the door and gives you the chance to prove yourself. More importantly, you can evaluate the company and decide if it's one you'd like to work for permanently.

Getting a temporary job tends to be easier than finding permanent work. The easiest way to find temporary work is to register with one or more temporary services agencies. Having your name on file with more than one agency helps ensure that you work consistently and you have more potential assignments from which to choose.

To find the right temporary agencies, ask friends and networking contacts for their suggestions, search the Internet, or check your local Yellow Pages. Also, you can call companies you'd like to work for and ask human resources employees which temporary services they use. If you're fortunate enough to be in such a field as technology, accounting, health care, or sales, you may find a temporary agency that specializes in that area.

Next, contact the temporary agency, and briefly describe your skills. Most services will invite you in for an interview, which consists of filling out a lengthy application form and meeting with a representative. Be sure to bring along a current copy of your résumé and any written references. If you're seeking a position in an office environment, you'll most likely be asked to take a battery of tests on the computer. Your keyboarding skills and knowledge of various software programs will be evaluated.

Be sure to specify for the representative the kinds of positions you'll consider. The better temporary services endeavor to offer you assignments that meet your criteria, but you have to communicate those criteria early in the game. Most temporary agencies specialize in clerical or industrial jobs. Although you may aspire to be a manager in a business, you're more likely to be placed in a secretarial job. Don't be discouraged. Remember that this is a temporary position, not your job for life.

During the interview, don't be shy about asking questions. Find out how the temporary service operates—that is, how the representative intends to match you with an employer. Don't be embarrassed to talk about money. Most likely, you'll be paid an hourly fee that will vary from one assignment to the next. Be clear with your representative about the pay scale you'll consider. If you have good skills, you'll be selected for higher-paying jobs.

Depending on the geographical area you're in, the specific temporary service, and the diversity of your skills, you could be offered a job immediately or not for months. Don't hesitate to call the temporary service on a regular basis to check job availability. Often, it's the most assertive workers who are placed first.

Once you're given an assignment, try to get as much information as possible about it from the temporary service. In addition to the basics of when and where to report, ask questions to get a sense of the type of work you'll be expected to do.

At the job, adopt a full-time mind-set. If you approach the position as though you are working there permanently, you'll make a good impression. A good attitude is vital.

While you're working, keep your eyes open for opportunities for full-time employment with the employer. Many temporary employees get offered full-time work if they prove to be capable and likable. If a position is not available, your immediate supervisors can pass your name along to supervisors in other departments that may be hiring or even give you the names of their own personal contacts outside the company.

While temping, don't give up your search for a permanent position. Try to use your lunch hour to make phone calls. Schedule interview appointments for after work hours or first thing in the morning.

Temporary work gives you income, puts you in the workforce, and exposes you to potential job opportunities. It's a great way to learn about different companies and industries, and it gives you the chance to polish your skills and meet new people. View temping as part of your education and the job hunting process, and the experience will be worthwhile.

# Working in a Related Position

You may have your heart set on a specific job, but the reality is no openings exist at the moment. That's when you need to think creatively. Are there jobs that might be related to the position you really want and are more easily attainable? For example, if you're seeking a position as a nurse, investigate all types of health care jobs. There are many technical and administrative positions available that allow you to contribute to a patient's well-being—even if in a less direct manner. From health information technician to home health aide to legal nurse consultant, health care jobs run the gamut of professional roles. And many of these positions are considered ideal for long-term growth.

To find out about positions that might be related to the job you want, you should do several types of research. Search the Internet for ideas; read the want ads on career websites; speak to people already working in the field; and peruse trade journals—particularly those that contain job listings. Working in a position related to your field, even if it's not exactly what you initially had in mind, can open your eyes to new opportunities while also allowing you to gain experience and make contacts.

# Internships

Whether you are still in school or have already graduated, you may be able to obtain an internship in your field of study. Most internships are unpaid or include a small stipend. Some count as credit toward a degree. Although working for free may not seem appealing at first, consider this: Many top executives got their start through an internship program.

As an intern, you may be saddled with some of the less glamorous tasks of the job you aspire to, but you'll get firsthand on-the-job experience. A good internship is one that includes more than busywork. If making coffee is the only skill you learn while interning, your experience will have been a waste of time. Seek an internship that affords the opportunity to work on stimulating projects. You'll make contacts and develop the skills you need to succeed in your chosen career.

Many interns are hired once a position opens up (there's something to be said for being in the right place at the right time). If an internship is financially impractical for you, consider arranging a part-time internship that would allow you to hold a paying job at the same time.

## Finding an Internship

Your best chance of learning about internship opportunities is through college placement offices. They frequently receive and post notices about internships at local and national companies. In fact, many companies do their interviewing on campus, using the placement office to prequalify applicants. Some college placement offices don't even require that you be a student at their school to participate.

Also check out sources of internship possibilities on the Internet. Just as many companies list job openings on their websites, they also list internship opportunities. Some of the major career websites also include information about internships. And there are whole websites that are dedicated to promoting internship opportunities. An Internet search will help you quickly find them.

You should also do some networking to learn of internships. Many internships are not publicized. Rather, they are filled with people who heard of them through their contacts.

There are also some published directories that list internship opportunities across the country and even abroad. These books usually categorize internships by career field, location, and organization name. They may also offer details about duties, compensation, and competitiveness. Check your local library.

If a company you would like to work for has no current job openings, ask if it has an internship program. If so, you may be able to use an internship as a stepping-stone to a full-time job. If not, consider sending a letter that proposes an internship, clearly explaining how the company would benefit from bringing you on in that capacity.

# Volunteer Work

Although all students dream of earning large salaries when they graduate, depending on your career choice and the state of the economy, that may not be possible. In the first few years of your career, your focus should be on gaining valuable work experience, not earning a large salary.

One possible way to gain entry into your career field is through volunteer work. Offering your time to a company or an organization can help you gain entry and enable you to explore career options. As a volunteer, you'll probably be able to set your own hours, which would allow you to also hold a paying job.

Nonprofit or service organizations are usually the most receptive to working with volunteers. Some examples of organizations that often depend on volunteers are the United Way, the American Red Cross, libraries, and hospitals. Of course, every community differs, so you'll have to do research to find out the best volunteer opportunities. Whether you are seeking a career in computers, public relations, office management, accounting, or health services, there should be a volunteer position that would provide you with worthwhile experience and the chance to make contacts.

Although you won't receive a salary for your work, don't take your responsibilities lightly. To make the most of the situation, volunteer for an organization you are interested in or that has relevance to your career. Work closely with professionals who can serve as role models for you. Seek out training within the organization. Every skill you master makes you a smarter, more employable person. Ask to be promoted to tasks of greater challenge so your volunteer experience is filled with accomplishments.

Be sure to list your volunteer work on your résumé along with your paid jobs. Your achievements as a volunteer are significant. Potential employers will appreciate your initiative.

---

**EXERCISE**   **Think Creatively About Employment Options**

Take a moment to consider whether any of the strategies discussed in this chapter make sense for you. Complete the following:

List your career choice(s): _____

Brainstorm some practical ideas for work that could eventually help you land your dream position.

1. _____

2. _____

3. _____

List some specific steps you can take to find any of these get-you-in-the-door jobs:

1. _____

2. _____

3. _____

Interview some people with at least several years of experience in their chosen career. Ask them how they broke into the field. Discuss the pros and cons of their methods of entry. Consider how you can apply what you learned from their experiences to your particular situation.

## SUCCESS STORIES

Often, the greatest inspiration comes from those who have succeeded. Consider the following success stories from job hunters who were once just like you!

I did temporary work at a tourist bureau while I was job hunting for a permanent marketing position. The tourist bureau had no full-time openings. However, the vice president to whom I reported soon left the company to start his own marketing consulting business. Because we had worked well together, he asked me to join him.

Paul
*Marketing Consultant*

I taught high school math for several years, but my real passion was always physical fitness. I competed in two triathlons and many bodybuilding contests. I hoped to one day work full time in the fitness industry. I began counseling friends on how to lose weight and get in shape. They referred me to their friends, and eventually, I was able to get a little side business going. It was hard working days as a teacher and evenings as a personal trainer, but I felt like my career was heading in the right direction.

Once I had a strong client base, I decided to leave my teaching position, devoting all my time to a career as a fitness trainer. I love what I do and believe I've helped many people improve the quality of their lives by educating them on how to eat right and exercise for long-term health and fitness.

Russ
*Fitness Trainer*

I graduated with a degree in art but couldn't find a job in my field. Mostly to pay my rent but also as a creative outlet, I went to work in a local bakery as a cake decorator. Customers would often compliment me on my unique, artistic cake designs. One customer asked if I ever did any painting. When I told her I loved to paint and my degree was in art, she hired me to paint a mural on her daughter's bedroom wall. She loved the work and began passing my name around to her many friends. I was hired to do everything from painting family portraits to designing custom Christmas cards. Eventually, I was able to publish a couple of children's books I had written and illustrated. While I still can't wholly support myself on my artwork, my business is continually growing, and I hope one day to work full time as an artist.

Marty
*Artist*

I was looking for a computer programming position. While job searching, I managed to obtain a couple of freelance programming jobs, which led to additional work. After a few months, one company that I'd done a couple of projects for offered me a full-time job.

Sherry
*Computer Programmer*

I started as a secretary for a small real estate office. Over time, I became very familiar with real estate terminology and transactions. I enrolled in some real estate classes and then obtained my real estate license. Within weeks of getting my license, my boss hired a secretary to take over my clerical tasks and helped me transition into a sales position. Today, I earn a very good living and am one of the company's top producers.

Maria
*Real Estate Sales Associate*

After college graduation, I interned in the news department at a local TV station. I was envious of my friends who were making big money while I was essentially a volunteer, but I knew my time would come. I spent most days in the sports department. Because it was understaffed, I was frequently asked to do reporting assignments that might otherwise have gone to more seasoned reporters. Eventually, the sports department was given the budget to expand. I was hired full time as a sports reporter and am currently working toward becoming a sports anchor.

Dan
*TV Sports Reporter*

To keep busy when I was searching for an IT job, I helped my dad set up a website on the Internet for his company. He received so many compliments on it that some of his friends asked me to help design websites for their businesses. Before I knew it, I was in business.

Daniel
*Web Designer*

## Chapter Follow-Up

- Obtaining a job that satisfies your career goal may be difficult—particularly if you have limited experience in the field.

- Some of the paid ways to get your foot in the door are to seek out an entry-level position, part-time work, freelance work, temporary work, or work that is loosely related to your field.

- Some of the unpaid ways to advance your career are to obtain an internship or volunteer for a nonprofit organization.

- Whether your job is paid or unpaid and whether it meets your career objective or not, take advantage of the opportunity to gain experience and make contacts. It's all part of "paying your dues" as you advance up the ladder of success.

- When you hold a position that isn't your idea of a dream job, don't ever give up hope. Instead, continue your search for something better, and keep your eyes open for creative ways to drive your career forward.

# Part Four

# Beginning the Search

# Chapter 13

# Filling Out Job Applications

## What Do You Know?

### True or False

_____ 1. Completing the standard job application is a fairly unimportant step in the job hunt.

_____ 2. It may be acceptable to leave certain lines on the application blank.

_____ 3. Some employers require different applications for hourly and salaried positions.

_____ 4. If submitting the application online, it is not necessary to bring a hard copy to the interview.

_____ 5. Completing applications at hiring kiosks is rarely effective.

_____ 6. Never make negative comments on the application about previous employers.

## Chapter Focus

In this chapter, you'll learn to:

- Properly complete a job application form on paper, online, and at employment kiosks.
- Answer typical application questions.

## Real-Life Relevance

An employment application is a simple but often over-looked step of the job hunt. It is a way for employers to standardize the information they receive from applicants. Employers use it to get a fuller picture of your employment background but may also use it to evaluate your honesty and attention to detail.

# The Application Form

Many companies require a completed application form as well as a résumé from candidates before interviewing them. Some job hunters view the application form as annoying paperwork. In fact, it is truly an important step, and it's vital to do it right.

## Why Do Employers Require an Employment Application?

The application allows employers to standardize the information they receive from all applicants and to obtain more detailed information than might appear on the résumé. The application is often presented to the candidate just prior to the job interview and is used at every level and in every field of work.

## What Type of Employer Requires an Application?

Although application forms vary greatly, a surprising variety of employers—from small fast-food establishments to large Fortune 500 companies—begin the hiring process with this important step. Take the task as seriously as you would any of the other aspects of job hunting by being prepared, giving thought to your answers, and presenting your information in a neat, concise manner.

# Completing the Application Form

It's essential to follow certain general rules when completing an application form to avoid being eliminated from the field of contenders:

1. **If possible, obtain an application and complete it at home prior to the day of the interview.** If the employer will allow you to pick up or download the form ahead of time, you can complete it at your own pace, without distraction. If you go to a business to pick up an application in person, remember to dress professionally and make a good first impression.

2. **Read through the entire application first.** Reading through the entire application allows you to plan your time and get a sense of the length of the document and extent of the information requested.

3. **Write in pen.** Pencil smudges look unprofessional. Be prepared, and bring a pen with you. Because a job application is a legal document, be sure to use black pen, never other colors.

4. **Take your time.** The job application not only provides prospective employers with necessary information, but it also serves as a test of your neatness and attention to detail.

5. **Plan your time.** Some applications are lengthy. Allow thirty minutes or more to complete them.

6. **Print clearly, and be neat.** Imagine the frustration of an employer who is interested in your application but cannot decipher your name or phone number.

7. **Use one lettering style.** You can print or use script, whichever form of your penmanship is neater, but be sure to stick with your choice throughout the application.

8. **Complete every line.** If a section is not applicable, write N/A, or draw a line through the answer space. Check the side, top, and bottom margins and both sides of the paper for questions you might have missed. The employer needs to know that you did not overlook a section.

9. **Know your work history.** On an index card or a practice application, bring with you the names, addresses, e-mail addresses, and phone numbers of all your former employers, plus a list of people to contact as references. If your experience is limited, it is perfectly acceptable to include names of people for whom you've done odd jobs, such as yard work or babysitting.

10. **Keep your application consistent with the résumé.** Use same the exact version of your name (for example, not P. J. Dutton on one and Peter James Dutton on the other), the same job titles, company names, and dates.

11. **Choose references carefully.** Before you begin filling out job applications, it is a good idea to call or write to the people you wish to serve as references for you to ask their permission and to remind them of your current career goals. Do not list anyone about whom you have the least bit of doubt about getting a good reference. You may not have much space on the form, but an ideal mix would be two to three professional references who could discuss the quality of your work and one to two personal references (not relatives) who could discuss your character.

12. **Be careful when giving salary requirements.** If possible, avoid committing yourself to a specific number. If the form has a question labeled "salary requirements," it is best to write "negotiable" or "competitive."

13. **Use only recognizable abbreviations.** This will help maximize the readability of your application.

**Fill out job applications with care. A neat, properly completed form can help make a good first impression.**
(Fuse/Jupiter Images)

14. **Be courteous to everyone you meet at the job location.** Many people who go to job sites to fill out applications assume that because the application visit isn't a formal interview, they can be casual, rude, or unprepared. Remember that your first contact with an employer creates a strong impression. Dress as you would for a job interview. Be friendly and courteous, even to those whom you might consider "unimportant," such as clerks and administrative assistants. These people may have input in the hiring decision and could end up being your coworkers.

15. **Proofread.** In the rush of job hunting, it is easy to become nervous and careless. Show the employer that you pay attention to detail by handing in an application that represents a job well done.

## Typical Application Questions

Although every job application form is different, many questions are fairly common. Review the following list to prepare your answers:

1. **Name.** Follow the instructions in filling out this blank. Applications often require you to place your last name first and include your middle initial.

2. **Address.** Give your entire address, including your ZIP code.

3. **Phone number.** Be sure that the phone number you list will always be answered. If you provide a cell phone number, do not answer the phone unless you're in a location where you can have a clear, professional conversation.

4. **Social security number.** Your social security number often becomes your employee identification number, which companies then use to input and retrieve your file from their system. Be sure you write down the number accurately. If you are hired, this number is required so the employer can make contributions to your social security account and file tax forms. Some application forms will allow you to enter only the last four digits of your social security number, although they will require the full number once you are hired.

5. **Person to reach in case of emergency.** Name a person who can be reached during your work hours and who can respond quickly in an emergency situation—preferably someone local with his or her own transportation.

6. **Citizenship.** The employer asks for this information to ensure you are a U.S. citizen or an alien who has a legal right to hold the job for which you are applying. Be prepared to provide a work visa if necessary.

7. **Position you are applying for.** Be as specific as possible in naming the type of job you seek. Use the correct title of the job if you know it. Do as much research as you can before applying so you do not have to write "Any" as a response to this question.

8. **Salary desired.** Unless you know the exact salary being offered for the job you want, it is best to give a range that leaves you some room for negotiation. You may also use phrases such as "to be discussed" or "negotiable" if you think it would be to your benefit to avoid listing a figure.

9. **Salary history.** You do not have to disclose your salary if you feel uncomfortable doing so. You may write "Competitive" to complete this part of the form.

10. **Reasons for leaving previous job.** Never speak poorly of a former employer. If you were fired, write "sought other opportunities" or "career change." Other acceptable reasons for leaving include "moved," "resigned," or "education." Be prepared to have a tactful, truthful, and complete explanation for these reasons should questions arise in an interview.

11. **Date available.** Give the earliest possible date you could begin a job. If you are currently unemployed, write "immediately." If you are employed, give a date that allows at least a two-week notice period at your current job.

12. **Education.** List your high school, college, graduate school, and any specialized courses or certifications you've completed.

13. **Work experience.** Have this information prepared before you begin filling out the application form. You'll need to include the names of previous employers and their addresses and phone numbers as well as your job title, dates of employment, and supervisor's name. Be prepared to account for gaps in your employment. You might explain by saying you were returning to school, traveling, or looking for a position that was more suitable or offered more responsibilities.

14. **Military service.** List your military experience or write N/A if it is not applicable.

15. **Have you ever been convicted of a crime?** Answer honestly. Many employers routinely check for criminal records. If an employer hires you and then learns you lied, it is likely that you will be fired.

16. **Hobbies or interests.** Use this area to call attention to any of your specific interests that might make you a more valuable employee or demonstrate you have a well-rounded personality. Reading, traveling, and outdoor activities such as hiking or bicycling are all good choices. Do not list any hobbies that carry a negative connotation; do not mention religious or political affiliations.

17. **Foreign language ability.** List the languages other than English that you know. You may also be asked to assess your proficiency in reading, writing, and speaking the foreign languages you list.

18. **References.** List previous employers, teachers, or other professional contacts. Be prepared to provide their phone numbers and addresses. Do not use relatives. Character references need to have known you for at least two years.

19. **Signature and date.** This line is important. Your signature and the date confirm that you have, to the best of your knowledge, completed the questions accurately. An application is not considered valid unless it is signed and dated.

20. **For personnel use only.** Check out this section to get a hint about the kinds of information the prospective employer will seek in an interview.

# Hints for Online Job Applications

Many employers accept online applications in addition to or instead of paper versions. The basic rules still apply, but there are some important differences between the two formats. (Online applications can be found on job boards, on company websites, and at hiring kiosks.)

**Job Boards** may require you to register and build an employment profile. You can then apply for specific positions as they become available. You can also keep track of your applications and upload or copy and paste your cover letter and résumé.

**Company Websites** also post openings and accept applications on their "Careers" or "Employment Opportunities" sections. Be sure to follow the directions carefully and print out a spare copy of the application for yourself. Some job hunters have reported that their application or résumé couldn't be located by the person conducting the interview, so keep an electronic or hard copy handy for the interview. Some companies also have a different set of instructions about where to submit applications for part-time, full-time, or management positions. Before completing the application, it is also a good idea to peruse the company's "About Us" section. Research the company further and make note of the company's mission and vision, history, and plans as well as any the corporate culture and special language used to describe jobs or job skills.

**Hiring Kiosks** can be used in addition to or instead of other online job applications. They usually contain a typical job application form, but you are required to complete the form right in the workplace (often a store) or an other public area, such as a mall. Hiring kiosks are particularly convenient if you don't have access to the Internet at home. On the other hand, because completing applications can take thirty minutes or more, you need to begin entering your information at least a half hour before the business closes, and bring all your relevant information with you. The kiosk may be a freestanding unit or a cubicle that allows you to sit at a desk or table. Some employers only make their applications available at an in-store kiosk because they feel strongly that their customers make the best employees.

**EXERCISE**  **Sample Employment Application**

A sample employment application appears on the following pages. Fill it out for practice and to create a master document with all your relevant information. Refer to it when completing actual employment applications. After you have completed it, make a list of all the supporting documents you needed for reference, and assemble those documents before the interview. For example, you might need your social security card, a school transcript, or immigration documents.

# APPLICATION FOR EMPLOYMENT

PRE-EMPLOYMENT QUESTIONNAIRE
EQUAL OPPORTUNITY EMPLOYER

## PERSONAL INFORMATION

DATE _____

| NAME (LAST NAME FIRST) | | SOCIAL SECURITY NO. |
|---|---|---|
| PRESENT ADDRESS | CITY | STATE | ZIP CODE |
| PERMANENT ADDRESS | CITY | STATE | ZIP CODE |
| PHONE NO. (   ) | REFERRED BY | |

## EMPLOYMENT DESIRED

| POSITION | | DATE YOU CAN START | SALARY DESIRED |
|---|---|---|---|

ARE YOU EMPLOYED? ☐ YES ☐ NO       IF SO, MAY WE INQUIRE OF YOUR PRESENT EMPLOYER? ☐ YES ☐ NO

EVER APPLIED TO THIS COMPANY BEFORE? ☐ YES ☐ NO       WHERE?       WHEN?

## EDUCATION HISTORY

| | NAME & LOCATION OF SCHOOL | YEARS ATTENDED | DID YOU GRADUATE? | SUBJECTS STUDIED |
|---|---|---|---|---|
| GRAMMAR SCHOOL | | | | |
| HIGH SCHOOL | | | | |
| COLLEGE | | | | |
| TRADE, BUSINESS OR CORRESPONDENCE SCHOOL | | | | |

## GENERAL INFORMATION

SUBJECTS OF SPECIAL STUDY/RESEARCH WORK OR SPECIAL TRAINING/SKILLS

| U.S. MILITARY OR NAVAL SERVICE | RANK |
|---|---|

## FORMER EMPLOYERS (LIST BELOW LAST FOUR EMPLOYERS, STARTING WITH LAST ONE FIRST)

| DATE MONTH AND YEAR | NAME & ADDRESS OF EMPLOYER | SALARY | POSITION | REASON FOR LEAVING |
|---|---|---|---|---|
| FROM | | | | |
| TO | | | | |
| FROM | | | | |
| TO | | | | |
| FROM | | | | |
| TO | | | | |
| FROM | | | | |
| TO | | | | |

## APPLICATION FOR EMPLOYMENT

CONTINUED ON OTHER SIDE

**REFERENCES**    GIVE BELOW THE NAMES OF THREE PERSONS NOT RELATED TO YOU, WHOM YOU HAVE KNOWN AT LEAST ONE YEAR.

| NAME | ADDRESS | BUSINESS | YEARS KNOWN |
|------|---------|----------|-------------|
|      |         |          |             |
|      |         |          |             |
|      |         |          |             |

**AUTHORIZATION**

"I certify that the facts contained in this application are true and complete to the best of my knowledge and understand that, if employed, falsified statements on this application shall be grounds for dismissal.

I authorize investigation of all statements contained herein and the references and employers listed above to give you any and all information concerning my previous employment and any pertinent information they may have, personal or otherwise, and release the company from all liability for any damage that may result from utilization of such information.

I also understand and agree that no representative of the company has any authority to enter into any agreement for employment for any specified period of time, or to make any agreement contrary to the foregoing, unless it is in writing and signed by an authorized company representative."

DATE_____ SIGNATURE _____

INTERVIEWED BY _____ DATE _____

——————————————— DO NOT WRITE BELOW THIS LINE ———————————————

**REMARKS**

| |
|---|
| |
| |
| |
| |
| |
| |
| |

| NEATNESS | | CHARACTER | | |
|----------|--|-----------|--|--|
| PERSONALITY | | ABILITY | | |
| HIRED | FOR DEPT. | POSITION | WILL REPORT | SALARY WAGES |

APPROVED: 1. _____    2. _____    3. _____
                    EMPLOYMENT MANAGER                   DEPARTMENT HEAD                        GENERAL MANAGER

## SUCCESS STORIES

Often, the greatest inspiration comes from those who have succeeded. Consider the following success stories from job hunters who were once just like you!

The small town where I grew up had finally grown large enough to hire a recreation director for a new summer program. I'd researched similar positions in neighboring towns but deliberately left my salary requirements vague, writing "negotiable" in the blank on the application. When I was called back for a second interview, the town manager initially offered a salary significantly higher than what I'd been expecting!

Sal
*Recreation Director*

The day before my interview, I spent a long time on the phone reconnecting with all the people I'd listed as references. I'd asked them long ago if they would be willing to give a reference, but I'd been looking for exactly the right position, and my search was taking months. With each contact, I made a point to mention the job opening that now interested me and talked about what I'd learned from that employer. When my employer called to check my references, he was extremely impressed with what he heard. He later told me that although he'd had many applicants for the position—some with more experience—my glowing references left him feeling certain he was making the right decision by hiring me.

Hubert
*District Facilities Manager for a Large Retail Chain*

As soon as I approached the receptionist at the bank where I was applying for a position as a collections agent, she handed me an application. I quickly pulled my "cheat sheet" from my portfolio, sat in a chair in the waiting room, and completed the form in no time. What I hadn't realized is that all the people in the surrounding offices were watching and were impressed with my preparedness. Apparently, the woman who'd previously held the position I wanted was terribly disorganized, which had caused problems for many of her coworkers. Before I even began the interview, someone had commented to the manager how "buttoned up" I seemed. I was hired almost immediately!

Sasha
*Collections Agent*

## Chapter Follow-Up

- Completing the job application is a small but important step in the entire job hunting process.

- The care and attention to detail that you put forth on the job application are considered by many employers to be an indicator of the quality of your work overall.

- Each question on the application should be addressed, and many of the questions need to be answered carefully and with forethought.

- Online applications can be found on job boards, on company websites, or at hiring kiosks. Each type of online application presents its own challenges.

# Chapter 14

# Interviewing

## What Do You Know?

### Short Answers

1. List at least five steps a job hunter should take before interviewing for a job.
   _____
   _____

2. What do you think are the most common business etiquette mistakes a novice job hunter might make?
   _____
   _____

3. What's the best response to the question "Tell me about yourself"?
   _____
   _____

4. How is dressing for an interview on videoconference different from dressing for traditional interviews?
   _____
   _____

5. How would you describe the mind-set needed to search for employment when jobs are scarce?
   _____
   _____

## Chapter Focus

In this chapter, you'll learn to:

- Prepare for interviews.
- Identify the different types of interviews.
- Research the organization.
- Form questions to ask during the interview.
- Create a good first impression.
- Respond to questions like a pro.
- Manage your interview anxiety.
- Follow up on an interview.
- Avoid making major interview gaffes.
- Handle rejection.
- Ask for what you want.

## Real-Life Relevance

The more you learn about the interview process and the more you prepare by researching, dressing appropriately, and practicing questions, the more successful the interview will be. An interviewee who knows what types of questions to expect and how to best respond will present a more confident and more accurate picture of him or herself during the interview and increase the chances not only of being hired but also of being hired by an employer that's a good match for his or her skills and career goals.

# Preparation: The Key to Interview Success

Many people are underprepared for interviewing and therefore more nervous than they need to be. Think of an interview as a three-step process, and plan the execution of each step. There are critical points of preparation *before, during,* and *after* the job interview. Remember that you have only a short time to convey your experience, potential, and personality to an interviewer.

As you go through these interview preparations, envision the person with whom you'll be interviewing. Most likely, this individual will be of a different generation or background from you. Keep in mind that the interviewer may have conservative expectations about your dress and conduct as well as underlying expectations about what constitutes interview dress and behavior. Dress and act not as if you were with one of your peers but with someone who holds you to a higher standard than they do.

Prepare for the different types of interviewers you may encounter. Applicants are often interviewed first by a human resources manager and then by a department manager or direct supervisor. Sometimes, two or three people conduct the interview together. Learn about the different ways employers interview candidates (study the list of types of interviews). When the interviewer or an administrative assistant contacts you to arrange an interview appointment, be ready to inquire who will be present at your interview, and inform yourself about the wide variety of interview scenarios by reading as much about interviewing as you can so you can minimize stress.

As a job hunter, your goal is to get to the person to whom you'd be reporting. Human resources representatives often function as screeners, with the purpose of weeding people out. In some cases, human resources people have only a general knowledge of the available position; they may also be reluctant to describe the people with whom you'd be working most closely. Your objective is to either bypass the human resources department or be impressive enough to make it to the next step: your future supervisor.

Use the following guidelines to prepare for interviews. Review them frequently during your job search.

# Before the Interview

Many people think of job interviewing as sitting across a desk from a prospective employer and quickly trying to respond to the many questions being fired at them. The fact is that successful interviews are also the result of adequate preparation that occurs long before the face-to-face meeting. While employers do appreciate employees who think on their feet, they also recognize and value those who demonstrate thorough understanding and preparation for the task at hand. Use your interview to demonstrate your spontaneity and your preparedness!

Here is an overview:

- Understand the types of interviews.
- Dress properly.
- Plan your route to be on time.
- Research the organization.
- Prepare your questions.
- Bring the proper materials.
- Practice your responses.

## Types of Interviews

One of the first steps in preparing for the job interview is understanding that not all interviews are alike. You can prevent surprises by preparing for the different types of interviews. If the opportunity presents itself, try to determine which type of interview you'll be facing. Frequently, the administrative assistant who calls to arrange an interview appointment will be willing to tell you how many interviewers and how many candidates will be present during the interview. With proper preparation, you'll be able to demonstrate your skills and convey your personality effectively in any type of interview.

**Behavioral or Situational Interviews.**   An increasingly popular type of interview, the behavioral or situational interview is based on the premise that your past performance is the best predictor of your future performance. The interviewer typically asks specific, probing questions to tease out your past behaviors. The candidate's job is to briefly and specifically explain past situations, actions taken, and results achieved. Behavioral interviews encourage the candidate to tell a story in order to answer a question; it is to your advantage to give behavioral interview responses because these types of responses allow you to explain your strengths by providing examples. They also give interviewers better insights into your personality and your "fit" for the position.

**Board Interviews.**   In board interviews, the candidate meets several interviewers in a formal setting. These interviews are most often used for hiring at the corporate level, where several people may want to be directly involved in the decision process. Board interviews require special preparation and forethought.

**Directed Interviews.**    In directed interviews, the interviewer follows a prescribed set of questions. You may notice that the interviewer has a checklist. Directed interviews are usually used to prescreen applicants for another interview.

**Group Interviews.**    An interviewer may ask the job candidate to work with others on a particular task or topic, such as responding to a case study or building some sort of model or puzzle. Observers note your leadership abilities as well as your ability to work as part of a team. Group interviews are becoming increasingly common as managers learn the importance of teamwork in the workplace. It is important to note that not all employers are looking for team leaders and may instead be searching for "idea people," "peacemakers," "detail people," or "organizers" as part of their team. Be yourself while remaining as relaxed and professional as possible. If given the opportunity to ask questions during a latter part of the process, you might ask what type of team member the interviewer is hoping to find.

**Informational Interviews.**    Some job hunters use this type of interview to gain information from a person who works in a field of interest to them. This is the only type of interview in which the candidate does not ask for a job at the end of the session. (See the section on informational interviews in Chapter 3.)

**Meal Interviews.**    Held in a more casual setting, the breakfast, lunch, or dinner interview allows the interviewer and applicant to more easily develop a rapport. In such an interview, follow the host's lead in ordering food and in business etiquette, remembering that all other interview rules still apply.

**Nondirected Interviews.**    Nondirected interviews are less structured and less formal than other types of interviews. Not surprisingly, they are often used in informal workplaces. Nondirected interviews may allow room for expression. The questions asked tend to be open ended and spontaneous.

**Stress Interviews.**    Stress interviews are designed to see how well a job candidate holds up under pressure. If the position you're applying for involves a great deal of stress, don't be surprised to encounter a high-pressure interviewer. Even interviewers for nonstressful jobs may try to shake your poise by using rapid-fire or tricky questions. Recognize this type of interview for what it is—a test—and consider whether you'd feel comfortable working for an employer who uses this interviewing method.

**Speed interviews.**    Similar to speed dating, interviewers may arrange to meet many candidates at once, speaking with each for only a few minutes. Common at job fairs, this technique is based on the belief that the interviewer's first instincts about hiring are best. Prepare by learning as much as possible about the company, and be ready to present a brief summary of your objective and your skills and strengths. Conclude by trying to arrange a more traditional interview where you can discuss the position at length.

**Telephone Interviews.**    Telephone interviews may use a combination of interviewing techniques. For example, you may be interviewed by one person or by a group.

These interviews are typically used to screen out applicants, although they may also be used as a follow-up to an earlier conversation. The job hunter's primary goal in this type of interview is to secure a face-to-face meeting. Usually, phone interviews happen in one of three ways:

1. You cold-call the prospective employer to get information about job availability, and he or she begins asking you interview questions because you arouse his or her interest.

2. A company calls you unexpectedly as a response to a letter or résumé you sent.

3. You or a placement agency set up a specific time for a telephone interview.

No matter how the interview comes about, the bottom line is the same: A prospective employer is interested in you. It's vital that you seize the opportunity to get to the next step: an in-person meeting. Therefore, the telephone interview becomes a trial run for the real thing.

Effective telephone interviews, like face-to-face meetings, require preparation. Because you never know when a company might call you once your networking process is under way, keep a list of companies you've contacted handy. Be sure your information is organized (alphabetical order by company name usually works best) so you can quickly locate the information you sent the caller as well as any research you may have done about the company.

The most important point to remember is that phone interviews usually represent a weeding-out process. The interviewer is listening for any indication that you might *not* be the right person for the job or that it would be a waste of time to arrange a face-to-face meeting. Here are some tips to help you succeed in a phone interview:

1. **Take a surprise call in stride.** Although the call may come at the most inopportune time, try to sound pleased, friendly, and collected. If you receive the call on your cell phone and you are in an inappropriate environment, such as a noisy party, it is best to let the call be answered by your voice mail and then call back as soon as possible from a quieter location.

2. **Let the interviewer do most of the talking.** Keep your answers to the interviewer's questions brief and to the point. Rambling will bore the interviewer. However, try to avoid giving yes or no answers because they don't provide information about your abilities.

3. **Don't hesitate to ask some of your own questions.** This is an excellent opportunity to learn more about the company and the position in question. The information you gain will help you decide if you're interested in the job and, if so, will prove useful when you prepare for an in-person interview. However, under no circumstances should you ask about money or vacation time; these inquiries would be premature and inappropriate. Your focus should be on the responsibilities of the position.

4. **Speak clearly into the telephone.** Don't eat, drink, or smoke while on the phone. Turn down any background music, and eliminate other background noises as much as possible.

5. **Consider standing as you talk.** Standing may help you sound more alert, enthusiastic, and focused.

6. **Smile.** Smiling just as you would in a face-to-face conversation improves your tone, your telephone voice, and prevents you from sounding "wooden." The interviewer is trying to get to know you without the aid of nonverbal cues, so use every opportunity to convey your personality over the phone.

7. **Take notes of your conversation.** Keep your laptop or a pen and paper handy just for this purpose. Take down any relevant information the interviewer gives you about the position. You may also need to note a meeting time and address of the location of your in-person interview.

8. **Get a name and phone number.** If you have been invited to meet with the interviewer, write down his or her name and phone number so you can make contact should you have to change the appointment for any reason.

9. **Anticipate dialogue.** Rehearse your responses to possible questions. Create cue cards as prompts.

10. **Avoid salary issues.** If pressed, present a wide salary range that is acceptable to you, noting that you do not yet know enough about the position or its demands to be more specific.

11. **Try to reschedule if necessary.** Surprise interviews are difficult even for the most seasoned job hunter. Use the caller ID to avoid them whenever possible. If the call comes at an inconvenient time, see if you can make an appointment for another time so you can prepare your notes and create a calm and productive interview setting.

12. **Push for a face-to-face interview.** Ask something such as, "May we discuss this further next Tuesday afternoon?"

13. **Express thanks.** Close the conversation with appreciation for the caller's interest. Remember that your single objective at this point is to sell yourself so the interviewer requests an in-person meeting. It is unlikely you will be offered a position after only a phone interview. If the interviewer does not suggest a face-to-face meeting, take the initiative to ask for one. You have nothing to lose.

14. **Be sure to get follow-up information.** Get the interviewer's name, its correct spelling, phone number, e-mail address, and mailing address so you can follow up with thank-you notes and follow-up phone calls.

It is difficult to evaluate an opportunity over the phone. Even if the job doesn't sound right, go to the interview to get the practice. It may happen that the job sounds better when you get all the facts or that you learn of a more suitable position elsewhere within the company.

## The Videoconference Interview

Videoconference interviews, or video interviews, save employers time and travel expenses and are becoming more common, especially in today's global economy. However, they present unique challenges to the job hunter and require special preparation.

## Before the Videoconference Interview

Prepare for time difference, and be sure you understand which time zone applies when setting the appointment time.

Arrive early if you are using a public videoconferencing site, such as a large copy and shipping center.

If one is not built in to your laptop, purchase a webcam or download Skype and use it with a microphone headset.

Test your equipment, and practice using it well in advance of the interview.

If possible, log on early so you appear alert and prepared when the employer joins the conference.

If you will be interviewing from home, remove or limit distractions, such as those created by extraneous phones ringing, pets, and family members.

Clean up the background. Remember, the interviewer can see beyond your face, so use a home office or create a background that is as neat and professional as possible, eliminating toys and clutter from view.

Follow the basic guidelines for interview dress but also dress even more simply, avoiding busy patterns, loud colors, or noisy or fussy jewelry.

## During the Video Interview

Speak slowly and clearly, allowing for a slight time delay—when waiting for and replying to questions.

Make eye contact with the camera lens, just as you would with a person.

Finish your sentences clearly, without any trailing pauses.

Keep your answers brief and to the point.

Limit hand and body movements.

Smile and act as if you are in the room with your interviewers.

Try not to become disarmed by the fact that you may not be able to see all the interviewers.

## After the Videoconference

Be sure your connection is completely switched off, especially before making any comments about the interview.

Follow up with phone calls and thank-you letters, just as you would with a traditional face-to-face interview.

# Dress Properly

What is interview dress exactly? Why do employers and career professionals focus so intently on this particular part of the job hunt? Simply put, the first few seconds of the interview often weigh more heavily on the hiring decision than all the hours that follow. Many, many employers report that proper interview dress is still widely misunderstood, especially among first-time job hunters. Making a positive first impression is critical if you want to be hired. Many job hunters are incredulous that despite their impressive educational background or work history, something as trivial as a wrinkled shirt could portray them as unprofessional and cost them the perfect job. A smart job hunter will do what it takes to overcome this first step in order to get the opportunity to explain his or her more important assets in detail.

It is helpful for job hunters to think of the interview outfit as a job hunting uniform. The intent of the uniform is not to express your own particular style and personality; that can come later. The intent is to indicate to the employer that you understand the unwritten code of professional interview dress, that you are respectful, and that you are serious about landing the job. Your clothes should be neat, conservative, and professional, and if an interviewer is able to recall the specifics of your appearance beyond these general adjectives, it is likely that your interview dress is inappropriate.

# How Formally Should I Dress?

As a general rule of thumb, if you are unsure of how formal your interview dress should be, dress slightly better than you would to report to work each day. As in so many areas of the job hunt, conducting thorough research is key. Ask those who work in the field about the level of formality required. Visit the workplace or inquire at your college faculty or career office. If you are still unsure, dress conservatively.

It's also helpful to have a "dress rehearsal" the evening before a job interview. First, this gives you the opportunity to find missing buttons or fallen hems while you can still fix them. Second, you can ask the opinion of a good friend or relative. Finally, you'll see your put-together, professional self, which should build your confidence and poise for the interview.

### Interview Uniform for Women

*Interview Dress Do's for Women*

- Neutral-colored blouse, with or without a collar but with a conservative neckline and cut

- If blouse is sheer, flesh-tone undergarments should be worn underneath

- Knee-length, solid-colored skirt, preferably black, tan, navy, or gray

*Interview Dress Don'ts for Women*

- Low-cut blouses or snug-fitting blouses where the buttons pull. Ruffles.

- White undergarments under a white blouse

- Short skirts; skirts with flounced or asymmetrical hems

- Matching suit jacket or matching or color-coordinated blazer. Twin sets.
- Minimal jewelry: one pair of stud earrings, one ring per hand, no bracelets, dress watch
- Close-toed shoes with low heels
- Neutral hose in a shade lighter than your shoes
- Minimal makeup; little if any perfume (many people have environmental allergies)
- Neat, conservative hair, pulled back into a chignon or low ponytail, if longer than collar length
- Manicured fingernails with no polish or clear polish
- Small, professional-looking briefcase or small coordinating purse and portfolio

- Loud, patterned jackets, blazers, or sweaters
- Dangly earrings; several earrings on one ear; facial piercings
- High heels, open-toe shoes, sparkly shoes, or open-backed shoes
- Bare legs, black hose or patterned hose
- Bright makeup, strong perfume
- Big hair, long hair hanging in face, shaved or spiked hair
- Bright, sparkly, or long fingernails
- Carrying a purse and a briefcase
- Anything wrinkled
- Exposed tattoos or body piercings

## The Interview Uniform for Men

*Interview Dress Do's for Men*

- Matching suit in navy, black, or gray (pinstripe or solid) **or**
- Dress slacks in gray, tan, black, or navy
- White or light blue dress shirt with collar
- White undershirt
- Coordinating silk or silk-like tie with a simple pattern, properly tied and darker than the shirt
- Tie falls to middle of the belt
- Dress belt that matches shoes
- Clean, polished dress shoes that lace, in a color that matches or coordinates with slacks

*Interview Dress Don'ts for Men*

- Sweaters
- Cargo pants, baggy pants, or casual pants
- Dark shirts, collarless shirts
- Undershirts with colors or logos on them
- Cloth ties, leather ties, or novelty ties
- Tie falls above or below belt
- Not wearing a belt, belts with large buckles, or belts that don't match shoes
- Thick-soled or slide-on shoes, boots, sneakers

- Dress socks that coordinate with slacks and are calf length or above the calf
- Well-groomed short haircut, no facial hair
- One ring per hand, one dress watch, no other jewelry
- Small briefcase or portfolio
- Full-length dress coat

- Going without socks, sports socks

- Facial hair, ponytail, long sideburns

- Earrings, bracelets, pinky rings

- Backpacks
- Casual coats
- Exposed tattoos or piercings

## Common Questions About Interview Dress

1. **Why can't I just be myself?** Too much expression of personal style is considered immature or unprofessional. If you use your interview dress to make a personal statement, you risk losing the opportunity for an employer to discover the talents you possess.

2. **What if I'm overdressed? Won't I make a fool of myself?** The best way to avoid overdressing for the job interview is to research the standards for the field and the type of position you are applying for. Ask those who work in similar positions or someone who's familiar with your career field. Still, if you're unsure, it's always safer to be too conservative than it is to be too casual.

3. **In this day and age, isn't it okay for women to wear dress slacks to a job interview?** Casual clothes are in style and can be seen in all parts of society—from the classroom to some workplaces—and for some interviewers, a woman wearing slacks to a job interview would not be an issue. Unfortunately, a job hunter has no idea of how conservative the interviewer might be, and anyone who has been part of an interview committee could remember when a hiring committee did not advance a female candidate to the next step in the hiring process because her appearance—in other words, her slacks—was considered too unprofessional. In most cases, the candidate never learns the reason she was not hired. Again, it is always better to wear a classic interview outfit than to risk being eliminated from consideration for such a superficial reason.

4. **What if I can't afford new interview clothes?** An interview outfit does not have to be expensive or even new, as long as it's clean, neat, and conservative. If you have nothing appropriate to wear, try to borrow items from friends. Another option is to scout a thrift shop, which is likely filled with good-quality suits at inexpensive prices. There are several organizations that are devoted to helping job hunters find interview clothing. Dress for Success (Dressforsuccess.org) is a nonprofit organization devoted to advancing women's economic and career development and providing interview suits to women seeking to enter the workforce.

5. **What can I do if my tattoo or piercings are in a spot that is visible?** Tattoos and piercings have become more and more commonplace but still carry negative connotations for many. If at all possible, try wearing a higher collar, longer hemline, or longer sleeve to cover them. Women have also been successful at minimizing the appearance of tattoos by wearing opaque hose or hose that are slightly less sheer than typical. If your tattoos seem to be in the way of your career advancement, you may also want to speak with your health care provider to explore ways of removing them. If at all possible, body and facial piercings should be removed before the interview.

6. **I am very uncomfortable wearing pantyhose and never wear them. Do I *have* to?** In many professions, bare legs are considered unprofessional at a job interview. Investigate to find out how conservative the dress requirements are in your field.

7. **How do I know if it's acceptable to wear a sports coat and dress slacks instead of a suit?** Research is very important when determining how conservative your interview dress should be. A suit is usually the best choice. Ask those who are familiar with the company or field of interest to you. As a worst-case scenario, the interviewer may envision you for a position more advanced than the one for which you're applying!

## Practice the Trip to Arrive on Time

Punctuality is a cardinal rule of interviewing. Before the day of the job interview, practice getting to the business the same way you will on the big day. Don't rely solely on a global positioning device or an online map service. Although both can be extremely helpful, they are not foolproof. Make note of the traffic at the time of day you will be traveling to the interview, and find the most efficient route. Determine whether finding parking will be problematic, as it is in many cities, and be sure to bring enough cash for parking garages or plenty of change for meters. If you will be using public transportation, check the schedules of the trains or buses, and make sure you can locate the interview from the stop you'll be using. Time how long it takes you to walk from your stop. It is a good idea to arrive about ten to fifteen minutes before the interview. If you arrive any earlier, you may appear overly anxious; any later, and you seem disinterested.

**EXERCISE**   **Interview Dress Rehearsal**

Choose a day to wear your interview clothes to class. Ask your classmates or instructor for feedback. Can they guess your desired career field or position? What do they notice first? Solicit constructive criticism. Make notes about this for future interviews.

## Research the Organization

Researching the organization accomplishes two goals. First, you can find out if the company is right for you. Would the position for which you're applying meet your career goals and be a good match for your values and skills? What about potential for advancement? What is the reputation of this company in your area? Develop a list of questions, and use all the means at your disposal to learn the answers. Conduct research online; ask your instructors, family, and friends; and use the local library to find other resources that may not be available online. (See Chapter 3 for more ideas on researching organizations.)

The second goal you achieve by conducting thorough research is the sense of confidence and preparedness you'll convey in the interview itself. Your questions will be appropriate, and you'll be able to respond well should the interviewer ask you "What do you know about us?" or "Why do you want to work for us?"

### Sample Research Questions

- How large is the company, and when was it established?
- Exactly what product or services does the company produce? What are its future plans?
- How many employees work there? What is the reputation for being a worker-friendly establishment?
- Are there satellite locations?
- How is the company performing financially? What are its plans and projections for growth?
- Where does the position for which I'm applying fit into the management structure of the company?
- How is the company viewed in its community? Does it have a reputation for any types of community service?
- Who are its major competitors?
- What political, legal, or ethical issues is this company or field facing?

## Prepare Your Questions

Remember that you are interviewing prospective employers at the same time that they are interviewing you. Ask questions that will help you determine whether the position is a good fit for your skills, desires, and career goals. Asking a few intelligent questions makes you appear interested and enthusiastic. Here are some suggested questions:

1. Tell me about the nature of the position. What are the specific duties and responsibilities? Is a written job description available?
2. How do you define successful performance in this position?
3. What type of person have you found does best in this position?
4. What type of training can I expect in the first six months? Down the road?

5. Are there any travel requirements?

6. To whom would I report? Can you tell me something about his or her background?

7. Is this a newly created position? If not, who was the last person to occupy this position, and what is he or she doing now?

8. Does this organization encourage professional growth activities, such as participation in business societies or seminars?

9. How long has the company been in business? Tell me about the company's history.

10. What types of customers does the company service? What types of products does it sell?

11. What are the company's plans for the future?

12. How do you envision this company changing in the next five years?

11. What are the future prospects for promotion within the company?

13. Can I provide you with any other information about myself?

14. What is your feeling about how I would fit into this organization?

15. What skills are you looking for on your team?

16. What is the next step in the decision process? When will a final decision be made regarding the position?

It's best not to inquire about salary during the first interview. With careful research, you should have an idea of the salary range of similar positions. In addition, you want to demonstrate that you are more interested in the company and the position than in the money, so delay your questions about salary, benefits, and perks until the second interview or until the company makes you a job offer.

## Bring the Proper Materials

One of the final steps in interview preparation is assembling copies of all your interviewing documents: your résumé, list of references, working papers, transcripts, and any other items you have included in your portfolio. Have electronic and hard copies ready. Have a laptop or a pen and some paper for quick notes.

## Practice Your Responses

Although every interview will be different, you can still prepare. Think of the movie stars and politicians you often see interviewed on television or in magazines and newspapers. You can be sure that most of their answers are somewhat scripted. Although their delivery might seem natural, there's no doubt that they've given thought to the questions they might be asked and the best possible answers to them. Learn from the experts, and carefully plan this important aspect of the job hunting process.

**EXERCISE**

## Questions an Interviewer Might Ask You

As always, practice makes perfect. Read the following list of questions, and answer them aloud. Focus on answering the question succinctly while offering specific examples. This exercise will lessen your chances of being caught off guard in an actual interview:

1. Tell me about yourself.

2. What is your grade point average?

3. What is your major?

4. What courses do you enjoy in college?

5. What courses don't you enjoy?

6. What do you know about our organization?

7. What can you do for us? Why should we hire you?

8. What qualifications do you have that make you feel you will be successful in your field?

9. How did you hear about this position?

10. What types of jobs have you had in the past?

11. In what part time or summer jobs have you been the most interested?

12. What have you learned from the jobs you've held?

13. Have you participated in any volunteer or community work? What did you learn from those experiences?

14. How do you feel about routine work?

15. What are your future vocational plans?

16. If you could write your own ticket, what would be your dream job?

17. Are you willing to travel?

18. What have you done that shows initiative and willingness to work?

19. Are you involved in any extracurricular activities?

20. Do you hold any positions of leadership at school?

21. What are your special skills, and how did you acquire them?

22. Are there any work or school achievements you are particularly proud of?

**23.** Why did you leave your most recent job?

**24.** Do you have any geographical restrictions or preferences?

**25.** How do you spend your spare time? What are your hobbies?

**26.** What percentage of your college expenses did you earn? How?

**27.** What do you consider to be your strengths? Your weaknesses?

**28.** What books have you read recently?

**29.** If you were fired from a previous job, what was the reason?

**30.** Discuss five major accomplishments in your lifetime.

**31.** When can you start work?

**32.** When can you visit our headquarters for further interviews?

**33.** What kind of boss would you like?

**34.** If you could spend a day with someone you've known or known of, who would it be?

**35.** What personality characteristics rub you the wrong way?

**36.** Define *cooperation.*

**37.** How do you show your anger? What types of things make you angry?

**38.** Have you ever quit any activities? If so, what were they?

**39.** Have you ever experienced discrimination?

**40.** What does "9 to 5" mean to you?

**41.** With what type of person do you spend the majority of your time?

**42.** Do you consider this position a lateral or vertical career move?

**43.** What questions do you have for me?

Remember that "questions" can take many forms. You may be asked to perform a task during an interview—anything from composing a letter to working on a project. Be prepared to demonstrate your expertise.

**How to Respond to Interview Questions.**    As you reviewed the list of possible interview questions, you might not have been certain how to respond. First, remember to be truthful but not self-deprecating. If you need to discuss an area of weakness, do so, but follow up immediately with your plan for addressing that weakness. Second, practice, practice, practice. Rehearsing your responses will enable you to answer readily and prepare you to highlight your strong points. It will also reduce your level of nervousness. Some of the questions in the list require special reflection about why an employer would ask them in the first place. Below are some of the questions job hunters find most difficult and some strategies for answering them.

*Tell me about yourself.*    This is perhaps the most common of all interview questions. Don't view it as vague and intimidating but as a gift. After all, there are no wrong answers, and this question gives you the opportunity to begin the interview by presenting your most important strengths. The interviewer is trying to determine what kind of person you are and is leaving the parameters of that definition up to you.

Think of your three strongest qualifications for the job at hand and begin by listing those; for example, "I am a recent graduate of *X* University, and I have recently completed an internship with a company in this field. I've also lived in this area for the past ten years and have a good sense of the local economy." Or "I'm a mature employee with fifteen years' work experience. I have strong work habits and ethics, and I have recent training in the software used in this field." If the interviewer seems to be waiting for a more complete response, follow up with "Does that answer your question?"

*What courses did you enjoy and not enjoy in college?*    This question is another way of asking "What are you good at?" or "Would you be happy performing the duties that are integral to this position?" If you can do so honestly, list the courses that relate to your intended position. If you enjoyed courses that strengthened your communication or technical skills, be sure to list those too. Keep the list of courses you didn't enjoy small. Every manager fears hiring a negative person with a long list of dislikes.

*What types of jobs have you held in the past?*    What did you learn from them? Or, more aptly put, *did* you learn? Many interviewers are not as troubled by a job hunter who has held fairly menial jobs in the past as they are by one who has not learned any new skills from past experiences and therefore brings little to the new job. To respond to these questions, briefly list the areas of your former jobs, but spend the most time explaining your transferable skills; for example, "I worked my way through college as a server in a local restaurant, and I learned a lot about working under pressure and interacting with the public." Of course, if you have held jobs in a field related to the one to which you are applying, it is appropriate to explain your specific skills in detail.

*What books have you read recently? What are your hobbies?*    The worst possible answer to the first question is: *"Books?"* Questions such as these seek to ascertain whether you are a bright, well-rounded individual whose personality will fit on the employer's team. Answer simply and honestly. There are no wrong types of books or hobbies, as long as you do indeed name some. However, do be careful to avoid mention of any political, religious, or controversial topics that could be used to discriminate against you.

*What can you do for us? Why should we hire you? What do you know about this organization?*   These questions evaluate your knowledge of yourself, the company, and the position. Answer by describing a few things about the company, such as how large it is or what it does, and then explain how your skills fit the company's needs. The more homework you've done on the company and on identifying your own skills, the easier it will be to answer these questions. Express confidence in your abilities without being arrogant.

*What do you consider to be your strengths? Your weaknesses?*   If you have done a thorough self-assessment, you can easily cite as strengths such work habits as organizational skills or the ability to work independently. You should also mention several concrete skills that relate directly to the job.

Weaknesses are a bit trickier to deal with. Don't deny having weaknesses. Think in advance of a weak point *that is not integral to the job*; for example, "I need to work on my keyboarding speed" is a fine response if you are seeking a position in education. Many of us could safely respond that we are always trying to learn new software programs. Be sure to follow up with an explanation of how you are working to correct the problem you've cited. Finally, some people can honestly cite weaknesses that aren't very negative at all. "I tend to take on too much," or "I can be a perfectionist" are examples of this type of "weakness."

*Why did you leave your most recent job?*   Many people struggle with explanations of why they've left past positions. Remain tactful and diplomatic, but be honest. Never speak negatively about a former employer but instead explain career moves in terms of your overall skills or plans. For example, you might respond with "My former employer and I decided that the position was not a good match for my skills" or "The position turned out to be incompatible with my new career goals." Of course, if a life event, such as a move, birth of a child, or enrollment in college, caused you to leave a job, it is perfectly acceptable to say so.

*Discuss five major accomplishments.*   The trick to responding to this question is remembering that you are the one who can interpret the word *accomplishment.* Few of us can list conquering Mount Everest as an achievement, but many of us have overcome barriers such as limited knowledge or experience. Think of small but meaningful achievements: overcoming shyness with the help of a public speaking course, completing a particularly difficult project, participating in a civic organization that linked you to your college or community, or mastering a new skill.

*What questions do you have for me?*   Surprisingly, one wrong answer to this question is "None." It is also a bad idea to ask about salary, benefits, or vacation time at this stage of the interview process. Rather, employers want to know that you are curious and thoughtful and have a good sense of the position for which you are applying. No matter how thorough your research was, there is always more to learn about the company and the job. Ask the interviewer to explain more about the duties of the position or about the role on the team that the company is trying to fill.

**Illegal Interview Questions.**    There are some things an interviewer shouldn't ask—usually information of a personal nature; however, it is not uncommon to be asked an illegal question. Usually, interviewers ask these questions not out of malice but out of simple ignorance of the law. Although laws vary from state to state, interviewers should not ask questions or make comments about your sex, marital status, race, color, religion, housing, physical data, or disabilities.

A smart job hunter is aware of the questions that he or she is not obligated to answer and knows his or her options when responding. You have three choices when confronted with an illegal question:

1. Answer the question and ignore the fact that it is not legal.

2. Ask "I wonder why you would ask that question?" Then, on hearing the interviewer's response, decide whether to answer.

3. Contact the nearest Equal Employment Office. Be aware, however, that although you may have a legitimate claim, it is difficult to prove you have been the victim of discrimination. Hence, this may not be your best option.

Whichever option you choose, consider whether you'd like to work for an employer who is so interested in your personal life. (After you are hired, of course, your company may need personal information, such as your marital status and the names and ages of your children for insurance purposes.)

Seemingly illegal questions are legitimate if they are related to genuine job requirements. For example, it is perfectly acceptable for a shipping company to inquire about your physical condition if the job you are applying for requires heavy lifting. It is also appropriate for a company to ask your age if the position requires the handling of liquor.

**EXERCISE**   ## Preparation Worksheet

If you think through your skills, you will be better prepared to explain them to the interviewer and to relate them to the position you want:

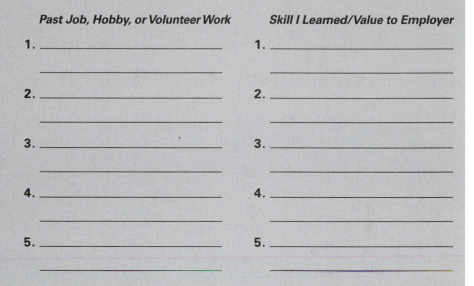

*Past Job, Hobby, or Volunteer Work*

1. _____
   _____
2. _____
   _____
3. _____
   _____
4. _____
   _____
5. _____
   _____

*Skill I Learned/Value to Employer*

1. _____
   _____
2. _____
   _____
3. _____
   _____
4. _____
   _____
5. _____
   _____

Here is an alternative way to organize your thoughts before an interview:

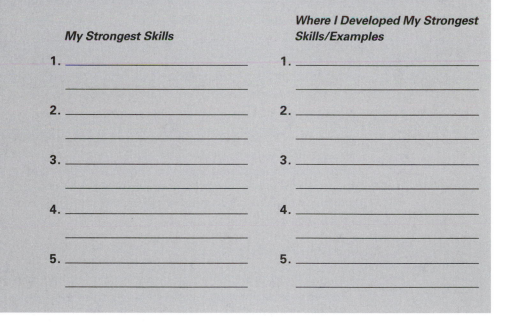

*My Strongest Skills*

1. _____
   _____
2. _____
   _____
3. _____
   _____
4. _____
   _____
5. _____
   _____

*Where I Developed My Strongest Skills/Examples*

1. _____
   _____
2. _____
   _____
3. _____
   _____
4. _____
   _____
5. _____
   _____

**Identifying Your Interests.**    As several of the sample questions already listed indicate, it is common for employers to ask how you spend your spare time. Although this information may not seem directly relevant to a particular job, it can give the employer additional insight into your personality and your preferences.

Take time to identify your interests before going to an interview. In the space below, list the five interests or hobbies you pursue most frequently, and briefly describe your participation. Your answers may range from sports activities to volunteer work to club memberships. In an interview, it may be best to avoid mentioning any political or religious affiliations that could count against you. Use your best judgment in making that decision.

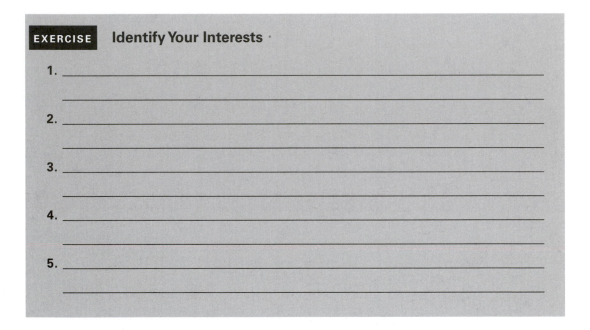

**EXERCISE    Identify Your Interests** ·

1. _____

   _____

2. _____

   _____

3. _____

   _____

4. _____

   _____

5. _____

   _____

**Personality Traits and Skills Most Sought by Employers.**    Despite the formality of the interview process, the hidden agenda for most interviewers is to get to know you. Although your education and skills are the major deciding factors, it is also important to employers that your personality be a good fit for the job and the company. Employers are also wary of any personality traits that could be problematic in the workplace.

*Most Desired Personality Traits*

- **Strong Work Ethic.** Employers want to leave an interview assured that the candidate could contribute to the company's productivity, do more than is asked without being pushed or coddled, and show up on time each day, with "sleeves rolled up."

- **Positivity and Enthusiasm.** Negativity is toxic and destructive in any work environment. On the other hand, optimism, a sense of humor, and a self-starting attitude are equally infectious. While they can't be taught, they definitely make everyone's job easier.

- **Professionalism.** Practice good business etiquette, be prompt and efficient, manage cell phones appropriately, and dress and act respectfully. Even entry-level employees are more likely to be considered as potential candidates for positions of more responsibility if their professionalism sets them apart.

- **Persistence and Grit.** Employers indicate that one of the most important things about hiring candidates with a college degree is that, if nothing else, it indicates that a person has set a goal, overcome obstacles, and persisted until that goal has been achieved. Challenging tasks on the job require the same sort of determination and focus.

*Most Desired Skills*

- **Strong Communication Skills.** Employers want to hire candidates who can listen carefully, ask questions, follow directions, speak articulately, and write well.

- **Computer/Technical Literacy.** Most careers now require at least a basic understanding of technology, and many require knowledge of software particular to the field.

- **Leadership Skills.** Experience motivating, leading, organizing, and communicating with others on the team is valued. While not every candidate is applying for a leadership position, employers want to see that employees have the potential for promotion in the future.

---

**EXERCISE**   **You've Got Personality**

Go through the lists of desired personality traits and skills to check the ones you think apply to you. Then, select one trait from each area and briefly write about a situation in which you demonstrated that trait—whether at school, at home, or on the job. You should end up with at least two different stories.

*Example:* From the list of desired personality traits, choose strong work ethic: "Once when a coworker called in sick, I worked a double shift to complete an important project before the deadline."

Once you have identified specific situations in which you applied these positive traits, you'll be prepared to share these anecdotes with an interviewer should the appropriate opportunity present itself.

**EXERCISE**   ## Mock Interviewing

Do a mock interview with a friend while a silent third person looks on outside your line of vision. (Better yet, videotape yourself.) Have the observer take notes, listing any nervous signals you display.

Once you've identified or viewed on video the ways your anxiety manifests itself, focus on eliminating these tendencies and continue to practice your interview skills at home. However, the best remedy is simply doing as many interviews as you can—even for jobs for which you are not that interested. The real-world practice you receive from these interviews will help you perfect your presentation, gain self-confidence, and eventually minimize—if not altogether eliminate—your feelings of anxiety.

# During the Interview

Your preparation has finally allowed you a chance to make a good first impression, discuss your skills and your experience, and learn more about the position and the employer. Maximize each moment of the job interview to accomplish all three of these goals. Here is an overview:

- Create a good first impression.
- Respond like a pro.
- Manage your interview anxiety.

## Create a Good First Impression

Studies have shown that people form an opinion of someone they meet in the first two to four minutes. For that reason, it is vital that you pay attention to detail to create the best possible first impression. Give a positive initial greeting by using a firm handshake, good eye contact, and a smile. Display a positive, upbeat attitude, and try to relax as much as possible. Some other factors that affect the impression you make are your age, sex, appearance (hair, clothes, hygiene, jewelry, makeup), movement, mannerisms, personal space, and manner of speaking. Good manners play an important role.

**When meeting a prospective employer for an interview, be sure to make good eye contact and give a firm, confident handshake.**
(© P. Windbladh / zefa / Corbis)

## Rules of Business Etiquette

To enhance the likelihood of making a favorable impression, follow these basic rules:

1. Arrive ten to fifteen minutes early for your interview.

2. Introduce yourself politely to the receptionist, and state the first and last names of the individual you are to see.

3. If the receptionist offers coffee or tea, you may accept it, but be sure you won't have trouble juggling the cup and your résumé materials when you shake hands with the interviewer. It might be best to politely pass on the offer.

4. If you accept a soft drink from the receptionist or your interviewer, pour it into a cup, if available, rather than drinking it from the can.

5. Do not chew gum.

6. Do not smoke. It is also best not to smoke just before an interview; many people find the residual smell offensive.

7. Introduce yourself to the interviewer by clearly stating your first and last names. Make eye contact and smile.

8. Say something to the effect of, "It's nice to meet you" in your initial greeting.

9. Address the interviewer by using Mr. or Ms. unless you are asked to do otherwise. Don't assume that if the interviewer calls you by your first name that you are both on a first-name basis.

10. Be willing to make a bit of small talk—possibly about the weather, the traffic on the way to the interview, or the interviewer's good directions.

11. After the interviewer has led you from the reception area to an office or conference room, do not take a seat until the interviewer motions you to a particular place.

12. Sit straight and relatively still. Avoid distracting movements of your hands or legs.

13. Fold your hands comfortably in your lap or on top of your résumé materials. Do not cross your arms over your chest (you will appear disagreeable) or spread them across the back of the chair or couch (you will appear too relaxed, lazy, or uninterested).

14. Be attentive when the interviewer speaks. Avoid interrupting—even if the interviewer does most of the talking. Maintain good eye contact with the interviewer.

15. Shut off and conceal your cell phone. Never check messages or text, even if you are in a waiting room.

16. Don't hesitate to ask for clarification if you don't understand something.

17. Be positive and upbeat in your remarks.

18. Avoid complaining about a previous job or employer. Even if your remarks are true, you won't appear professional if you harp on these subjects.

19. Avoid criticizing, contradicting, or disagreeing with the interviewer.

20. If you are offered a tour of the facility, the interviewer will indicate whether you are to walk ahead or to follow. Women should know that male interviewers often encourage them to pass through doorways first.

21. At the end of the meeting, thank the interviewer for his or her time and extend your hand for a strong parting handshake. Don't forget to smile and make eye contact one last time.

## Respond Like a Pro

By now, you have reviewed and rehearsed your responses to the most common interview questions. While you may know *what* you want to say, *how* you say it is equally important. Did you know that people show 55 percent of their feelings and emotions nonverbally? Thirty-eight percent of a message is carried by tone of voice. Only 7 percent of your feelings and emotions are conveyed by the actual words you use.

Your "silent" message is conveyed through signals in your body language. Positive signals can indicate agreement, openness, acceptance, and interest. Negative signals can reveal disagreement, suspicion, rejection, and defensiveness. Become attuned to the nonverbal signals you give off, and watch others' body language to determine their receptiveness to you.

## Mind Your Body Language

| Positive Signals | Negative Signals |
|---|---|
| Good eye contact | Poor eye contact |
| Leaning forward | Slumping or turning away |
| Uncrossing arms or legs | Crossing arms or legs |
| Nodding head in approval | Shaking head in disapproval |
| Smiling, occasional laughing | No response |
| Unbuttoning jacket | Buttoning jacket |
| Rapt attention | Doodling or blank stare |
| Palms or wrists turned outward, open | Hands in pockets |
| Raised eyebrows | Narrowed eyes, sideways glances |
| Steepling fingers | Making a fist |

In an interview, it is helpful to monitor not only your own but also the interviewer's body language for instant feedback on how you're doing. If you receive positive signals while discussing a certain area, continue the discussion in the same vein. If you detect negative signals, try to modify your approach. You may find that the interviewer also begins to imitate your signals. For example, when you lean forward, the interviewer may do the same. This copying of signals usually indicates agreement, and you may even encourage a good reaction from the interviewer by subtly copying his or her signals.

As you observe and interpret body language, remember that each separate signal may not be a definitive indicator of a person's emotions. People have their own mannerisms or habits, so it is most meaningful to evaluate clusters or groups of signals to decipher the true message.

Here are some more pointers for responding to interview questions:

1. Be truthful, but never put yourself down.

2. Speak distinctly. This is especially important if English is not your first language or you have a different accent from your interviewer. Take care to speak slowly and clearly.

3. Help the interviewer. In many companies, the interviewer is not a human resources professional with training and experience conducting interviews. He or she may be a manager or supervisor whose skills lie in a different area and who is unsure of which questions to ask. Be ready to explain your experiences and skills, and relate them to the job for which you're interviewing.

4. Don't be too serious or too humorous—common responses to interview stress. Try to strike a balance somewhere in between.

5. Listen carefully, and make good eye contact. Do not stare down an interviewer in an effort to make good eye contact, but do show your attentiveness and respect. Do not get distracted by your surroundings, but watch your interviewer for cues about his or her response to your questions and your answers to his or her questions.

6. Be concise. Take a moment to compose your responses. Answer briefly without rambling, and check whether you have answered thoroughly enough by noticing the interviewer's response.

7. Do not oversell yourself. If you do not have one of the requirements for the position, it is best to remain honest and upbeat. Try a response such as, "I haven't learned that particular software program yet, but I have mastered several others, so I'm sure I could learn it quickly." That kind of honesty is usually much more welcome and impressive than an outright lie or a blustery or evasive answer.

## Manage Your Interview Anxiety

Many people consider a job interview to be one of life's most stressful events. Some become so overwhelmed they jeopardize their own success. If you feel overly threatened by job interviews, try the exercises described in the following sections.

**Put Things into Perspective.**    Some people place so much importance on each interview that the pressure to succeed becomes crippling. When you catch yourself thinking terrifying thoughts that start with the word *if,* stop and redirect yourself. "If" thoughts have a tendency to pile up and weigh you down.

A nonproductive train of thought might proceed this way: "*If* I don't do well at this interview, I'll be so disappointed. I'll never have the confidence to do well at another interview." Another might be: "*If* I don't land this job, my parents [spouse, friends] will think I'm such a failure. How will I pay for the rent [car, mortgage]?" These thoughts are self-defeating and negative. They focus on the future, which you can't control, at the expense of the present, which you can control.

Instead of terrorizing yourself with "what *if*s," be your own best friend. Say nothing to yourself that you wouldn't say to a good friend to whom you were trying to lend confidence. Say everything to yourself that you'd say to a friend who needed a little extra support going into a stressful situation. *Instead of thinking,* "What *if* I become tongue-tied during the interview and ruin my chances?" *tell yourself,* "Of course it's natural for me to feel nervous at first, but I'm sure I'll relax and do fine."

---

**EXERCISE**    **Preparing Positive Statements**

In the spaces below, write down a few positive, calming, and confidence-producing thoughts. (If you have trouble doing this, think of things you would say to a good friend.)

1. _____

_____

2. _____

_____

3. _____

_____

If you need to, read these over just before you go to interviews. Why should you give yourself any less support and respect than you would your best friend?

# Combating Interview Anxiety

Sometimes, even though you succeed in calming your stressful thoughts, your body does not cooperate. Sweaty palms, a nervous stomach, and a dry mouth are symptoms that nervous job hunters occasionally feel. Don't let this type of physical discomfort throw you. Try these relaxation techniques before the interview:

1. **Use nature's original relaxation device: the sigh.** Allow yourself a few huge sighs, and notice how tension leaves your body.

2. **Focus on your breathing.** While sitting in a waiting room, take long, slow, deep breaths through your nose. If you have the opportunity, close your eyes, sit comfortably, and imagine that your breath has a color. In your mind's eye, watch your breath as it enters and leaves your body. The resulting deep breaths will prevent you from focusing on nervous thoughts, relax your muscles, and oxygenate your brain. (Try it now and see.)

3. **Slowly and sequentially, tense and release each muscle group in your body.** Start with your toes and work up to your head. Some people also imagine their body as a vessel filled with warm sunshine.

Bookstores and libraries offer many books about relaxation techniques. Many gyms and hospitals offer yoga or meditation classes. Information can also be found on the Internet. Do some experimenting to find a few relaxation tricks that work for you.

Remember that stress is not all bad. We all need a little stress to be productive. Think of adrenaline as an asset, and use the extra zip to project more energy, think clearly, and speak distinctly. Focus on the ways stress can work for you and not against you.

---

**EXERCISE**   **Do You Have Interview Anxiety?**

|  | Never | Sometimes | Always |
|---|:---:|:---:|:---:|
| Before an interview: |  |  |  |
| I have trouble sleeping. | ❑ | ❑ | ❑ |
| I get a headache. | ❑ | ❑ | ❑ |
| I get a stomachache. | ❑ | ❑ | ❑ |
| I lose my appetite. | ❑ | ❑ | ❑ |
| My palms sweat. | ❑ | ❑ | ❑ |
| I have cancelled an interview because of panic. | ❑ | ❑ | ❑ |

| | Never | Sometimes | Always |
|---|---|---|---|
| In an interview: | | | |
| My hands shake. | ❑ | ❑ | ❑ |
| I have trouble remembering things. | ❑ | ❑ | ❑ |
| My mind keeps going blank. | ❑ | ❑ | ❑ |
| I tap my hands or feet constantly. | ❑ | ❑ | ❑ |
| I crack my knuckles frequently. | ❑ | ❑ | ❑ |
| I can't think clearly. | ❑ | ❑ | ❑ |
| I can't wait to get out of the room. | ❑ | ❑ | ❑ |
| I feel nervous and jittery. | ❑ | ❑ | ❑ |
| I worry that I'm doing poorly. | ❑ | ❑ | ❑ |
| I have a hard time understanding directions. | ❑ | ❑ | ❑ |
| I can't remember things I said. | ❑ | ❑ | ❑ |
| I feel like crying. | ❑ | ❑ | ❑ |
| I feel exhausted. | ❑ | ❑ | ❑ |

Tally your check marks. If you have more than five checks in the Sometimes or Always columns, plan a strategy for extra interview practice.

**Hide Your Nervousness.**    All interviewers expect interviewees to be a little nervous. However, you don't want your nervous actions to detract from your appearance and the impression you make. By becoming aware of the nervous signals you give off, you'll be able to eliminate them and present yourself more confidently in interviews. See if you find yourself exhibiting any of the following behaviors:

- Playing with your hair
- Wringing your hands
- Cracking your knuckles
- Clearing your throat
- Tugging at your ear
- Playing with your jewelry
- Touching your neck
- Picking or pinching your skin

- Jingling money in your pocket
- Covering your mouth with your hands when you speak
- Tapping your hands, feet, or pen
- Swiveling in your chair

# After the Interview

Once the interview is over, your job isn't done. Use each interview as a learning opportunity to prepare for the next one or to follow up on a few action items that may ensure that you are offered the position. Here is an overview:

- Make concluding notes.
- Assess your interview skills.
- Follow up with phone calls and thank-you letters.

## Make Concluding Notes

The interview is over, and you can finally breathe a sigh of relief. But your work is not over yet! While the interview is fresh in your mind, summarize information and discussion points about the organization and the position. Write the names of each person who participated in your interview—double-checking the spellings by using the company literature or website. Note any mention of job responsibilities, travel requirements, or other topics that troubled or intrigued you. When you are interviewing with several companies at once, it is easy to confuse the topics mentioned at the interviews, so writing a good summary of each one is important. Refer back to your concluding notes before going on a second interview or engaging in salary negotiations.

## Assess Your Interview Skills

Now is the time to assess your performance so every interview—good or bad—can be a learning experience. Determine what you did right and what aspects you could improve. Put in writing some suggestions for your next interview. Be sure to conduct your self-evaluation within a day of the interview; otherwise, you're likely to forget portions of the conversation.

**EXERCISE**    ## Interview Self-Evaluation

Photocopy this interview self-evaluation form for future use. Then, complete the following statements about your interview.

1. I would describe my initial greeting with the interviewer as _____.

_____

2. I was good at _____.

3. I would improve _____.

4. My appearance was _____.

5. The next time I dress for an interview, I'll _____

_____

6. I was _____ on time _____ late _____ early.

7. When I spoke during the interview, my voice was _____

_____

8. My body language and eye contact during the interview could be described as _____.

9. The interviewer was more interested in _____ talking _____ listening.

I adjusted my interview style accordingly by _____.

10. I conveyed the following points about my skills: _____

_____

11. The toughest question I faced was _____.

I handled this question _____.

The next time I'm asked that question, I'll _____.

12. My overall mood and degree of relaxation was _____

_____

13. Here is a list of things I need to do next to land this job:

   a. Thank-you letters _____.

   b. Follow-up phone calls _____.

   c. Other _____.

# Follow Up with Phone Calls and Thank-You Letters

Even after the interview is over, the interviewer is still evaluating an important job skill: follow up. Do not wait passively for the interviewer to get back to you about the status of the hiring decision; instead, call after several days. Some employers wait to see which applicants demonstrate good follow-through. Ask if any decisions have been made and if you can provide any further information. Make a note about those you contacted and when, and if the employer has no news, politely ask if you could follow up again in a week.

You should also follow up every interview with a letter of thanks. Surprisingly few job hunters write a letter of thanks after the interview, so seize this opportunity to demonstrate your professionalism, follow-through, and good manners, and get your name on the interviewer's desk one more time. This small gesture has a big impact and should be considered essential after every interview.

### Suggestions for Wording Follow-Up Phone Calls and Letters

- "I'm very interested in the position. Are there any questions I can answer or anything I can do to make this work for you?"

- "I was thinking about what you said regarding the X project, and I have some ideas that I think could help. See attached."

- "I've been offered a job with another company. However, your firm is my first choice. I wanted to check with you on the status of the position we discussed before I accept this other offer."

- "I enjoyed our conversation about X. I saw an article on the subject in [insert publication name] and thought you might be interested in it. See enclosed."

Few job hunters remember this important step. Those who do will stand out; they also succeed in putting their names in front of the employer one more time while creating goodwill and a lasting positive impression. Notice the sample letter that follows. Although it is brief, it is effective. Thank-you notes may be e-mailed, typed, or handwritten.

14 Hill Street
Middletown, KY 83103

March 3, 2011


Ms. Sonia Pratte
President, Technopro, Inc.
672 Charles Avenue
Bedford, KY 83102

Dear Ms. Pratte:

Thank you for taking the time to meet with me on Monday. I enjoyed touring Technopro and learning more about your business.

As I mentioned in the interview, I would be very interested in the bookkeeper position and feel I could be an asset to Technopro. Thank you for your consideration. I look forward to hearing from you soon.

Sincerely,

*Lawrence Dempsey*

Lawrence Dempsey

**Sample 12.1    THANK-YOU LETTER TO FOLLOW UP IMMEDIATELY AFTER INTERVIEW**

# Nontraditional Ways to Get an Interview

Occasionally, the job hunter needs to try something unique to get a foot in the door. Although networking, telephone calls, and letters are the traditional approaches to securing an interview, you may reach the point where you're ready to become more creative and assertive.

**Warning:** Not all employers endorse these approaches. Consider how conservative your career field is, what traditional methods you haven't yet tried, and what you have to lose. Also remember that some career experts swear that unorthodox approaches are the best. Use your best judgment, and when you've carefully considered your options, make a plan:

- Send your résumé to the person you'd like to work for by express mail or courier marked "Personal and Confidential."

- Get creative with your résumé. Make it very large or very small, make a puzzle out of it, or print it on neon orange paper. In your cover letter, explain your unusual presentation. For example, you might start out, "I'm the piece of the puzzle Brown, Incorporated, has been looking for." Accompany a tiny résumé with a letter that begins, "Sometimes, it's easy to overlook the obvious choice."

- Create a business card giving your name, phone number, and a few of your best qualifications. When you meet potential contacts, give them your card.

- Post a position wanted ad.

- Learn whether the prospective employer belongs to any local clubs or organizations. Go to a meeting to network and introduce yourself.

- Send a clever e-mail to your prospect.

- Send a series of postcards. The first might read "Wish I were there." Send more information on each one.

- Learn what the employer's hobby is. Send a small but appropriate item, such as a small button, magnet, or keychain with a note of thanks. For example, you might send an avid sailor a small model sailboat. You may need to enlist the aid of a secretary to find out this information. These small tokens might be most appropriate after the interview.

- Send an object related to your name. Reginald King might send a crown; Dawn Greenleaf might send a pressed four-leaf clover.

- Send a photograph with your résumé printed on the reverse.

- Send an unusual object with an explanation. For example, send some shoelaces with a note that reads "I'm sorry you've been tied up, but I'm hoping we can get off on the right foot."

- Send a jar of cinnamon with a few words about how you can add spice to the company.

**EXERCISE**  **Brainstorming Interview Access**

Brainstorm two or three other nontraditional methods to obtain an interview that might be suitable for your career field or position. Write them here.

1. _____
   _____

2. _____
   _____

3. _____
   _____

When you've committed yourself to one of these unusual tactics, carry it off with confidence and enthusiasm. It may turn out to be the most profitable and memorable of your job hunting experiences.

# Reasons for Unsuccessful Interviews

Job applicants are frequently rejected because of the following behaviors or characteristics that become apparent during interviews:

- Too interested in starting salary
- Uncertainty about job/career or long-range goals
- Poor personal appearance
- Overbearing, overly aggressive, conceited, or "know-it-all" behavior
- Inability to express self clearly—poor voice, diction, grammar
- Lack of interest and enthusiasm—passive, indifferent
- Lack of confidence and poise—nervous, ill at ease
- Poor scholastic record—just got by
- Unwilling to start at the bottom—expects too much too soon
- Makes excuses—evasive, hedges on unfavorable factors in record
- Lack of tact
- Condemnation of past employers
- Lack of maturity
- Lack of courtesy, ill mannered
- Marked dislike for schoolwork

- Lack of vitality
- Fails to look interviewer in the eye
- Limp, fishlike handshake
- Loafs during vacations
- Unhappy married life
- Friction with parents
- Sloppy application form
- Merely shopping around
- Wants job only for a short time
- Little sense of humor
- No interest in company or industry
- Lack of knowledge in field of specialization
- Parents make all major decisions
- Emphasis on who he or she knows
- Cynical
- Lazy
- Intolerant, strong prejudices
- Narrow interests
- Inability to take criticism
- Lack of appreciation of the value of experience
- Radical ideas
- Late to interview without good reason
- Knows nothing about company
- Fails to express appreciation for interviewer's time
- Asks no questions about the job

**EXERCISE**   **Considering Interview Errors**

See if you can come up with a few reasons of your own that someone might "fail" an interview:

1. _____

2. _____

3. _____

Select three inappropriate interview behaviors or characteristics from the list above or from your own responses, and brainstorm ways to remedy these negatives. For example, if you select "lack of vitality," you might think of extending a firm handshake and giving an enthusiastic greeting as ways to convey your energy and vitality to an interviewer.

1. _____

2. _____

3. _____

# Handling Rejection

Nobody likes rejection, but it happens to everyone at some time in his or her career. Remember that as you seek employment. Many people spend months searching and interviewing for dozens of jobs before they receive an appealing offer. When the economy is depressed, months can turn into years before the right position turns up. So, don't get discouraged if you don't achieve quick success.

When you're first making the rounds, try not to be personally offended if potential employers don't return your calls. Realize that they may be busy and that your call represents an interruption—and certainly not a priority—in their day.

## What You Don't Know

Try not to take it personally if you are not offered a job after having what you consider a successful interview. You may feel that you are perfectly suited to a particular position, but the employer may not think that. There may be other candidates who have more experience, skills that more precisely match the job's responsibilities, or a personality more compatible with management practices.

You may be rejected for reasons that have absolutely nothing to do with you. For example, there may be an in-house candidate who has a leg up on the job, but nonetheless, company policy dictates that outside candidates must be interviewed. Or perhaps a current employee has a personal connection to one of the other candidates.

Sometimes, it's a salary issue; the employer knows you're the best candidate but nonetheless settles for a lower-salaried, less-qualified individual. Or you may be overqualified, leading the employer to conjecture that you won't want to stay in the position long term but are using it as a stepping-stone to a job at your level.

Most likely, you'll never be privy to the real reason you weren't selected. Employers are careful not to divulge any hiring information that could result in a lawsuit. The important thing is to look at every rejection as a learning experience. Make your most educated guess as to why the outcome was not what you wanted. Look for specific ways to improve your presentation.

Finally, remember that finding a job is a numbers game: The more people you contact and the more interviews you have, the more likely you are to land a job.

## The Right Frame of Mind

Rare is the individual who begins job hunting and is immediately offered the quintessential dream job. Most job hunts take time and effort. You'll be better equipped to handle a challenging job search if you maintain a positive attitude. Keep these tips in mind:

1. **Believe in yourself.** You've worked hard to get where you are today. You've acquired the skills you need. Now it's just a matter of time until you find an opportunity to put them to use. Dare to dream. Pursue ideas and opportunities that are of interest and value to you. Exude confidence in all you do.

2. **Look at the big picture.** Don't let the little things get you down. Learn from your mistakes. Keep your perspective, and focus on what's important.

3. **Don't feel angry or bitter.** It's easy to be upset when employers don't recognize the wonderful asset you could be to their companies, but don't internalize the rejection. Besides being self-destructive, your anger will come through in future interviews.

4. **Be creative.** Don't give up. Find unique solutions to problems. Keep generating new ideas. Think beyond the traditional answers. Look for a market niche, and develop a creative way to fill that niche.

5. **Be flexible.** Plan your job search, but re-evaluate and change your plan as you learn new things and meet new people. Expect the unexpected. Develop contingency plans to handle different situations.

6. **Be optimistic.** Focus on the positive aspects of all occurrences—even negative ones. If one approach fails, be prepared to try another.

7. **Don't be afraid to take risks.** Accept the fact that finding—and eventually accepting—a new job involves an element of risk. Learn to manage the risks by identifying them and then limiting their downsides.

8. **Be persistent.** Keep your attention focused on the task at hand. Don't give up until you've found an avenue to success. Keep exploring solutions until you find one that works.

9. **Adopt an action orientation.** Be a doer. Be a decision-maker. Take control of a situation, and propel yourself toward success.

10. **Have a "Plan B."** If your career path is not a smooth one, perhaps it's time to reassess your strategy and goals.

# Ask for What You Want

Some job hunters make the mistake of forgetting to ask for what they want. Either because they are too timid or because they assume the employer knows their intentions, they find themselves unpleasantly surprised and disappointed during different phases of their job hunt.

At each step of the search, keep your goal in mind, and be sure to clearly communicate it to the appropriate people.

In your cover letter, remember to ask for an interview. Also, specify what you plan to do next; that is, follow up with a phone call or a visit. Don't wait for the employer to call you. Follow up each letter promptly.

In an interview, close by asking for the job (assuming that you still want it). Tell interviewers that it's been a pleasure meeting them and that you'd enjoy working with them. Make it clear that you want the position. Be enthusiastic and positive. In your thank-you notes and in all other follow-up letters, state that you are well suited to the responsibilities and challenges of the position.

At each phase of your job hunt, a small goal should be clear in your mind. Sometimes, stating these goals aloud or writing them down can help you achieve them.

## SUCCESS STORIES

Often, the greatest inspiration comes from those who have succeeded. Consider the following success stories from job hunters who were once just like you!

I was seeking an entry-level position with an engineering firm. The owner of one of the companies I applied to was an alumnus of my college and agreed to interview me for that reason. As it turns out, we hit it off so well that I was completely relaxed during the interview. He hired me almost immediately.

**Ross**
*Engineer*

I had applied for numerous teaching jobs by using conventional methods and had been unsuccessful. One day, in a fit of desperation, I walked into a local college, located the chairperson for the English department, and hastily explained why I would be an excellent candidate for her next open position. As luck would have it, she did have an opening and interviewed me on the spot! I walked out with a job offer in less than thirty minutes.

**Melissa**
*English Professor*

I was applying to be a copywriter for a small advertising agency in my town. I searched online and read everything I could find that made mention of the company name or the names of the owners. During the interview, they asked what I knew about the company, and I talked at length. I mentioned their generous contributions to a local college's scholarship fund and some of the awards they'd recently won. I knew by the expressions on the interviewers' faces that I'd hit the nail on the head. After I was hired, they both told me that one of the major reasons they hired me over the other candidates was because I demonstrated my understanding of the field and of their particular company.

Fern
*Advertising Copywriter*

# Chapter 15

## Evaluating Job Offers

## What Do You Know?

### Short Answers

1. What kinds of things do you need to know about an employer before considering a job offer?

_____

_____

2. What kinds of things do you need to know about a specific position before considering a job offer?

_____

_____

3. How do you compare several job offers?

_____

_____

4. How can you avoid scams when job hunting?

_____

_____

5. Give five tips for negotiating a better salary.

_____

_____

240

## Chapter Focus

In this chapter, you'll learn to:

- Evaluate a job offer.
- Negotiate your salary.
- Write a job acceptance letter.
- Write a job rejection letter.

## Real-Life Relevance

For a while in your job hunt, it may feel as though your entire focus is on finding potential employers and winning their favor. But eventually, you'll move on from that phase into a decision-making mode. It will be time for you to choose your course and determine which job is right for you. Researching each company that makes you an offer and learning the specifics of each position are the first steps when deciding between several offers. Finally, learning what things to do before, during, and after salary negotiations can improve your chances for financial success.

# Choose the Best Job for You

Congratulations! Your hard work and professionalism have resulted in several job offers. Now you are faced with a decision that many people would envy. Before you can compare offers, learn all you can about the employer and the job itself:

- Is the company known to be a good employer? What is its reputation?
- What is the culture of the company and the management style of your supervisor?
- Do the company's mission, vision, and values statement align with your own values and goals?
- Is the company on solid financial footing? And what about its plans for the future?
- What does a search reveal about the company's past?

And what about the position itself?

- Does it offer the compensation you require?
- Are the skills and temperament required in this position a good match for your own?
- Does the position offer enough challenge, variety, or autonomy for you?
- What role will you play in the organization?

Research the company with the help of your local library, and search the Internet and the company's own website and public relations office if possible. Ask your contacts with knowledge of the field or of the area. Learn all you can so you can weigh the factors in this important decision.

**EXERCISE**    ## Comparing Job Offers

To help choose the job that is right for you, complete the following exercise step by step. The process may be time consuming, but good decisions require careful consideration.

**Step 1:** The chart below will help you evaluate your career options. It lists a number of job variables. Fill in the blank spaces at the bottom of the left-hand column with other factors that are important to you in weighing one position against another.

| | | *Job Option 1:* _____ | *Job Option 2:* _____ | *Job Option 3:* _____ |
|---|---|---|---|---|
| *Rank* | *Job Variables* | *Company Name* | *Company Name* | *Company Name* |
| _____ | Title | _____ | _____ | _____ |
| _____ | Status | _____ | _____ | _____ |
| _____ | Responsibilities | _____ | _____ | _____ |
| _____ | Challenges | _____ | _____ | _____ |
| _____ | Creativity | _____ | _____ | _____ |
| _____ | Potential satisfaction | _____ | _____ | _____ |
| _____ | Opportunities to learn and grow | _____ | _____ | _____ |
| _____ | Salary | _____ | _____ | _____ |
| _____ | Benefits | _____ | _____ | _____ |
| _____ | Hours/schedule | _____ | _____ | _____ |
| _____ | Commute | _____ | _____ | _____ |
| _____ | Work environment | _____ | _____ | _____ |
| _____ | Training | _____ | _____ | _____ |
| _____ | Educational opportunities | _____ | _____ | _____ |
| _____ | Supervisor | _____ | _____ | _____ |
| _____ | Coworkers | _____ | _____ | _____ |
| _____ | Potential for advancement | _____ | _____ | _____ |
| _____ | Service to others | _____ | _____ | _____ |
| _____ | Location | _____ | _____ | _____ |
| _____ | _____ | _____ | _____ | _____ |
| _____ | _____ | _____ | _____ | _____ |
| _____ | _____ | _____ | _____ | _____ |

**Step 2.** Rank each job variable according to its importance to you. Careful, honest self-evaluation will help you decide which aspects of employment you value most. Would you endure a long commute to earn a higher salary? Do you need a company that provides in-house child care? Is being able to work outdoors extremely important to you? You might have added these factors to the bottom of the variable list. If you decide that a factor is unimportant to you, rank it last or cross it off the list.

**Step 3.** Circle your top five variables.

**Step 4.** Open your mind to any feasible options to which you haven't yet given full consideration. Returning to school, traveling, joining the military, or return-ing to a former position are examples of such options. Don't rule out any of them yet. If you think of options other than the immediate job offers, create columns for them.

**Step 5.** Examine each job variable in the light of each job option. Go to the blank under Job Option 1 and across from your number one job variable. Mark the blank with a check, a check plus, or a check minus, indicating, respectively, whether the job meets your needs, exceeds your expectations, or falls short of your requirements. Examine every job variable under Job Option 1 in this way. Do the same for the other job options. You may discover you aren't sure how a particular employment offer meets your requirements with regard to one of the variables. Mark that blank with a question mark, and be sure to include the relevant variable on a list of questions to ask your contact person later (see the fill-in items below).

**Job Option 1   Questions to ask _____ (contact person)**

1. _____

2. _____

3. _____

**Job Option 2   Questions to ask _____ (contact person)**

1. _____

2. _____

3. _____

**Job Option 3   Questions to ask _____ (contact person)**

1. _____

2. _____

3. _____

**Step 6.** Now you have carefully considered what is important to you in your career and you've also examined all your job options. Look carefully down the column under each option. Which column has the most check pluses for your top five priorities? This is probably the option to choose.

**EXERCISE**    ## Using a Pro/Con List to Evaluate a Job Offer

Here's a simple alternative to the previous method of considering job options. You may even want to use both methods if you're truly having trouble deciding whether to accept a particular job or trying to compare multiple offers.

Divide a sheet of paper in half or create two columns on your computer screen. Title the left side "Pros" and the right side "Cons." Now begin to consider every variable you can think of. You can use the list of job variables from the previous exercise as a starting point. Place each variable either in the pro category or the con category.

For example, consider the issue of job location. Ask yourself if the company's location is convenient for you. Will the commute be easy or difficult? Will you be forced to move? Depending on your answers, place the variable of location in the pro or con side.

After you've gone through every variable that you can think of, answer the following questions:

**1.** Are there more pros or cons to this job?

_____

**2.** Are there any pros or cons that are so significant that they should be given more weight in my decision?

_____

**3.** Is there a way that any of the cons could become pros? For example, if the salary is in the con column, what might it take to make it into a pro? Perhaps there is room for some salary negotiation or a commitment from the employer to implement a raise after six months versus the traditional one-year mark.

_____

_____

_____

**4.** If you are choosing between jobs, compare the pro and con lists for both. Which job offers more pros? Are the pros for one of the jobs more important variables to you than the pros of the other?

_____

_____

Doing one or both of the two exercises should give you insight into whether a job is right for you or which job of several possibilities to select. If you're still finding it difficult to make a choice, share the results of these exercises with a trusted friend, relative, or career professional for help in evaluating the answers and arriving at a decision.

Job decisions don't have to be permanent or irreversible. Should you choose a position that ultimately doesn't suit you, you now have the job hunting skills to search for another. Also, whereas your parents or grandparents may have worked for the same company for much of their lives, in today's fast-paced career world, it's not uncommon to change jobs every couple of years or even every year.

## Tips for Avoiding Scams

Part of selecting the right job for you is determining the quality of the employer and the legitimacy of the position being offered. Unfortunately, there are fraudulent business opportunities that target job hunters. Follow these tips to avoid becoming a victim:

- Don't get involved with an employer that can't make its business model perfectly clear to you.

- Be suspicious of a company that's willing to hire you without even a phone interview.

- Do not give your bank account, PayPal, credit card, or social security numbers to an employer whose legitimacy you cannot independently verify. These numbers can be used to steal from you or launder funds stolen from others.

- Do your own research by using the Internet or with a business librarian's help on any employer that makes you feel at all uncomfortable.

- As the old adage says, "If it sounds too good to be true, it probably is."

Finally, it's important to recognize that even the most rational people can make irrational decisions when under stress. If you are in financial trouble, recognize your vulnerability and think carefully before you make matters worse by getting involved with a suspicious employer.

# Negotiate Your Salary

Discuss salary with your prospective employer only after all other items have been firmed up because this is likely to be the biggest negotiating point. Also, you don't want to give the impression that you consider salary to be the most important aspect of your employment; rather, you want the employer to believe you are genuinely interested in the job and its responsibilities. Discuss and firm up all aspects of the position, including title, duties, and how it fits into the company before you discuss salary. However, don't ever accept a job without knowing the salary. In fact, you should go into an interview knowing how much you want to make and then work toward that goal.

## Before Discussing Salary Requirements with Your Potential Employer

1.  **Have a salary figure in mind.** Research the typical salary range for the position you're considering, including the geographical consideration of what this type of position pays in your area. There are several ways to do this. Search the Internet; many career websites and job boards have salary charts you can view. However, be sure that the descriptions of the jobs you are using for comparison are comparable in skill and experience levels to position for which you're applying. Seek out online trade journals, which often do salary surveys for their industry. Call or e-mail trade associations, which may be able to provide you with data or direct you to other sources. Make use of the network of contacts you have developed and ask others in the field. Read online classified ads, which often list salaries along with job requirements.

2.  **Decide whether salary is a priority.** How important is salary to you at this stage in your career? Does this job represent a good stepping-stone or entrée into the company? If so, is that more important than salary at this time?

3.  **Is the salary negotiable?** Some jobs have flexible salaries, and some do not. Try to ascertain into which category your position falls. Jobs requiring more advanced skills usually have more pay flexibility because people's varied experience, and credentials have to be taken into consideration.

4. **Consider the health of the local economy.** If the economy is weak and jobs are scarce, you'll have less negotiating power. If the economy is strong and employers must compete for skilled workers, you'll be able to exercise more clout.

5. **Know your worth, and assess the demand for your skills.** If they are highly specialized, you may have an edge in negotiation. If they are more general and are shared with numerous other applicants, you may not. For example, a programmer with knowledge of industry-specific software will be in a better position to negotiate than a programmer who knows only popular software. An advertising copywriter who is comfortable writing for high-tech or industrial clients might be in a stronger position than a writer with only generalized consumer account experience. A paralegal with experience in worker's compensation cases may be able to leverage his or her expertise into a higher-paying job with a law firm that specializes in these cases. Sometimes, that specialized niche knowledge is the something extra that helps you stand out and become an employer's first choice. Years of experience and a personality that fits the organization also increase your value to the organization.

## During Salary Negotiation

1. **Negotiate with the appropriate party.** Try to determine if the person you're negotiating with actually makes the salary final decision. Whenever you're able, deal with the manager who has the final say. If possible, research the salary level of the person you are negotiating with so you gain a psychological advantage and can be aware of how he or she may perceive the salary you're discussing.

2. **The first offer should come from the employer.** Let the employer say the first number. Realize that this initial offer is most likely below what the company is actually willing to pay.

3. **If pressed, give a salary range.** If you must state a figure, give a range you would consider. Aim high, but be realistic. Researchers have found a strong correlation between people's aspirations and the results they achieve in negotiation. Observe the employer's body language and overall response to judge whether your range is in the ballpark. Also remember that many employers are good actors when it comes to negotiating salaries.

4. **Be firm and confident.** When stating your salary requirements, don't be wishy-washy. Say "I want $X$" instead of "Well, I know this is probably too much, but I'd like to make $X$. Is that a problem?"

5. **Don't be dissuaded from negotiating.** Everything is negotiable. Even standard positions with fixed salary scales, union positions, entry-level positions, and commission-only positions have areas of negotiation. Don't assume you have to accept the salary offered; instead, negotiate different job title, job responsibilities, vacation times, perks, or bonuses.

6. **Don't be so fast to say yes.** When the employer throws out a number, don't just accept it. Respond with, "I was hoping for something closer to $X$." Make sure that $X$ is an amount higher than you think you can actually get. This leaves room

for compromise. Also keep in mind the lowest salary you can accept, and be prepared to walk away if necessary.

7.  **Talk in terms you understand.** You can discuss your salary in weekly, monthly, or annual terms, as long as you know how the numbers add up or break down.

8.  **Focus on the present.** Avoid mentioning what you made at your previous job, especially if you are seeking a large hike in pay. If it becomes apparent that you must provide that information, answer honestly, but explain that your responsibilities in the new position sound as if they would be much more challenging than you had in your previous job.

9.  **Use objective criteria.** It will be easier to win the employer's agreement if he or she sees that your expectations are firmly grounded on objective information, such as what similar firms pay people with similar experience.

10. **Tout your skills.** When negotiating, focus on the qualities you bring to the job more than on the salary. Provide documents that demonstrate your skills and accomplishments and provide the manager with facts that he or she can use to justify the salary you're requesting. Bring documentation of salaries of similar positions in your geographical area. You will be most persuasive if you make the employer feel you are worthy of the salary you want.

11. **Consider affordability.** Think about whether you can afford to live on the salary being offered. Be sure to account for state and federal taxes, which will come out of your pay. Remember that the cost of living varies from place to place. A terrific salary in Boise, Idaho, might not be enough to subsist on in New York City.

12. **Be strong, now.** Don't be lulled into accepting less now in return for an offer to renegotiate your salary in three to six months when you've proven yourself. When that day comes, you'll have no leverage, having already invested time and energy into your current position.

13. **Count perks.** Take into consideration such benefits as health and life insurance, stock options, retirement investment programs, and vacation time. They can add significant value to a modest salary.

14. **Ask about health insurance deductions.** Find out how big a premium is deducted from your salary for health insurance, as nearly all employers today require at least a minimum contribution from their employees. In some cases, the employee contribution is substantial. Also, evaluate the quality of the health insurance plan. With medical costs skyrocketing, a good insurance plan can be an important benefit.

15. **Year-end bonuses are bonuses, not guaranteed payouts.** Don't consider year-end bonuses as part of your salary. You'll receive a bonus only if the company is doing well and only at the discretion of the employer. In addition, you don't want to have to wait until the end of the year to get your money.

16. **Be realistic about commissions.** If commissions are part of your salary, get an indication of what you can expect. Recognize that the employer will probably highlight the earnings of people who make the highest commissions while downplaying those of people who earn average or below-average commissions.

17. **Find out about future salary reviews.** Ask how often salary reviews are conducted and how large raises tend to be in percentage of overall salary. As with estimates of commissions, the employer may exaggerate this claim, so be wary.

18. **Get promises in writing.** If the employer is sincere about following through on verbal promises (e.g., "We'll review your salary in six months"), he or she will have no problem putting your agreement in writing.

19. **If you can't upgrade the salary, try to upgrade the job.** If the compensation offered seems more appropriate for a lower-level position, consider offering to accept more responsibilities.

20. **Avoid ultimatums, threats, and other coercive behavior.** If you reach a critical impasse in the discussion, ask whether you can think about the salary and get back to the employer. This will provide an opportunity for tensions to subside and for you to assess your options.

21. **Take your time.** Don't feel pressured to make a decision on the spot if you haven't had time to double-check the offer and examine the numbers carefully. If you need more time to think over an offer, ask for it. You might try "I'm really interested in this position, but this is such an important decision. Would you mind if I think this over until tomorrow?"

## After Salary Negotiation

1. **Schedule a follow-up meeting.** If you have asked for time to review an offer, be sure to make an appointment for the following day or two to finalize the arrangement.

2. **Review your results—whether good or bad.** The best way to improve your negotiating ability is to learn from your experiences. After you finish negotiations, reflect on what you did that worked well and what you might want to do differently the next time.

---

### Humorous Negotiations

Reaching the end of a job interview, the human resources representative asked the young engineer fresh out of college, "And what starting salary were you looking for?"

The engineer said, "In the neighborhood of $150,000 a year, depending on the benefits package."

The human resources representative said, "Well, what would you say to a package of five weeks vacation, fourteen paid holidays, full medical and dental insurance, company-matching retirement fund to 50 percent of salary, and a company car leased every two years—say, a red Corvette?"

The engineer sat up straight and said, "Wow! Are you kidding?"

The human resources representative said, "Of course . . . but you started it."

*Source:* **www.jokemaster.com**

## Negotiation Is a Learned Skill

Savvy businesspeople know that most salaries and benefits are at least somewhat flexible. Every situation needs to be gauged in terms of your bargaining position versus the position held by the other side. As you become more advanced in your career, your position will be strengthened. Negotiation is a skill you develop. Keep the following premises in mind to achieve a successful outcome:

1. **Everyone should feel like a winner.** Negotiations should not be battles. Most likely, the person with whom you're negotiating is someone with whom you'll later be working, so it's best not to treat the negotiation as a win-lose proposition. The art of negotiation is to find a solution that constitutes a good result for both sides. Successful negotiations occur when both sides are satisfied and feel they received a fair deal. Remember, good negotiators never gloat; they always leave the other side feeling like a winner.

2. **Every item is open for discussion.** If someone tells you "Policy does not allow . . ." or "That is not how we do business," then they are either bluffing or not senior enough to know better. You may need to be more persistent for the other side to either reconsider their policy or bring in a more senior company representative who can make the decision.

3. **Show them you're serious.** A negotiation that is important to you may not be as important to the other party. Get their attention by letting them know that you are serious. Be blunt, and clearly spell out what you are negotiating and what the pros and cons are for the other party.

4. **Never believe opening claims.** Opening offers are usually low. Don't be offended or confused by this. Simply come up with your reasons to justify an equally outlandish opening offer. Then, let the negotiations begin.

5. **Have a silent partner.** If you think it would help your position, explain that there is another party (e.g., a spouse, a parent, a trusted mentor or teacher, accountant) with whom you must confer before making a final decision. This other person and his or her influence on your decision can be real or imagined. Either way, the existence of the other party helps prevent you from making a rash decision and can be used as a bargaining strategy. A silent partner gives you time to think and strategize ways of improving your decision.

6. **Give yourself multiple options.** While your intent may be to get the best salary, other options on which the employer may be more flexible could be the amount of vacation time or benefits. The more options you create, the better your bargaining position will be. Never show that you are desperate. If there is something that you must have, don't let on what it is.

7. **Be patient.** No one wants to put time and effort into negotiations only to have the deal disintegrate at the last minute. Take advantage of the other's impatience. Let them dread the thought of going through the same negotiating process with another candidate. Brilliant negotiators are patient. Let them be the ones to cave in.

8. **Prepare for the negotiations.** Skilled negotiators know what they want and as much as possible about what the other side wants. Knowledge is power, especially in negotiations. With each successive offer and counteroffer, you learn more about what the other side desires. The more that you know at the outset, the less you need to be revealed during the negotiation process.

9. **Let the other person do the talking.** It is better to speak less and think more. The less the other side knows about your position, the more he is forced to offer to learn what you want. Let the employer be chatty. Don't confess "I really need this job" or "This is my dream position." Leave him or her wondering, and you'll have more power in your negotiations.

10. **Don't undernegotiate.** Most people give up too much and agree too readily. Practice will help make you a better negotiator. So look for opportunities in your work and your life to hone your skills. Then, when faced with a job offer where the stakes are high, you'll have the confidence to negotiate effectively.

## Negotiating Strategies

Most employers use negotiation tactics to acquire the employees they want at the lowest possible salary. By becoming familiar with some of the maneuvers they use and possibly even using some of them yourself, you'll be a more effective negotiator and will likely land a position that meets most or all of your terms.

**Tactic #1: The Wince.**   The wince is a visibly negative reaction to someone's offer. When an employer tells you the salary for a position, you might act stunned or surprised. This tactic tells the employer that you reject his or her offer and expect him or her to try again.

**Tactic #2: Silence.**   Silence can be an extremely strong tool in negotiations. If the employer throws out a salary number that you don't like and expects a response, try sitting back and waiting. Most people feel uncomfortable in the ensuing silence and start talking to fill the void. Often, they'll respond with a concession.

**Tactic #3: The Good Guy–Bad Guy Routine.**   You've probably seen this tactic employed in the movies where two detectives are interrogating a suspect. In the case of job negotiations, you might find yourself dealing with a supervisor and a manager or a manager and a human resources representative. One person acts as if he or she had like to do whatever it takes to bring you on board, while the other person cites objectives to meeting your employment requests.

If you find yourself in a good guy–bad guy situation, recognize it and ignore it. Don't let the good guy influence your decision. Let them play their game while you watch out for your own interests.

**Tactic #4: Limited Authority.**   If you're asking for a higher salary and the person with whom you're negotiating says he or she can't approve the new numbers without the consent of an unseen higher authority, realize that this may or may not be the case. Just because he or she says "It's out of my hands" doesn't necessarily mean that's true.

In this situation, your strategy can be to ask to deal directly with this other person or encourage him or her to get the other person involved. You may find that although he or she has used this tactic to force you into backing down, if you stand firm, he or she does in fact have the authority, and you may very well get what you want.

**Tactic #5: The Red Herring.**    The name for this technique comes from fox-hunting competitions: One team drags a dead fish across the fox's path to distract the other team's dogs. In a negotiation, a red herring means one side tries to distract the other side from the most important issues by focusing on minor points of contention. For example, the employer might focus on your request for two weeks of paid vacation per year, when what he or she is really after is reducing your proposed salary. He or she will subsequently withdraw his or her objection that you get two weeks vacation per year, but only after he or she has received your concession to work for less pay. If your negotiations get bogged down with minor problems, suggest setting those issues aside and work on the details on which you can agree.

**Tactic #6: The Trial Balloon.**    Sometimes, the employer will throw out an idea or a salary just to see your reaction. He or she will then use that reaction to gauge how to proceed with the negotiations. Trial balloons are questions designed to assess your opponent's position without giving any clues about your plans. An example might be the employer who says "What if I were to tell you we could create a new position for you?" This type of question puts the ball in your court, but it isn't really an offer. In this type of situation, a possible response might be "If you could create a new position, what type of job would it be, and what would it pay?"

**Tactic #7: Future Promises.**    In this tactic, the employer gives you a less-than-satisfactory offer but makes nonspecific promises that he or she will "make it up to you" in the future. For example, he or she might offer you a lower salary than you deserve but will promise you pay raises "down the road." Or he or she might offer you a less prestigious title with promises that after a short while, you'll be given the higher title you aspire to. The problem with future promises is that once you are already working for the employer, you'll have limited clout to force his or her follow-through. It's always best if you can get the position and salary you want before you become an employee. If that's impossible, then be sure to request that promises be put into writing and be associated with specific fulfillment dates.

**Tactic #8: Outrageous Behavior.**    Outrageous behavior can be any form of unacceptable conduct intended to force the other side to accept a concession. It can range from yelling and angry outbursts to tears or threatening to walk out of the room. The most effective response to outrageous behavior is none at all. Just wait for the employer to calm down before reacting because emotional negotiations likely won't result in your favor. If you encounter someone who uses outrageous behavior to elicit your compliance, ask yourself if you really want to work for this type of individual.

**Tactic #9: The Written Word.**    Occasionally, an employer will provide you with a written offer instead of a verbal one. If that's the case, don't assume that just because the offer is written that it's nonnegotiable. You can challenge the terms by opening up a discussion about them one by one. Or you can play the game by submitting a counteroffer in writing.

Before you rush into a negotiation situation, become familiar with these tactics and how they affect the process. When you learn the uses of these negotiation techniques and how to defend against them, you can reach more mutually beneficial agreements.

# The End is in Sight

It's time to take a huge breath, give a sigh of relief, and pat yourself on the back. You've come a long way to get to this point—the crossroads where you must decide to accept or reject an offer. Because you cannot predict the future, be sure you handle this final task with as much professionalism as you did earlier job hunting activities, such as writing your résumé and interviewing. You want the employer to like and respect you regardless of whether you choose to accept the position. Now go sit down at your keyboard; you've got at least one more letter to write.

## The Acceptance Letter

Once you've decided which job you want to take, it's time to wrap things up. The acceptance letter serves several purposes. It is an opportunity to thank the hiring party, express enthusiasm for the position, and, most importantly, define the terms of your employment as agreed on in your negotiations. Send letters to every person who was directly involved in the hiring process. (There may come a time when you'll be glad you put this information in writing.) Your acceptance letter should include a statement of the following issues (see Sample Letter 13.1):

- Job title
- Salary
- Contract terms
- Starting date

## The Rejection Letter

You may have thought employers were the only ones who get to write rejection letters. Not true. Here's your big chance. If you have decided against accepting a position you've been offered, take the time to formally decline in writing. You never know if one day you may be calling that employer again for a job; you want to be remembered positively. Your rejection letter should cover these issues (see Sample Letter 13.2):

- A courteous thank you for the employer's time and consideration
- A brief explanation of why you are not accepting the position
- A statement of any hopes you may have to work with that employer in  the future

131 East Robin Street
Milville, Virginia 23331
May 21, 2011

Mr. John Michaels
Medco Ltd.
14 Collie Street
Kingston, Virginia 23332

Dear Mr. Michaels:

I was very pleased to receive your letter of May 17, 2011, offering me the job of Executive Assistant for Medco's southern division. The conditions of employment meet my requirements, and I would like to accept the position.

As per our agreement, I will begin work on June 15, 2011, at a starting salary of $43,000. I look forward to working with a company as dynamic and progressive as Medco.

Sincerely,

*Mary Carlson*

Mary Carlson

**Sample 13.1    Letter to Accept a Position**

10 Cypress Avenue
Hollywood, CA 91472
September 30, 2011


Ms. Sandra Miles
Marketing Director
Quistron Corp.
17 W. 4th Avenue
Hollywood, CA 91473

Dear Ms. Miles:

After much thought, I have decided not to accept the job of account representative in the
Marketing Department of Quistron Corp. I have accepted another position that I feel is more
in line with my goals at this stage in my career.

Thank you for taking the time to meet with me and consider my qualifications. Should my
situation change, I will certainly contact you.

Cordially,

*Janet Massi*

Janet Massi

**Sample 13.2   LETTER TO DECLINE AN OFFER**

# SUCCESS STORIES

Often, the greatest inspiration comes from those who have succeeded. Consider the following success stories from job hunters who were once just like you!

I applied for about ten sales positions and had interviews at three companies. Much to my surprise, all three ended up making me offers. I carefully weighed the pros and cons of each job and even spoke with one of my teachers to get her input. In the end, I picked the job that seemed to offer the most potential for my future. It was a thriving company and was adding to its product lines. The salary was slightly less than the other two jobs, but the potential to increase my income with sales commissions and bonuses made it the most appealing option.

Aditi
*Sales Representative, Business Publications*

I was about to graduate with a degree in architectural engineering technology when I came to the realization that I didn't enjoy the field and was not looking forward to my career. Fortunately, I had a couple of professors who liked me and recognized my work ethic. Using their contacts, they helped me get a job in computer software development for a major defense contractor. My new career choice is much better suited to my personality and interests. Best of all, my employer is paying for me to continue my education in the computer field.

Ray
*Software Developer*

I received a degree in medical technology but wasn't exactly sure what type of job to pursue. After talking with a couple of people who worked in doctors' offices and hospitals, I decided to seek a position with a medical lab. I obtained a job performing tests to help diagnose diseases and other health problems. I find the work fascinating. Additionally, medical technology is a growing field with an increasing demand for trained personnel. I was able to get a job right out of college and have always been able to easily find a job wherever I chose to live.

Heather
*Laboratory Technologist*

I've always loved reading. I would have liked to become a children's author, but after several failed attempts, I faced the reality that I didn't have the literary talent necessary to be published. I wasn't ready to completely give up on my dream, however. I applied for and obtained a job as a sales representative for a major publisher of children's books. I truly believe in the quality of the books that we sell. And I get a great deal of personal satisfaction knowing that I am introducing literature to children through selling my company's books to schools, libraries, and bookstores.

Antonio
*Sales Representative for Book Publisher*

I studied liberal arts in college and wasn't quite sure exactly what career I was going to pursue. I joined a club of women entrepreneurs for the purposes of networking and learning what types of careers other women had. I became friends with a woman who owned a vocational school. One day, she mentioned that she was in a jam because her communications skills teacher had just quit and classes were scheduled to start in two days. Since I was unemployed and felt I had good communications skills, I offered to substitute until she could find a replacement. The first class went so well that she offered me the job full-time and started me on a fulfilling career as a teacher.

Diane
*Teacher*

## Chapter Follow-Up

- Before deciding on a job offer learn all you can about the employer and the position offered.

- When comparing offers, consider all job variables and how important each variable is to you. Weigh one offer against another, using a thoughtful, systematic process.

- Educate yourself to avoid falling victim to job hunting scams.

- Take time before negotiating a salary to research salary ranges for your position in your geographical area. Also develop an honest assessment or reflect on your own worth to the employer, the local job market, and the relative importance of salary at this stage in your career.

- During salary discussions, be sure to negotiate with the appropriate party, have ample proof of your worth, and negotiate professionally yet tenaciously.

- After salary negotiations, assess your negotiating skills so you can improve on them in the future. Like any learned skill, negotiation can be improved with practice.

- Learn different negotiating strategies so you can use them as needed and be aware of when they are being used by another party.

- After an offer has been made, write a follow-up letter either accepting or rejecting the position.

# Chapter 16

# Learning Your New Job

## What Do You Know?

### True or False

_____ 1. One of the most important things you can do on the first day on the job is make others aware of your skills and knowledge of the field.

_____ 2. Asking questions when training makes a new employee appear ignorant.

_____ 3. Recent college graduates rarely have to work on their written and oral communication skills when beginning a new job.

_____ 4. Kissing up to the boss isn't a good idea.

_____ 5. The person who trains you about the policies of the workplace is usually called a mentor.

_____ 6. When you are newly hired, it is important to research your field to stay current.

## Chapter Focus

In this chapter, you'll learn to:

- Adapt to your new job in the first few days, weeks, and months.
- Be successful in your position.
- Work productively with managers.
- Manage relationships on the job.
- Become a team player.
- Find a mentor.

- Stay current in your field.
- Be evaluated in your position.

## Real-Life Relevance

Until now, your only objective has been to obtain a job. Now it's time to switch focus: learning how to succeed in your new position. How exciting! Here are some strategies and words of inspiration to help you get through those first few weeks and months and ultimately achieve your highest potential.

# Before You Begin

1. **Adjust to your new schedule.** Many new graduates are unaccustomed to the early start time and to working for eight hours straight after a long commute. Get to bed earlier than usual, and set an extra alarm until you adjust to the new routine. Don't make a poor first impression because you're late or exhausted.

2. **Do your homework.** There's no reason that you, as a new employee, need to walk in clueless. Through the Internet and other sources of information, it's easy to research companies and industries. Take it on yourself to research anything that is new to you.

3. **Learn about the company.** Find out how this company is different from others in the field and find out what it values. Read through the company's website and its clients' websites. The more information you learn, the easier it will be to find your place in the company.

# Your First Few Days on the Job

Your first few days at a new job are a lot like your first days in a new school: You look forward to a new beginning filled with exciting possibilities, but you're a bundle of nerves. What if they don't like you? What if you say the wrong thing? What if the job isn't what you thought it would be?

It's not surprising that starting a new job is frequently listed as one of the top ten most stressful events in a person's life. Here are some suggestions to help you fit in and succeed:

1. **Be ready for anything.** Some new employees aren't even given any introductions, a desk, the proper keys, or even enough work to do on the first day. Others are thrown into a whirlwind of activity and expected to catch on.

2. **Write it down.** Bring a pad of paper wherever you go, and jot down important information. You're likely to be overwhelmed with details—everything from where the restroom is located, to coworkers' names, to your specific job responsibilities. If you take good notes and review them during downtime, you'll quickly commit the important information to memory.

3. **Learn names quickly.** You will make a strong first impression and will fit in more quickly. Use memory tricks or jot down notes until you feel confident.

4. **Just ask.** Don't be afraid of sounding uninformed—you *are* uninformed! The quickest way to find out what's going on is to ask and better now than later when you're in the midst of a project with a tight deadline and don't have a clue what to do. Ask specific, legitimate questions. Asking good questions makes you appear interested in your job and intent on doing it right.

5. **Listen.** Some new employees are so eager to demonstrate their new skills that they appear to be arrogant know-it-alls. Being a good listener is often more important and helpful than excessive talking.

6. **Be enthusiastic.** Show eagerness to do the task at hand. You're excited to be in this new position and open to the many opportunities it will present. It doesn't hurt to let some of that natural enthusiasm show through.

7. **Hold your opinions.** Every company has its own way of getting work done. Most likely, the policies and procedures that governed the work flow at a previous job don't apply here. Don't think that you'll change everyone over to your way of thinking. First, learn their methods, be flexible, and adapt.

8. **Be optimistic.** Don't get discouraged if you feel overwhelmed. It doesn't matter if you're a secretary or a CEO; everyone experiences a learning curve when starting a new job. The first days are the hardest, but rest assured: Your anxiety will soon diminish. Before you know it, you'll no longer be the new kid in school!

**When starting a new job, it's important to be receptive to help from coworkers and to quickly learn as much as you can about the company and your individual responsibilities.**
(© Spencer Grant / PhotoEdit)

The first few weeks on the job are sure to be challenging. If you're like most other people, you'll feel a bit unsure of yourself for a while. But don't let your fears take over; it won't take long until you feel comfortable and even confident in your role. Here are some things to keep in mind as you familiarize yourself with your new position:

1. **Learn your company's policies and procedures.** Some companies have a formal orientation program for new employees, whereas others expect you to learn as you work.

2. **Study the company's mission statement.** Find out how your job fits into the company and its mission. Consistently read the internal job postings so you can become clearer on the full scope of what the company does and what role your position plays.

3. **Become aware of the corporate culture.** Be alert to how people communicate most often (meetings, memos, face-to-face, voice mail, or e-mail). Note how the company handles its communications with customers and vendors. Observe the dress code—whether written or implied—and be sure your clothes are appropriate. Become aware of how many hours people work. Some companies are strictly 9 to 5, whereas others expect workers to put in longer days or take short lunch hours. (Be advised that most companies don't pay salaried workers for overtime.) Adapt your style to that of the company. Be vigilant for written and unwritten rules.

4. **Don't try too hard.** Nobody expects you to accomplish miracles overnight. Give yourself time to learn the ropes or you'll risk making serious gaffes. You may also offend people whose support you'll later need.

5. **Send thank-you messages to the people who helped you job hunt.** Write or type short notes to all the people you contacted when you were unemployed. Tell them about your new job, and thank them for their support. They will appreciate and remember your efforts.

6. **Be discreet about your salary.** It's unprofessional to discuss salary. Never ask or tell your coworkers or colleagues about pay; it will inevitably come back to haunt you. That kind of news travels fast. You don't want everyone knowing what you make, and you don't want your managers thinking you're the source of salary information that has the potential to cause discontent and conflict among employees.

7. **Clarify expectations.** Identify immediate priorities that need to be addressed. Talk to your boss to learn what he or she expects from you.

8. **Identify the winners.** Figure out who the superstars are at your company. That's usually easy to do because they're people who are well known and respected. Observe the company's movers and shakers, and learn their secrets to success. Do they have a good attitude? Do they work harder than others? Are they more reliable? Are they committed to quality? When you determine what helps them stand out, you'll be able to emulate their good qualities.

# Your First Year on the Job

Your first year of employment will have both ups and downs and successes and failures. Here are some strategies you can employ to ensure that your initial year represents a solid beginning:

1. **Learn your job.** Become proficient in the tasks and responsibilities that you were hired to handle. Some people concentrate on getting promoted without focusing on the tasks at hand. For true on-the-job success, you need to do a great job—no matter how trivial your tasks might seem to you.

2. **Accept that you will make mistakes.** As you learn on the job, you will make your share of fumbles. Don't be too hard on yourself. What's important is how you learn from those mistakes.

3. **Focus on performance and results.** Excuses, even the best ones, are not what managers and supervisors remember at review time. You're not in school anymore, where an A was often rewarded for effort. Solid, consistent performance is the only thing that matters now. Be conscientious and enthusiastic about your work, and ask for regular feedback about your performance and then use it. Also, keep a "kudos" file of any achievements that have been recognized.

4. **Meet deadlines.** In school, you were probably accustomed to having someone else set deadlines—due dates for papers, final exams, final projects, and so forth. At work, you're often responsible for setting your own deadlines or at least for recognizing when intermediate tasks need to be completed to meet final deadlines. Set parameters and then be sure to meet them.

5. **Persistence pays off.** In the beginning, a task may seem hard or overwhelming. Stay with it. Eventually, you'll get the hang of it.

6. **Take initiative.** Don't be afraid to assume responsibility. Ask questions if you're unclear about an issue or task. Request assistance if you need it. Take on projects that others don't want. By stepping up, you'll be proving to your manager that you're not afraid to take on a challenge or do whatever else needs to be done to help the company. You'll be demonstrating that you are a good team player.

7. **Go the extra mile.** Always do more than what's expected of you, never less. Do it without being asked or expecting recognition for your efforts. Remember that attitude is key.

8. **Use common sense.** Try to figure things out on your own before asking for help. Work on developing your own instincts. Be a good listener, and you'll accelerate the learning process.

9. **Pay attention to detail.** Detail-oriented people get the job done right, leaving nothing to fall through the cracks.

10. **Make a good impression.** The tendency is for everyone to watch the new employee. The impression you make during the first year will stick with you and set the course for your career.

11. **Dress appropriately.** Wear clothes and jewelry that demonstrate your professionalism. Dress at or above the conservative median within the company. Until you are sure what is acceptable, remove or hide tattoos and piercings. Practice good personal hygiene and grooming. Be sure you are clear on what "business casual" means at your workplace and when it's acceptable. Be sure to dress professionally for all business events and client interactions.

12. **Earn the respect of your coworkers and superiors.** Establish your professional image from the outset of your employment. Let people know you're serious about your work by being honest, responsible, and ethical. Once you prove yourself, you'll gain acceptance among your peers and be acknowledged as a valued part of the team. Resolve any conflicts in a professional manner.

13. **Hone your communication skills.** Ask questions, and listen well. Continually strive to improve your speaking and writing abilities.

14. **Practice proper phone and e-mail etiquette.** Answer your phone with a professional greeting; a simple "hello" just doesn't cut it in a work environment. You may want to ask your manager how he or she would prefer that you answer the phone or if there is a company standard. Different companies and positions within companies may have their own requirements for phone etiquette. Be pleasant no matter how tired or exasperated you may be. Speak slowly and distinctly; do not mumble. When you place a call, be sure to identify yourself and state your business in a clear manner. The office is not the place for personal calls. If you must make or receive an occasional personal call, keep it short and to the point. Use proper e-mail etiquette, such as avoiding writing in all capital letters, using cute colors or fonts, emoticons, or foul language. Only send e-mail to the people involved, and remember that the quality of your writing helps establish your professional reputation.

15. **Use technology professionally.** Use your phone and computer for company business only. As tempting as it may be, you shouldn't be checking Facebook, instant messaging with friends, or texting while at work. Visiting sexually explicit websites is a definite no-no, as is downloading any material that could be deemed questionable. Save personal calls for your lunch hour, and use your cell phone, not your work phone.

16. **Watch your language.** In most business settings, profanity and slang are considered unprofessional. Learn office jargon, and use it when appropriate. Focus on being clear in your communication—written and verbal. Any type of racial or ethnic slur or a comment that could be perceived as sexual harassment is totally unacceptable. Any deviations from this policy can result in serious legal ramifications that go beyond being fired from your job. Also remember that employers have the technology and the right to monitor your phone calls, voice mail, e-mail, and Internet activities.

17. **Behavior counts.** How you conduct yourself, how you interact with coworkers, and the way you approach your work all affect your success. Superiors considering you for a promotion usually take into account not only your work performance but also how you deal with stress, how motivated you are, and how much other employees and managers like working with you.

18. **Act mature.** Prove that you can work well without supervision and are dependable, responsible, and professional at all times.

19. **Keep your workspace businesslike.** In most workplaces, it is acceptable for offices to reflect the personalities of their occupants, as long as the overall decor is not offensive or unprofessional. A few personal touches are fine—photos, diplomas, awards, a few healthy plants. Avoid racy posters and calendars or posted slogans that reflect a negative attitude, such as "I love my job; it's the work I hate" or "Is it Friday yet?"

20. **Be organized.** Set up a filing system that works for you for paper and electronic files. If an appropriate system is not obvious, ask a coworker for assistance or get a book on developing organizational skills. The time you invest in getting organized will result in increased productivity. To avoid accumulating office clutter, you may want to set aside a few minutes at the beginning or end of each day to do housekeeping—clean your desktop, put files away, update your calendar. Also, take time to set daily, weekly, and long-term priorities.

21. **Stay informed.** Unlike in school, where you were assigned reading material, on the job, it's up to you to find and read material related to your position. You might consider reading industry blogs and newsletters, competitors' sales literature, and a daily newspaper, among other resources. Check the Web regularly to see what's new and exciting in your field. Include in your searches sites of professional associations in your field, competitors of your company, companies in related fields, and vendors to your industry.

22. **Be receptive to new ideas.** Be willing to learn new skills and new ways of doing specific tasks. When introduced to a new skill or procedure, do your best to complete the task efficiently, without balking or unnecessary hesitation.

23. **Keep your personal life personal.** Relationship problems, personal health issues, and financial difficulties should be dealt with outside the office. Involving coworkers in personal problems is unprofessional.

24. **Be careful what you post online.** Don't post anything negative about your job, any proprietary information about your company, or any sexually explicit material on social networking sites, such as Facebook, or on a blog, even if it's your own. Assume that it will eventually be discovered. If you wouldn't want your employer or coworkers to see it, then it doesn't belong online.

25. **Draw a solid ethical line, and never cross it.** Integrity means doing what is right, even if it is difficult or unpopular. Don't lie, cheat, or steal, even when you're unlikely to be caught. Develop a reputation for honesty and integrity.

26. **Share credit with others.** When you are personally complimented for something that was a team effort, be sure to share the glory with everyone who contributed.

27. **Learn to accept criticism.** Try not to become defensive when criticized. Instead, learn from your mistakes.

28. **Know your strengths and weaknesses.** What do you enjoy? What gives you a sense of satisfaction? What types of tasks make you uncomfortable? Position yourself to take on those responsibilities for which you are best suited.

29. **Write down short-term (daily, weekly, and monthly) and long-term (one-year, five-year, and ten-year) goals.** Make the goals realistic and measurable. Evaluate yourself periodically. Revise your goals when necessary.

30. **Accept all responsibilities graciously.** Realize that in your first job, you may be asked to do entry-level tasks that do not fully use your education and skills. Complete those tasks with a good attitude, but seek opportunities to take on more challenging work.

31. **Accept the fact that you won't love every aspect of your job; few people do.** View each task as part of a bigger process aimed at accomplishing your goals. Also, first jobs are just that—first jobs. Rarely does someone stay in a first job for life. Gain all you can from the experience.

32. **Remember that you won't be new forever.** Eventually, you'll get to know the ropes, just as your coworkers did. With a little enthusiasm, professionalism, and common sense, you'll be well on your way to success.

**EXERCISE**   **First Days Interviews**

Talk with at least three individuals (friends, family, teachers, and others), and ask them about their first few days, weeks, and year at a new job. Obtain answers to the following questions:

1. What themes emerged?

2. What were their biggest fears?

3. Looking back, how do they feel now about those fears? Were the fears justified? How did they confront and eventually eliminate their fears?

4. What was their biggest success and their biggest failure in their first year on the job?

5. What was their most memorable experience of that first year?

6. If they had to do it all again, what would they do differently?

7. What can you learn from the experiences of these individuals?

8. How might you apply what you've learned?

## Tips for Working with Your Manager

There are likable people and unlikable people, and managers can fall into either category. If you're blessed with a good manager, you'll have the opportunity to learn from someone with experience and develop a long-term professional relationship. If you find that getting along with your manager is a challenge, swallow your pride, and consider this an educational experience. Here are some tips for working with your manager:

1. **Understand your manager's position.** He or she most likely answers to another boss, who is interested only in performance and results. Be aware of your manager's position in the company and your position relative to others whom he or she manages.

2. **Communicate with your manager.** As in any other relationship, good communication is important. Don't be afraid to tell your manager of your successes, failures, and goals. He or she can't help you if you don't make known what you want.

3. **Take the ball, and run with it.** Most managers prefer that their staff assume some responsibility so they don't need to micromanage. Find ways to help your manager get the job done. Instead of asking for guidance on every aspect of a task, take the initiative to gather information and make decisions.

4. **Accept criticism without becoming defensive.** Work on improving deficiencies, and learn from your mistakes.

5. **Show respect for your boss in everything you do.** Don't join in when others are boss bashing, even if you're tempted. It's unprofessional, and it may come back to harm you in the future.

6. **Don't be a complainer.** When others begin to grumble, fight the urge to join in. Make the best of the situation, and learn from it.

7. **Consider the situation as short term.** At some point in your career, you're likely to encounter a manager with whom your personality clashes. If you see no hope for developing a good working relationship with that person, begin quietly looking for your next job. Continue to act professionally and responsibly—even if the situation gets rough. Don't treat this glitch in your career as a personal failure. Instead, see it for what it is, learn from the experience, and move on.

## Managing Relationships on the Job

It would be a mistake to think that success in a job depends wholly on your level of expertise and performance. Good interpersonal skills can be just as important—if not more so. If your personal attributes and the culture of the hiring company don't merge, you may be in the wrong place. A situation of "bad chemistry" has serious ramifications. If you can't adjust to the corporate culture or it to you, you could be out of a job again.

The term *right chemistry* refers to the match of an employee's behavioral style and the required style of an employer and of a particular job—in addition to having the requisite skills. Interpersonal characteristics and cultural fit are highly important elements of professional success. Good social skills, a positive attitude, enthusiasm, and a sense of humor are vital. Here are some tips to help you establish successful relationships with your coworkers:

1. **Develop relationships in which you have mutual respect for those around you.** Mutual respect based on mutual gain is vital.

2. **Learn to manage the small-group relationship.** In school, for the most part, you learned to work as an individual, but in companies, teamwork is the direction of the future. You'll need to share information and create a fair distribution of tasks.

3. **Make a point of getting involved with other people in the organization and their work.** Be friendly but not to the point where talking takes time away from your work and harms your productivity. It's good to have people on your side.

4. **Develop good interpersonal and communication skills.** Cultivate relationships with others through good verbal and written communication.

5. **Ask everyone questions.** Absorb information from all people you work with. Be respectful of other people's jobs.

6. **Pay attention to the actions and responses of others.** Listen and observe. What are people saying and doing? Involve others in your day-to-day decisions.

7. **Steer clear of office politics.** How effectively you deal with politics is just as important as how well you do the job. It can greatly influence whether you succeed or fail.

8. **Tips for becoming a team player:**
   - **Develop a "team mentality."** Exhibit a good attitude.
   - **Participate in group activities during company time and after hours.** Such group sports as softball and bowling can provide great bonding experiences. Social gatherings can help make work settings more comfortable, but remember that your off-hours conduct should never be inappropriate.
   - **Show your team spirit; take pride in the team.** Support your coworkers. Contribute to team success. Share credit for accomplishments, and congratulate others on their successes.

9. **Traps to avoid:**
   - **Forming cliques.** Participating in a clique makes a statement to people outside the group that they don't belong, possibly alienating and hurting the feelings of people whom you may one day need on your side.
   - **Sexual and racial comments.** Sexual harassment and bigoted language are not acceptable—even behind closed doors.
   - **Passing judgment.** Avoid being critical of others. Your judgments could be wrong, and your comments could get back to the person you criticized.

- **Kissing up to your boss.** You'll alienate coworkers and eventually management if you take this tack. It's appropriate to let your manager know how you're doing, but use suitable forums, such as a monthly report.

- **Breaking a trust.** This is the quickest way to lose friends in the work environment. Betraying someone who has confided in you or passing along information that should not be broadcast is as inappropriate in the work environment as it is in social circles.

- **Gossiping.** Talking about others is unprofessional. Talking about business issues outside work could be harmful to the business. Discretion is important. In business, gossip can get back to competitors, vendors, and suppliers. Be careful of what you say.

- **Socializing at work.** Have fun, but strike a balance between socializing and serious work. Also, balance your work life with your personal life. Having only coworkers as friends may be too limiting.

- **Inappropriate Internet use.** Use the Internet only for work-related tasks. If you should ever you find yourself concerned that someone might look over your shoulder to see what you're doing, then you probably shouldn't be doing it.

# Failures Who Became Successes

Gain inspiration and motivation from these "failures":

- Albert Einstein was four years old before he could speak.

- Isaac Newton did poorly in grade school and was considered "unpromising."

- Beethoven's music teacher once said of him, "As a composer, he is hopeless."

- When Thomas Edison was a youngster, his teacher told him he was too stupid to learn anything. He was counseled to go into a field where he might succeed by virtue of his pleasant personality.

- F. W. Woolworth got a job in a dry goods store when he was twenty-one, but his employer would not permit him to wait on customers because he "didn't have enough sense to close a sale."

- Michael Jordan was cut from his high school basketball team.

- Boston Celtics Hall of Famer Bob Cousy suffered the same fate.

- A newspaper editor fired Walt Disney because he "lacked imagination and had no good ideas."

- Winston Churchill failed the sixth grade and had to repeat it because he did not complete the tests that were required for promotion.

- Babe Ruth struck out 1,300 times, a major league record.

# Finding a Mentor

Find a good mentor, and you'll greatly accelerate your on-the-job learning and increase your potential for success. A *mentor* is someone you respect, admire, and like—someone to whom you can look to set good examples, teach procedures, help you see the big picture, solve problems, guide you toward your future, and provide perspective and emotional support.

What's in the relationship for the mentor? Many professionals see mentoring as an opportunity to give back for their success. Some are flattered to have a new recruit admire them. Mentors also get the benefit of loyalty and dedication. Your success may help ensure their success. They may look to you for assistance with special projects and tasks. You may also provide them with creativity and new perspectives in dealing with work situations.

To find a mentor, identify someone with solid experience and good interpersonal skills. Some companies have established mentoring programs through which you are paired with a willing coworker. Although it would be best to have a mentor within your own organization, you can also tap professional groups, such as SCORE (Service Corps of Retired Executives) and BPWA (Business and Professional Women of America); service organizations, such as Rotary Club; and civic groups, such as your local chamber of commerce as sources of mentors. You may even be able to find a mentor online, who can give you guidance and the benefit of his or her experience through meaningful e-mail correspondence.

---

### Can You Guess Who . . . ?

| | |
|---|---|
| Failed in business | age 22 |
| Ran for legislature and was defeated | age 23 |
| Failed again in business | age 24 |
| Was elected to the state legislature | age 25 |
| Mourned the loss of a sweetheart | age 26 |
| Had a nervous breakdown | age 27 |
| Was defeated in a bid for Speaker of House | age 29 |
| Was defeated for Congress | age 34 |
| Was elected to Congress | age 37 |
| Was again defeated for Congress | age 39 |
| Was defeated for Senate | age 46 |
| Was defeated for Vice-President | age 47 |
| Was again defeated for Senate | age 49 |
| Was elected President of the United States | age 51 |

That man was Abraham Lincoln.

Permission to reprint granted by Ann Landers and Creators Syndicate

Be sure you are sensitive to your mentor's time constraints. Don't just take from the mentor but also find ways you can help him or her do his or her job better. Realize that even mentors have a human side, and recognize their shortcomings while appreciating their positive attributes. Finally, when you eventually outgrow your mentor, don't forget who helped you get to that stage.

# The Importance of Staying Current

In today's fast-paced, competitive market, it is essential to stay current and informed—even when you have a job. By continuing to improve your skills and education, you not only improve your job performance (and your career advancement and compensation), but you also greatly enhance your marketability should you need to resume a job hunt. In addition, by keeping an active and curious mind, you increase your job satisfaction and prevent burnout. Depending on your field, there are many avenues to self-improvement.

The Internet is one of the easiest ways to stay informed. Search the Web on a regular basis for news about your field, related businesses, and your company's competitors and vendors. Subscribe to e-newsletters and blogs for your industry. Seek out articles about advances and trends. Set aside a portion of every week to catch up on your online reading.

Formal education is another option. Take courses through your local college or your city's adult education program. Many colleges now cater to working adults by offering courses in the evenings or on weekends and also online courses. You do not have to complete a degree but instead can dabble in a class or two to brush up on your writing, speaking, or computer skills. You will be surprised at how many others like you are taking classes and how understanding most professors are regarding the needs of working adult students. Returning to school can be a frightening experience for some, but most find the rewards well worth the initial apprehension.

In some cases, employers team up with local educators and corporate trainers to design appropriate courses or seminars to offer in the workplace. This is something you may want to inquire about or suggest to your supervisor or human resources manager. Of course, if your employer already offers some additional training, you would be wise to jump at the opportunities they present.

Other opportunities for formal education include seminars, conferences, and webinars—online seminars—sponsored by professional organizations or trade associations. These events are often designed to meet a need common to people in your profession. They tend to be brief, focused, and highly informational—a good choice for busy employees with little time to spare. They often provide the most current information, covering subjects that colleges and universities haven't yet developed programs for. These classes offer another hidden but invaluable asset: the opportunity to network with other people in your field and learn through word of mouth about relevant news and technology. When attending seminars, avoid the temptation to be a wallflower or to take a wait-and-see attitude. You may learn more by making small talk with the person next to you in the coffee line than you might have expected.

Networking groups represent a more formal way to reap the benefits of networking. These groups usually meet once a month and offer members the opportunity to exchange business cards, develop contacts, keep track of developments in their field, and get to know their competitors.

You can also join trade associations or professional organizations to keep on top of important developments in your field. Virtually every profession has a national association that offers a publication on developments in the field as well as updates on relevant legislation and technology. Even if you choose not to join your national or local professional or trade organization, it is still a good idea to check out these publications at your local library or on the Internet. When considering whether you should become involved, keep in mind that trade and professional organizations typically offer discounted student memberships and are often looking for leadership at the local or national level.

These same organizations also hold trade shows, where leaders in the field show off their latest products and rub elbows. You may find that after attending a few trade shows, you begin to recognize the names and faces of key industry players. They may even get to know you!

Finally, it is important to keep an open and curious mind. Read newspapers and trade magazines—in print or online—to keep abreast of issues that affect your field. Offer to cross-train at your place of employment or to assist your coworkers whenever you're able. By continuing the lifelong process of listening and learning, you will find that you become a sought-after and indispensable member of the workforce.

## How You Will Be Evaluated

In school, you were accustomed to receiving midterm and final grades. In the world of work, you'll most likely have performance reviews. The larger the company is, the more formal the process tends to be. A performance review evaluates the quality of your work over a specific time period—usually a year.

Objective and subjective qualities are evaluated. For example, a review might assess your achievement of short-term goals and progress made on long-term goals as well as your attitude, ability to get along with others, and professionalism. Most likely, you will be rated with some form of grading system.

## These Employees Won't Go Far

The following humorous statements were taken from actual employee performance evaluations. Whether the comments were shared with the subject of the assessments is not clear.

- "Since my last report, this employee has reached rock bottom—and has started to dig."
- "This employee is not so much a 'has-been' but more of a definite 'won't-be.'"
- "Works well when under constant supervision and cornered like a rat in a trap."
- "He sets low personal standards—and then consistently fails to achieve them."
- "This employee should go far—and the sooner he starts to pack, the better."
- "He would argue with a signpost."
- "He has a knack for making strangers—immediately."
- "He brings joy whenever he leaves the room."
- "If you see two people talking and one looks bored—he is the other one."
- "He has a photographic memory with the lens cap glued on."
- "Donated his brain to science before he was done using it."
- "Gates are down and lights are flashing—but the train's not coming."
- "He has two brain cells: one is lost and the other is out looking for it."
- "If you gave him a penny for his thoughts, you'd get change."
- "The wheel is turning, but the hamster is dead."

A performance review usually includes a salary review. However, raises at most companies are not guaranteed. Poor individual performance, rough times for the company, or management changes can all influence a potential raise. Try to focus on your contribution to the company as the reason for a raise. Your "need" for more money is not really relevant in the company's eyes.

The most important part of a performance review should be a discussion of areas for improvement and the setting of new goals. Your task as an employee is to clarify any areas of your review you don't adequately understand, accept constructive criticism with grace, and express willingness to improve any problem areas.

# Advice from Those Who Have Made It

Many of the people we spoke with while writing *The Ultimate Job Hunter's Guidebook* were willing to share advice about job hunting and career success. Here are some of the thoughts that emerged from those conversations:

- To succeed, choose a career you love.
- Keep your eyes open for any and every opportunity. Then, go for it!
- Make your own breaks.
- Learn something from every task and every job. It all comes in handy someday in some way you often can't foresee at the time.
- Nobody is indispensable, especially you.
- Learn from all the people you meet. Everyone has some special quality, skill, or talent.
- Every problem is an opportunity in disguise.
- Don't sweat the small stuff, and remember, it's almost all small stuff.
- Seek out challenges. Your greatest personal satisfaction will come from difficult achievements.
- Take setbacks in stride. Learn from your failures, and move on.
- Don't make the same mistake twice.
- Cultivate your talents. Work on improving your deficiencies.
- Practice your skills. Even the best artists, performers, and athletes need to hone their expertise.
- Persistence will get you almost anything eventually.
- Try to make the right decisions in life. Rectify wrong decisions as hastily as possible.
- Don't get caught up in the day-to-day stresses. Focus on the positive aspects of the big picture.
- Work toward long-term goals, but enjoy life today.
- Take responsibility for your actions—good or bad.
- Don't spend time worrying about past mistakes. Live in the present.
- Become the most positive, enthusiastic person you know.
- Be decisive, even if it means you are sometimes wrong.
- Find a comfortable balance between work and family.
- Commit yourself to becoming a lifelong learner.
- Character counts.
- Be a nice person.

## SUCCESS STORIES

Often, the greatest inspiration comes from those who've succeeded. Consider the following success stories from job hunters who were once just like you!

My first day on the job was a disaster. I hadn't slept at all the night before because I was so nervous. Getting ready for work, I tore a contact lens—something I hadn't done in years. It meant I had to wear my old glasses to work. I felt unattractive and self-conscious. When I got into work, I learned that the supervisor who had hired me was out sick. Fortunately, a coworker offered to show me around and help me get started on some projects. The good news is that after that first day, I quickly got up to speed. I was given a lot of interesting responsibilities. I really liked my job, my coworkers, and my company.

Delia
*Geologist*

I remember my first day at work. Just thinking about it gives me butterflies. I literally shook as I rode the elevator up to my new office. Even though it was a job I had wanted very badly, it took everything I had not to run back to my car, drive home, and hide under the bed. Somehow, I managed to make it through that first day, and every day from then on got easier. I learned about my company's product lines, procedures, and vendors. Within weeks, I began to feel comfortable in my job, and within months, I became quite skilled at it and began to really enjoy my work. I'm proud of myself for hanging in there even when everything seemed so new, so scary, and so overwhelming.

Lorraine
*Clothing Buyer*

I'll never forget my first job. It's where I first learned the importance of providing excellent customer service. I would take dictation of classified ads over the phone for placement in the newspaper. I had quotas to meet and supervisors who monitored the calls. Every day, I talked with thirty to fifty customers. Some were really nice; others were curt and even rude. I learned how to be polite and helpful but also firm. Even though I'm in a completely different field now, the skills I mastered working those phones on that first job still come in handy almost every day.

Cara
*Research Analyst for Financial Services Firm*

I started out as a secretary, but as the company grew, so did my responsibilities. Because I was a fast study with computer programs, I soon learned how to manipulate the company's websites and became the in-house webmaster. When the company began aggressively advertising on the Internet, I took on administration of all the online ad campaigns. When the company bought customer relations management software, I took over the tasks of data transfer, employee training, and ongoing program administration. With each passing day, I grew in my role. I enjoyed my job, and the company appreciated and rewarded my efforts.

Tamara
*Computer Information Specialist*

My first year as a television production assistant was hard but fun too. At first, I felt overwhelmed by all the different equipment and the time-pressured environment. But eventually, I became familiar with how things worked and what tasks I was responsible for. When I look back on my career, that first year was actually one of the most fun because I felt like I was learning something new every day. I had so many interesting experiences—from assisting on the daily newscasts to producing holiday special shows to working on location at sports events. The hours were long and the pay was low, but the experience was priceless.

Jamal
*TV Producer/Director*

## Chapter Follow-Up

- The first few days and weeks on the job offer a chance for tremendous professional growth and are the beginning of establishing your professional reputation.

- Before you start your new job, adjust your schedule, and research to learn more about the company.

- In the first few weeks on the job, continue to learn more about the written and unwritten rules of your new workplace while learning about your coworkers and thanking all who help you as you're becoming oriented.

- In the first year on the job, exercise good common sense about workplace behavior, focusing on deadlines and results and earning the respect of your coworkers.

- Seize the opportunity to learn from your manager, and adjust your work habits to make the relationship productive.

- Managing relationships at work can be as important to the job as the hard skills you possess. Avoid common workplace relationship traps, and develop a team mentality.

- Finding a mentor can be an invaluable factor in your own personal and professional growth.

- Staying current in your field helps you remain valuable and marketable.

- Learn how you will be evaluated during your first year.

# An Invitation to Share

As you embark on your career, you'll be creating your own success stories and developing your own ideas about how to find jobs and advance in the workplace. Write to us about your experiences. We'd love to hear about them and possibly even include them in the next edition of *The Ultimate Job Hunter's Guidebook*. Be sure to include your name, address, phone number, and e-mail address so we can contact you.

Send submissions to:

South-Western, Cengage Learning
College Business
5191 Natorp Boulevard
Mason, OH 45040
college_bus@cengage.com

# Answer Key

## CHAPTER 1
## Planning Your Job Search

### What Have You Learned?

*Answers to short answer quiz*

1. What do you think are the first three steps of the job hunt?

   The first three steps of the job hunt are choosing a direction, setting goals, and deciding on a strategy to reach those goals.

2. What tools do you think a job hunter needs?

   In addition to a large network of contacts, a job hunter will need also need a flawless résumé, effective cover letters, strong references, and a powerful portfolio.

3. What role do social networking sites play in the job hunt?

   Social networking sites enable job hunters to expand their circle of contacts and build their personal brands.

## CHAPTER 2
## Conducting a Self-Assessment

### What Have You Learned?
Review your answers to "What Do You Know?" All the questions, with the exception of number 5, are false. Which of your answers were incorrect? How much did you improve your understanding of self-assessment?

## CHAPTER 3
## Targeting and Strategizing for the Hunt

### What Have You Learned?

*Answers to short answer quiz*

1. List three ways to research a career that interests you.

   Three ways to research a career involve using online research on career databases, such as those found at the Bureau of Labor Statistics website; conducting informational interviews of people whose jobs interest you; or job shadowing and observing part of the workday of a person with a job you're considering.

2. How does an informational interview differ from a job interview?

   The purpose of an informational interview is solely to gather information about a potential career. The job interview occurs much later in the job hunting process, and its purpose is to gain a job offer.

3. What is job shadowing? What's the best way to make a good impression when job shadowing?

Job shadowing is the technique of learning about a potential career by quietly observing the workday or part of a workday of a person in the field.

# CHAPTER 4
## Organizing the Job Hunt
### What Have You Learned?
### *Answers to short answer quiz*

1. How much time per week should a job hunter use to look for employment?

The most effective job hunts consume 30–40 hours per week, which is a full-time job in itself!

2. List all the ways a cell phone could become a job search tool.

The cell phone is not only useful for contacting potential employers, but the calendar, reminder, notepad, data storage, and text alerts features and Internet access can all be very helpful when you are job hunting.

3. How could disorganization sabotage the job hunt?

Losing documents and losing time equal lost opportunities. On the other hand, being able to quickly find your job search tools or to locate information about company or position that interests you is invaluable.

4. Under what circumstances might it be acceptable to quickly check a text message during an interview?

None. It is never acceptable to take a phone call or check a text during an interview.

# CHAPTER 5
## Preparing Your Résumé
### What Have You Learned?
### *Answers to the True or False quiz*

1. *False.* In certain liberal or highly creative fields, outrageous résumés are acceptable and may even be welcome! However, most traditional professions require a traditional résumé.
2. *True.* Sometimes, less is more. Try not to overwhelm your reader with an overly busy résumé full of bold print, numerous fonts, and excessive graphics. Use a few different tools judiciously to carefully call your reader's attention to the key headings and the job titles or dates you wish to highlight.
3. *False.* The most important thing an employer needs to keep in mind after reading your résumé is your name. Without that recollection, all the other information is useless.
4. *False.* The résumé is designed to convey the most relevant information in the most condensed format possible. For this reason, it is important to use telegraphic phrases, starting with carefully chosen action verbs, to describe your skills.
5. *False.* Years ago, one's health as excellent was an accepted résumé practice. These days, references to one's health are unnecessary.
6. *False.* Your work experience will never come before the résumé heading and should be near the top of your résumé only if you believe it is your strongest selling point.
7. *False.* Résumé language is unique in that it contains few complete sentences and uses phrases starting with action verbs instead.
8. *False.* Most employers expect to see only your most recent and relevant work experience on your résumé. While some job applications may require you to list a more extensive job history, the résumé is not the place for an exhaustive accounting of your employment.
9. *True.* Some job hunters feel that it is deceitful to list a college from which they did not receive a degree, but all educational experiences could be beneficial to an employer and should be listed accurately (minus a graduation date if you did not graduate).

10. *False.* Standard résumé software can help job hunters create an excellent first draft and gives a good picture of what a résumé should look like. However, few are perfect as is. Any résumé created with the help of a software package will need to be carefully rearranged and individualized to make your résumé stand out and to showcase your particular strengths.

# CHAPTER 6
# Writing Cover Letters

## What Have You Learned?

### *Answers to the True or False quiz*

1. *True.* You should always send a cover letter with every résumé.
2. *False.* You should include a call to action in your cover letter. That's being professional and pro-active, not pushy.
3. *True.* You should personalize the cover letter if possible, addressing a specific individual, as opposed to a generic approach, such as "To Whom It May Concern."
4. *False.* Your cover letter should be one page and should mention only a couple of the most important and relevant highlights of your resume.
5. *True.* It's perfectly acceptable to send your cover letter by e-mail, unless the employer has specifically requested that applicants use postal mail.
6. *True.* A referral cover letter mentions a mutual contact as a means to persuade the employer to give you consideration.
7. *True.* The main purpose of the cover letter is to get you an interview.

# CHAPTER 7
# Obtaining References

## What Have You Learned?

### *Answers to short answer quiz*

1. Can you obtain any references if you've never before held a job in your field?

   Yes. You can ask for references from previous employers and coworkers even if they're not in the field you're currently pursuing. Additionally, guidance counselors, teachers, coaches, neighbors, and supervisors from internships or places where you've done volunteer work can serve as character references.

2. What purpose do letters of recommendation and references serve?

   Employers want to be confident in their hiring decisions because it's costly and time consuming to hire and train the wrong individual. In addition to the interview, your letters of recommendation and references help the employer get to know you by providing informed assessments of your job or school performance and your character.

3. Why is it important to let people whom you list as references know that you're providing their name and contact information to your prospective employers?

   You want to make sure the people you list as references are comfortable providing a strong recommendation. If you sense any hesitation, you may want to cross that person off your list of references; remember, you want only enthusiastic recommendations. When you speak to your references, remind them of the work you did and mention qualities you would like them to tell prospective employers about you. Taking these steps will help ensure you get a positive referral.

4. Why should you never provide your originals when giving an employer letters of recommendation?

   You can't be sure the employer will follow through on returning those letters to you. Therefore, only provide photocopies or electronic scans of your letters, and put your originals in your files for safekeeping.

## CHAPTER 8
### Building a Portfolio or Personal Website
**What Have You Learned?**

*Answers to short answer quiz*

1. List at least four items that you think are appropriate for inclusion in a portfolio.

   Examples of portfolio contents are: letters of recommendation, work samples, documentation of any awards won, certificates of completion for any conferences or workshops attended, and any other items that could help to persuade an employer that you are qualified for the particular position you're seeking.

2. When should you present your portfolio to an employer?

   If you've created an e-portfolio or personal website, you can include a link to it in your cover letter and on your résumé. At an interview, you can present your portfolio of hard copies in a binder, a folder, a file, or a portfolio case. Another option is to leave behind a digital copy in CD or DVD form to be viewed at the employer's convenience.

3. What are some of the benefits of creating an e-portfolio or personal website as opposed to a more traditional portfolio containing hard copies of your documents?

   An e-portfolio or personal website can be referenced in your cover letter and résumé; thus, the employer has an opportunity to view it early on in the selection process. If your information is compelling, you're more likely to be offered an interview. Additionally, an electronic version of your portfolio demonstrates your comfort level with technology to an employer. Finally, an e-portfolio or personal website can be easily updated as you gain exhibits you wish to share.

## CHAPTER 9
### Finding Potential Employers
**What Have You Learned?**

*Answers to short answer quiz*

1. What is networking?

   Networking involves getting in touch with your personal contacts to see if they can offer you any job leads. Contact friends, former classmates, former work associates, suppliers, vendors, relatives, neighbors, fellow professionals, organization members, and anyone else you can think of who might be able to connect you to an employer.

2. Why is networking an important part of job hunting?

   One of the most common ways to get a job is through personal contacts—also known as your network. Networking can help you learn about job openings that aren't being advertised.

3. What are some different ways to find out about job openings?

   Among the ways to learn about open positions are classified ads in newspapers, career websites, industry blogs, alumni placement offices, employment agencies, professional organizations, and networking.

4. What is a job fair?

   Participating companies set up tables staffed by representatives who will greet you, tell you something about the company, and, most importantly, assess whether you might be a potential candidate for employment.

5. Where can you search online to find job openings?

   Start with career websites—most of which have help wanted ads. Local newspapers also publish their classified ads online. You can also check individual company websites.

6. What are some ways you can you research employers?

   Check resources such as Hoover's (www.hoovers.com), which gives background and competitive information on companies. You can also go to individual company websites. You can also Google the company name to see if any relevant news items are posted online. And don't forget your city library, which likely has a wealth of resources about individual companies—particularly if they're local.

# CHAPTER 10
# Social Networking and Your Online Reputation

## What Have You Learned?

### *Answers to short answer quiz*

1. What is online social networking?

   Social networking online is the practice of expanding your business and social contacts by making connections through individuals via the Internet. It's a way to meet more people, which increases your chances of finding a potential employer or someone who can refer you to one.

2. Can you name at least two online social networks?

   LinkedIn, Facebook, Twitter, Plaxo, and XING are some of the more popular social networks online.

3. How might social networks be useful in your job hunt?

   Use social networks to access other professionals who might be able to offer job leads or contacts. Social networks can also help you to gain visibility and credibility in your field.

4. Can you think of a way to combine online social networking with offline networking?

   When you get to know someone through social networking and find there may be value in connecting further with them, you can reach out either by phone or request an in-person meeting over coffee or lunch. The situation can work in reverse too. Anyone you meet in your job search you can also connect with on your social networking sites as a way to stay in touch.

5. What is your online reputation, and why is it important?

   Many employers search the Internet to see if the picture you've painted for them in your résumé and interview matches the person displayed on social networks and other online sources. Also, recruiters and HR professionals routinely use online reputational information in their candidate review processes. For better or for worse, the search engines find content you produce or that mention you and index it.

## CHAPTER 11
## Have You Considered . . . ?

### What Have You Learned?

#### Answers to the True or False quiz

1. *False.* The vast majority of government jobs aren't for politicians. They're for such positions as teachers, law enforcement officers, park rangers, lawyers, accountants and much more.
2. *False.* Not all government jobs are based in Washington, D.C. There are federal jobs in every state.
3. *False.* Nonprofits do have paid employees, just like a traditional, for-profit business.
4. *True.* Working for a small company versus a larger company could be a great learning experience in that you may get to wear many hats and have diverse responsibilities.
5. *True.* Starting your own business is a viable alternative if you have a good idea, the means to implement the idea, and the desire to "give it your all."
6. *False.* Difficulty finding a job in your field is not a good reason to return to college. Only seek a more advanced degree or different degree if you think it is truly necessary to succeed in your career.

## CHAPTER 12
## Job Hunting in Tough Times

### What Have You Learned?

#### Answers to the True or False quiz

1. *False.* You should consider taking an entry-level job if it will help you to learn more about your field and could serve as a steppingstone to a more advanced position.
2. *True.* A part-time job is worthy of your consideration if it gives you entry into your field and you can afford to live on the salary you'd earn—at least temporarily.
3. *False.* Freelancing is an option for people in many fields. Architects, writers, artists, secretaries, photographers, computer programmers, software engineers, nurses, and television producers are among the many types of professionals who freelance.
4. *True.* Temporary work can give you income, put you in the workforce, and expose you to potential job opportunities.
5. *True.* Most internships are unpaid or include only a small stipend, but they can give you college credit toward your degree and valuable on-the-job experience.
6. *False.* Volunteer work can provide meaningful experience and also provide opportunities to network with individuals who may be able to guide you toward paid employment.
7. *True.* When the economy is down, you should be open to any and all potential sources of employment, and you may have to think creatively to generate your own opportunities.

## CHAPTER 13
## Filling Out Job Applications

### What Have You Learned?

#### Answers to the True or False quiz

1. *False.* Because the job application may be the first item a potential employer sees about you, it's important to complete your application with care. Otherwise, you might never get a chance to provide your resume or be given an interview.
2. *False.* Complete every line on a job application. If a section is not applicable, then write N/A or draw a line through the answer space.

3. *True.* Some employers require different applications for hourly and salaried positions.
4. *False.* Even if you've submitted your application online, you should bring a hard copy to the interview, just in case the interviewer doesn't have it handy.
5. *True.* Completing applications at hiring kiosks is rarely effective.
6. *True.* Never make negative comments on the application about previous employers.

# CHAPTER 14
# Interviewing
## What Have You Learned?

### *Answers to short answer quiz*

1. List at least five steps a job hunter should take before interviewing for a job.

   Before interviewing, a job hunter should research the profession, research the employer, practice responses to interview questions, prepare his or her own questions for the employer, assemble electronic and hard copies of all employment documents, understand the types of interviews, and prepare an appropriate interview outfit.

2. What do you think are the most common business etiquette mistakes a novice job hunter might make?

   Most novice job hunters underestimate the importance of business etiquette. Some fail to use a firm handshake, make good eye contact, and speak clearly. Other common mistakes include interview dress that is too casual and poor listening and handling of cell phones during the interview.

3. What's the best response to the question "Tell me about yourself"?

   The best response is a brief summary of the candidates three strongest skills or personality traits, followed by a clarifying question, such as "Does that answer your question?"

4. How is dressing for an interview on videoconference different from dressing for traditional interviews?

   Videoconference interviews require proper interview dress, but colors, patterns, and accessories must be kept simpler.

5. How would you describe the mindset needed to search for employment when jobs are scarce?

   While searching for employment, job hunters must focus on remaining physically and mentally strong. They must remain optimistic and avoid bitterness or negativity while working diligently and creatively on unearthing job leads.

# CHAPTER 15
# Evaluating Job Offers
## What Have You Learned?

### *Answers to short answer quiz*

1. What kinds of things do you need to know about an employer before considering a job offer?

   Before considering a job offer, it is important to know about the reputation of the company, including its treatment of its employees, its vision and values, and its financial standing. It is also important to learn as much as possible about the corporate culture and the management style of your potential supervisor.

2. What kinds of things do you need to know about a specific position before considering a job offer?

   Before accepting a specific position, be sure you are informed about the compensation. Also try to ascertain whether the skills and temperament required for this job are a good match for your own and whether the position offers enough challenge, variety, and autonomy for you.

3. How do you compare several job offers?

To compare several offers, align the variables side by side and consider which are most important to you. Consider things such as title and status but also such factors as creativity, potential satisfaction, and potential for advancement.

4. How can you avoid scams when job hunting?

To avoid job hunting scams, you must have a healthy skepticism and be willing to conduct research so you can be clear about the company's business model and background. Never give out bank account, PayPal, credit card, or social security numbers to an employer until you are certain of its legitimacy. Trust your own instincts if you feel an offer is too good to be true or that you have been hired without having properly presented your talents and credentials.

5. Give five tips for negotiating a better salary.

To negotiate a better salary, begin by having a salary figure in mind and deciding how important a priority the salary is to you. Consider whether you might be able to negotiate your salary again in the future and depending on the health of the local economy. You should also be clear on the demand for your skills and their worth. Be sure you are negotiating with the right party, and remain firm and confident.

# CHAPTER 16
## Learning Your New Job
### What Have You Learned?
### *Answers to the True or False quiz*

1. *False.* One of the most important things you can do on the first day on the job is listen and learn.
2. *False.* Asking relevant and intelligent questions when training is the best way to learn and show interest.
3. *False.* Recent college graduates often have to continue to improve their written and oral communication skills when beginning a new job.
4. *True.* Kissing up to the boss isn't a good idea.
5. *False.* While a mentor may help with some training, a mentor is a person who assists you in your career, providing guidance and advice.
6. *True.* When you are newly hired, it is important to research your field to stay current.

# INDEX